2⌐ ⌐EN

D0539263

Please return before the last
below
for lus

# TOP MANAGEMENT IN JAPANESE FIRMS

DR. RYÛEI SHIMIZU

PROFESSOR OF BUSINESS ADMINISTRATION
KEIO UNIVERSITY

CHIKURA SHOBO, TOKYO

1986

TOP MANAGEMENT IN JAPANESE FIRMS 1st Published in October, 1986.

ISBN4-8051-0542-9

# Preface

The modern business management is conducted centering on products; the development of new products helps promote growth of modern businesses. It is top management who make a decision on product strategies. Empirical researches on Japanese business enterprises conducted over the past 20 years have found that a corporate could be assessed by financial factors in the short term, product-related factors in the medium term, and top management factors in the long run.

Many of past studies on top management had the nature of historical studies or case studies which focussed on individual top business executives. In recent years, some researchers have taken a rather non-scientific approach to the subject; they discuss top management's abilities, comparing them with famous warriors of several centuries ago. Past historical studies had their own significance, however, they failed to identify top management's abilities in logical and systematic forms.

The present book is designed to examine, in logical and systematic manners, how top management's abilities contribute to corporate growth. For this purpose, a method of observing large numbers has been adopted.

First of all, three functions to be performed by top management ——thinking out future business visions, strategic decision-making, and business management and control——will be discussed. Then top management abilities to be displayed in the above three functional processes will be studied. Such abilities will include ambitions, insight, determination, persuasion and leadership.

To demonstrate top management abilities alone does not explain corporate growth. Instead, there are surrogates between top management abilities and corporate growth including strategic decision-making and consequences of decision-making. They are also considered as factors related to top management.

Factors required of top management may differ depending on business environment, business scale and type of business. It is therefore necessary to take this into consideration in identifying desirable top management factors.

This study will use both bibliographical and empirical methods. The former method, which refers to writings published both in Japan and other countries, will be employed to explore managerial functions and abilities required of the top management. The empirical method will be used to examine relative contributions of top management's abilities to the growth of firms, and desirable top managemnt abilities in different environments. The empirical study is based on results of interviewing surveys on approximately 220 top business executives of the big firms listed in Tokyo Stock Exchange conducted by the author over the past 20 years. Furthermore, the author's past questionnaire surveys covered a total of some 9,000 firms listed on the Tokyo Stock Exchange, and some 30,000 others. The data presented in this book were obtained from about 6,800 companies.

As to contents of this book, the first chapter, titled "Top Management's Decision-Making in Japanese Companies", clarifies: 1) factors which influence the devising of future business visions in the decision-making process, 2) the roles of the chief executive and other executives in the decision-making process, and 3) the pattern of decision-making in Japanese business enterprises. Chapter 2, titled "The Systematization of Top Management's Abilities in Japanese Firms", first points out that desirable abilities of the top management differ according to the environment surrounding them. It then deals with top management's abilities displayed in three functional processes. Chapter 3. "Interviewing Survey of Presidents in Big Firms" is the result of an empirical study on the top management in electrical machinery companies listed on the Tokyo Stock Exchange. Based on an interview survey on 64 presidents, it investigates their everyday living, behavior patterns at work, and views on business management, in a bid to analyse how these factors contribute to better corporate performance. Chapter 4, "An Empirical Research on Top Management's Abilities (in the Electronics and Chain Restaurant Industries)", examines how factors related to chief executives, such as their attributes, abilities and decision-making, and consequences of decision-making, contribute to the improved business results. It will be based on interviews with several chief executives and a questionnaire survey. Chapter 5, titled "An Empirical Research on Top Management's Abilities in the Sake Brewing Industry", analyses relative contributions of similar factors to those in Chapter 4 to better business results, using coefficients of correlation. Chapter 6, titled "Quantitative Research on Relationsihp between Top Management Factors and Corporate Growth in Japanese Big Firms", compares contributions of top management factors including attributes of the chief executive, decision–making, and consequences of decision-making, to the corporate growth, based on a large number of time series data. It also discusses differences in the above contributions by business environment, business scale, and type of business. Chapter 7 is a summary and conclusion.

If this book can contribute to academic as well as business circles in the world, it is not due to the work of this author alone but rather reflects the result of the enormous efforts and cooperation of the many people who participated in this undertaking. I should like to express sincere gratitude to the members and staff of the Study Group of Management Ability in Keio University, the Committee of Management Abilities in MITI where the author has worked as the head since 1974, the Japan Development Bank, the National Tax Agency, the Nikkei Business and the great number of firms that kindly gave answers to our questionnaire and interview surveys. Lastly I would like to thank Miss Miharu Hasegawa who helped me translate original work into English and, Mr. Takashi Chikura, President of Chikura Shobo, willingly published this book, and Mr. Satoshi Sekiguchi, editor, skillfully supervised the final preparation of this book.

1986 April

## Ryûei Shimizu

Dean, Professor of Business Administration in Keio University, Head of the Committee of Management Abilities in MITI

Contents

6

# 1

# Top Management's Decision-Making
## in Japanese Companies

## 1-1. The Japanese Top Management

The top management is a group of the highest ranking company executives who assume various managerial functions including: 1) Thinking out future business vision enabling the company to develop for an extended period of time, 2) Making strategic decisions for this purpose, and 3) Directing, coordinating and controlling the employees in line with a business vision.

In most Japanese companies, the highest decision-making body is also the highest executive organ; in many Japanese firms, the highest decision-making body is the managing directors' board unlike the board of directors in the United States and Britain. The larger the company, the stronger the tendency (see Figure 1-1).

The managing directors' board of a Japanese enterprise, that is called as *"Jômukai"*, made up of executives from managing directors on up, is the highest executive organ to assist the president, in addition to being the highest decision-making body. Even if the board of directors is the highest decision-making body, there are many cases in which each director is also a department head who has management responsibility. [1]

Japanese company top management usually consists of board chairman, president, vice-president, executive directors, managing directors and other directors. The average age of presidents of large U.S.

---

(1) Section 6-4-2.

**Figure 1-1.** Highest Decision–Making Body of Japanese Companies

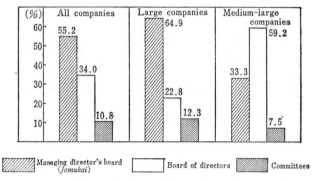

Source; Management Ability Indices, 1985, The Ministry of
International Trade and Industry (MITI)

enterprises is 58 and the average period of their being presidents is
eight years. Presidents of Japan's manufacturing industry are aged 62.7
on the average, which is about five years older than the U.S. level.
They stay in office for an average of eight years. Figures for presidents of large retail companies are 57.8 and 15.0 respectively. The
average age of company executives is 57.6 in the manufacturing industry and 52.3 in the retail industry. Many U.S. company presidents
are specialized in such fields as accounting, management, law and
sales. It is not easy to identify the specialization of Japanese counterparts because Japanese company presidents often experience many types
of work before becoming president. A study shows that there is no
significant relationship between the special field of the presidents and
business performances.

There are four types of presidents in Japanese companies; the founder, successor, company-bred and the *Amakudari* (retired high ranking
bureaucrat, or transferred from banks or parent companies). Companies
with a founder president record good business results irrespective of
type and size of business, and economic situations[2] (see Figure 1-2).

This is mainly because a founder-president is capable of developing
new products. However, I found that the growth of a company led

_____

(2) Sections 6-3-1 and 4-2-1.

**Figure 1-2.** Type of Japanese Company Presidents and Business Performances

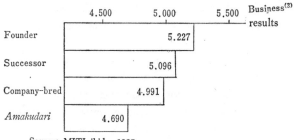

Source: MITI ibid., 1985

by a founder-president aged 65 and over slows down. Founder-presidents account for 6.8 percent of all presidents of large Japanese enterprises. This is compared with 5.3 percent in U.S. counterparts. In general, there is no significant relationship between ages of presidents and business results in Japanese businesses. As for the relationship between the average age of executives and business performances, under favorable economic condition, good business results are recorded by companies with young executives. On the other hand, when economic condition is unfavorable, businesses with elderly executives show good performances. [4] This is probably because in a high economic growth period, active way of management by young executives is desirable, while in a low growth period a prudent method of management by elderly executives is needed.

## 1-2. Decision-Making Process of Top Management in Japanese Companies

The principal function of the top management is to make decisions in a broad sense, the process of which is divided into three stages; thinking out future business vision, strategic decision-making (in a narrow sense), and managing and controlling a business(see Figure 1-3). The first stage involves personal contemplation, the second a process of harmonized unity in which decisions are made obtaining the

(3) Foot note (5) of chapter 4.
(4) Section 6-3-2.

consent of many company officers concerned, and the third a process of delegating authorities to trustful subordinates. The following are detailed explanation of each stage as shown in the left side of Figure 1-3.

The First Stage: Formation of future business vision

1) Presidents' understanding of problems

The president and other top management must always pay attention to trend of both external environment and internal conditions facing the company. They must also constantly be conscious of the company's traditional business philosophy as one of the company's creed. The top management build up future visions based on their own philosophy. With the recognition of objective conditions surrounding the company, the top management formulate future business vision and identify problems.

The Second Stage: Process of strategic decision-making

1) Decisions on business policies

In face of new business information, the top management with future business vision may specify problems, if there are any, using their intuition and insight. After gathering necessary information, they present the problems at their meeting and discuss measures to solve them. The president makes the final decision and draws up business policies or sets business goals.

2) Discussion and review within the top management

To implement the business policies, the president exchanges views with the executives on strategic plans mainly on products, and makes the final strategic decision. Since this process proceeds in parallel with formulating business policies, the top management at this stage aims at further confirming strategic concept and making related dicisions on, for example, distribution of financial sources needed.

3) U-shaped decision-making process involving middle lower management

The top management presents their strategic decisions to the middle lower management for discussion. The middle management coordinate their subordinates' views and submit their plans with specific target fugures to the top management. After further studying the proposed plans, the president makes final decisions on a long-range business plan.

The Third Stage: Management and control

1)   Managing and controlling a business based on a long-range plan

The top management works out an annual profit plan and compiles a yearly budget based on a long-range business plan. They delegate their authorities to execute the budget to the executives and department managers in charge. The budget then is allocated to each department and section so that the employees can perform better.

2)   Feed-back of business performances

Good business results can be achieved through company-wide demonstration of creativity from top management down to unranked employees. A year-to-year business performance is reflected in the next fiscal budget. If business results show no major improvement for a long period, it may lead to a revision of the long-range plan. If they are largely affected by external environment and internal conditions facing the company, it may result in a revision of business goals or strategy.

I will explain the items in the middle column of Figure 3-1 from top to bottom following from Section 1-3 to 1-8.

# 1-3.   Thinking out Future Business Vision and Background Factors

## 1-3-1.   External Environments and Internal Conditions

A characteristic of external environments facing modern Japanese businesses is their uncertain and discontinuous character. It is vital for companies to forecast such environments. In fact, it is possible to do so to some extent. The uncertain and discontinuous environments are generally caused by a lack of information on possible future phenomena. Some aspects of the external environments are: economy, technology, culture and international relations. Of the international relations, which are becoming increasingly significant in recent years, political factors are particularly important. For pent-up social, economic discomforts in a certain country sometimes cause a drastic change in international relations. In fact, many of the current changes in world politics are attributed to an unstable government facing people's discomforts. Japanese companies have so far attached importance to eco-

nomic factors, technology and international relations in this order,
but recently, the relative importance of economic factors is on the
decline, while technology is becoming increasingly important (see
Fiure 1-4).

Internal conditions here concern strengths and weaknesses of a company. The strengths include conditions that enable the company to
cope with discontinuous changes in external environmets, while the
weaknesses are conditions that prevent the company from doing so.
Some aspects of corporate strong points are: long-range viewpoint of
the top management, prompt decision-making, high levels of research
and technology, active attitude towards product development, stable
brand and customers, employees' high work morale, firm trust between labor and management, high ratio of owned capital, subcontractors with high levels of technology and firm trust between companies
and banking institutions, etc.. A weakness of a company, on the other
hand, is a lack of flexibility, i.e., inability to cope with the changing
external environments. As a company aims at mass production and
mass sales, seeking after an efficiency, such factors as workforce,
equipment and capital will become large in scale and fixed. This may
result in organizational rigidity of a company.

**Figure 1-4.** Trend in Important External Factors in Japanese Companies

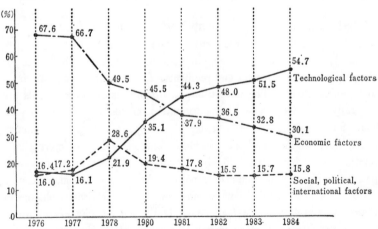

Source; Management Ability Indices, 1985, MITI

## 1-3-2. Business Philosophy

Business philosophy refers to the long-established sense of values on organizational management which provides a guideline for future business operation. Modern business philosophy places emphasis on: 1) profit-seeking, and 2) fulfilling social responsibility. Companies holding traditional capitalism and owner-company operators are inclined to profit-seeking, while modern businesses and specialist-operators are more conscious of social responsibility.

Business philosophy differs according to the time and size of industry. Japanese merchants in the *Edo* Feudal Era practiced family-patterned management. In the *Meiji* Era (1867–1911), public enterprises advocated business philosophy centered around national interests. On the contrary, *Zaibatsu* affiliated businesses have mainly held an Westernized business concept since the *Meiji* Era until now. By size of industry, smaller companies stress maintenance of their property, whereas large enterprises stress the importance of their social contribution. Business philosophy is expressed in company mottoes, but with only the framework. In other words, many Japanese company mottoes emphasize, for example, good quality products, social contribution, interpersonal trust, human efforts and creative thinking with little reference to profit seeking. The following are some examples of Japanese company mottoes:

"National service through industry, fairness, harmonious cooperation and gratitude", Matsushita Electric Industry Co.

"Harmony, sincerity, pioneer spirit", Hitachi Ltd.

"Maintaining internationalized viewpoint, supplying products of highest efficiency at reasonable prices, and satisfying customers all over the world", Honda Motor Co.

"Ideas and challenge", C. Itoh & Co.

However abstract business philosophy may be, it is very useful and indispensable for growth of a company if it is firmly held by the management and helps work out measures to cope with changing external environments.

## 1-3-3. Personal Philosophy of the Top Management

The top management formulates future business vision based not

only on external environments, internal conditions facing the company
and business philosophy but also on their personal philosophy that is
very subjective and of a human nature.    Such philosophy is greatly
concerned with the personal history of the top management: family
life, education, social class, health and experience in operating a
business. In particular, experience in philosophical thinking in his
youth helps the top management formulate his philosophy.    Generally
speaking, a company president who suffered adversity in his boyhood
such as unhappy family life and social environment or poor health,
often sets up an active vision very carefully. [5] A company's philosophy and the top management's personal philosophy are combined to
provide standards for drawing up of the company's future business
vision. For example, it is possible that the president of electronics
apparatus manufacturing company, born in a peasants' family, holds
his company creed, "social services", may draw up a plan to open
a factory in a rural district for the purpose of hiring local people,
and thereby raising standards of their living.    It is also likely that a
president, who once experienced uncomfortable hospitalization, may
aim at developing a new medical treatment system that can reduce
mental and physical sufferings of the patients.

## 1-3-4.  Thinking out Future Business Vision

Future business vision is one's view on how a company should
be ten years or 20 years from now.    What is vital to build it is the
management's sense of duty and understanding of what he should do.
These factors motivate the management to maintain or further develop
the company. Any future plan which is not based on the above factors
cannot get the workers to fulfil their duties better.    Some managers
formulate a whole vision through intuition, and others work out only
the framework of a future plan and then gradually complete the
whole by an analytical thinking process. In general terms, intuitive
thinking is needed under drastically changing business conditions,
while analytical thinking is important under stable environments. [6]
Anyway, a discontinuous and intutive thinking is particularly necessary

---

(5)   Hypothesis 3-31 of chapter 3 and section 4-2-2.
(6)   Sections 4-3-4 and 5-3-5.

to draw up an innovative future business plan.

## 1-4. The Strategic Decision-Making Process

1) Awareness of problems, Information gathering

The top management must constantly refine their sixth sense, identify problems, think flexibly and collect necessary information as well as having knowledge about the interrelatedness among collected informations. Sixth sense is refined by accumulated experiences and self-confidence. To collect much information, the top management must have a clear understanding of problems and renew their built-in memories. Otherwise, it is possible that they will overlook important information that may pose a threat to their company, and be unable to select key information. Also, unless the built-in memories which are criteria to select key information are constantly expanded or renewed, it may result in rigidity of the top management thinking. The knowledge of interrelatedness among collected informations may help top business executives not to miss information, though trivial and indirect they seem, on changing external environments, that may lead to a threat to their company. The creativity of the top management is demonstrated in their information gathering activities including building up the net-work to gather informations, which inherently comes from the interpersonal trust in his acquaintances; the top management must obtain information through contacts with leaders of various circles and discuss it at meetings with intimate friends. In addition, they must seek key information from newspaper[7] and magazine headlines and have experts study details.

2) Presentation and review of problems

The top management presents problems which they consider likely to pose a threat to their company in the future. In a company where there is no smooth communication between the young president, for example, son of the company's founder, and elderly executives, the president needs to call their attention by pointing out problems clearly. He sometimes must offer even solutions. On the other hand, in a big company where the president has big authority and responsibility, he

---

(7)  Section 3-2-1.

only suggests problems so that the executives can freely discuss them. [8]

Whether or not the executives take up proposed problems for discussion depends on such factors as the influence of the matters on their posts and their understanding of the problems. The executives would discuss in a very earnest manner matters that are likely to affect their post and promotion. But, they would not express their opinions clealy on matters that may result in demotions even if they think it necessary to discuss them. Instead, they oppose the discussion itself on one pretext or another that seem irrelevant to their demotions. It is also likely that a president who has technical backgrounds may attach importance to information on technical innovations, while his colleague executives majoring accounting may not do so.

3) Working out solutions, Decision-Making

The top management work out solutions to proposed problems and make decisions on step-by-step, and trial-and-error basis in a system approach. In other words, if the top management finds the proposed problems critical to the company, they try to work out a solution to them, using a systems approach. [9] This method aims at thinking a whole system of something, i.e., seeking a total optimum by taking into consideration a broad range of time and space.

Such an optimum selection is not made only by the president or a single executive. Instead, the president work out solutions and select an optimum by persuading the other executives participating in the decision-making. If the other executives oppose selected optimum for emotional reasons, the president postpone the final decision. But, their objections are logical, the president tries to further discuss the opposers using objective back-up data. Suppose such objections are aimed at retaining posts of the involved executives, the president should act accordingly. Anyway, the president should first determine the true reasons for any resistance of executives. It is not appropriate to persuade Japanese company executives only relying on objective data.

Generally speaking, innovative decisions are made mainly by the president, for a decision involving many executives may often result in a mediocre and uninnovative decision. In a growing company, it is

---

(8)  Answer of Hitachi's president of section 3-2-3.

(9)  Section 2-7.

desirable for the president to take initiative in making decisions rather than respecting executives' opinions. But, in a low growth and profit company which cannot afford even a minor failure, it is desirable that other executives participate in the decision-making and be held responsible for implementing decisions. [10]

## 1-5.  Business  Policies (Goals)

A business policy,  formulated on the consensus of  the top management,  shows the direction a company should take in the future. It is based on personal vision of the president and influential executives, and decided after vigorous discussions among the top management. Business policies in general terms incorporate business goals.

Business policies of Japanese enterprises attached imporiance to share expansion of main products and new product development in the high economic growth period(—1974). In a low growth period, cost reductions became relatively important(1975—1977). In the stable growth period(1978—1984), the relative importance of new product development became higher while cost reductions and share expansion became less significant(see Figure 1-5).

**Figure 1-5.** Trend in Important Business Goals in Japanese Companies

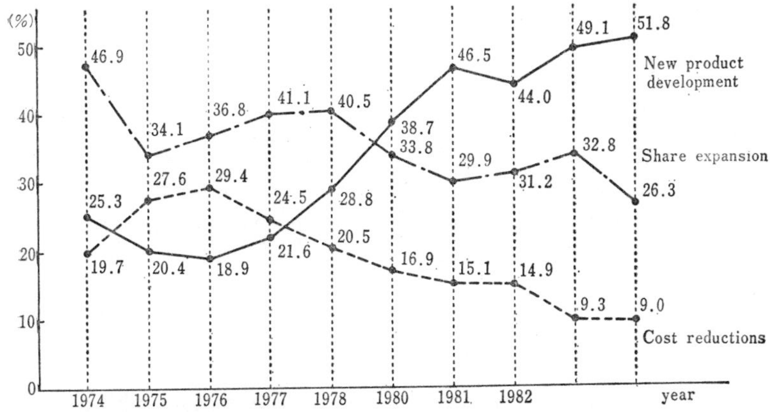

Source; Management Ability Indices, 1985, MITI

(10)  Section 6-4-1 and 4-4-3.

This is because in the high growth period, companies aim at share expansion by marketing newly improved products, but in a low growth period when sales slow down, they try to secure profit by means of cost reductions. In a stable growth period when business competition becomes intense, it is vital that companies develop innovative and competitive products. Three most important business goals of Japanese companies are: 1) new product development, 2) share expansion, and 3) cost reductions. This is followed by the other goals: business diversification, change of business and raising of owned capital ratio. Few Japanese enterprises attach importance to such goals as harmonious relations with the community, increased welfare for the employees and better consumer services. Companies citing new product development as one of main business goals always show high performances[11] (see Figure 1-6).

**Figure 1-6.** Important Business Goals and Business Performance

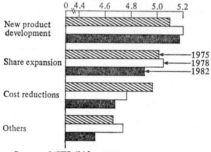

Source; MITI ibid., 1985

This is because such goal urges the employees to change their thought manner and develop their abilities. This in turn will enable a new product development. By this reciprocal process, the employees display their creativity in producing profit and thus contributing to the growth of their companies.

## 1-6. Business Strategy

Business strategy is measures for the company to cope with discontinuous changes in external environments. These measures are taken

(11)  Section 6-4-3, 4-4-2 and 5-4-3.

mainly for product strategy: companies cope with ordinary market changes with improved remodeled products. Amid discontinuous market and technology-related changes, technically innovative products are needed. If changes are too drastic to cope with only by the product strategy, diversification of business becomes necessary. If there are drastic discontinuous changes in international relations, new overseas strategy will be adopted.

There are two types of business strategy, offensive and defensive. The former includes new product development, business diversification and overseas strategy, and the latter business withdrawal. The "offensive" strategy needs technology and funds, while the "defensive" one careful treatment of personnel involved.

Business diversification is to start a new business which is encouraged by such factors as a drop in the growth rate of company's field of industry and in the profit rate of the company as well as existence of unutilized sources that is so called "slacks". However, most large Japanese companies are constantly diversifying their business in an attempt to cope with constantly changing environments. The strategy of business diversification can be classified as that of; production-related, market-related and expansion into unrelated fields.

In the past, many Japanese enterprises diversified business using their sales market. But now (in 1985), diversification into unrelated fields by redistributing sources is most popular. This is followed by the diversification of market-related by using established sales channels, and company's brand name. This is because companies can no longer grow only with the conventional-product-related diversification amid the drastically changing environments. In fact, an increasing number of Japanese enterprises are attaching importance to technological factors (see Figurg 1-4). Although there is little relationship between type of business diversification and business results, the starting time of such diversification affects business results: the earlier a company starts it, the better performance it gains. Business diversification is said to contribute to growth of a company, and to profitability to a lesser extent, but excessive diversification is said to negatively affect both factors.

Overseas strategy[12] concerns international trade and overseas investment. Overseas investment strategy of Japanese companies have mainly aimed at securing: 1) sales markets, 2) raw materials and 3) cheap labor. Sales markets have been explored in the United States and other advanced countries to deal with import restrictions imposed by Japan's trade partners and to prepare for fluctuations of exchange rates. Among exporters of raw materials to Japan is Australia. Cheap labor has been available mainly in Southeast Asian nations. But now (1985), the rate of Japan's overseas investment to secure cheap labor is very small. Expansion of sales market tops the list of purposes of Japanese overseas investment, accounting for 60 percent. Next is securing raw materials with 16 percent, and stock dividend plus royalty with 12 percent. Securing cheap labor only accounts for three percent.

As for method of overseas strategy of Japanese enterprises, almost 40% of Japanese companies export products through trading companies and/or agencies, and 20% of them through the company's overseas offices or affiliated sales companies. The companies which carry out positive overseas investment are about 30%. Only a little more than ten percent of Japanese enterprises have not any overseas strategy. Investment through overseas production facilities concentrates in fields of electrical machinery, chemical and transportation equipment.

Business withdrawal strategy is to abandon the company's main line of business, which is vital to promote the "offensive" business strategy involving new product development and business diversification. A conventional economic theory that as long as marginal revenues are more than marginal expenses, a production increase results in a maximum profit, only holds under a stable business environment. Amid largely changing business environments like today, there are chances for more profitable products. In order to start production of more profitable products, companies might need to withdraw from some line of business due to limited sources especially in medium-sized companies. In this light, defensive business withdrawal can be regarded as positive as well. What is most important in business withdrawal strategy is to maintain the trust of the people concerned; ranging from those in charge of production and sales of products included in a

---

(12)  Section 6-4-4.

withdrawal plan to the customers and clients.

Employees in the manufacturing and sales divisions, in particular, will oppose the planned withdrawal for fear that their accumulated know-how will become useless and they will be virtually demoted. Unless the company deals with these people properly by, for example, rewarding them for their past contributions, it will not only deteriorate work morale of the involved employees, but also affect work morale of the constituents as a whole. A successful example is a bankrupt company called Kojin which has filed an application for the Corporate Rehabilitation Law. With the closure of main line of business, Kojin's receiver set up an employment-promotion-committee and helped surplus workforce of 5.000~6.000 to find jobs in the Daiei super-market store chain and other companies. This helped Kojin expedite reconstruction of its management.

Both retail and wholesale sales channels operate based on interpersonal trust established in long years of business deals. If a company withdraws on simple grounds such as a fixed cost increase, it is possible that the dealers may transfer to sales channels of its rival company, giving a hard blow to the withdrawing company.

## 1-7. Long-Range Business Plan

Long-range plan is indicated with figures. It is set by the following process: First, general staff in the planning and/or president's office draws up a draft plan on the basis of business goals and strategy set by the top management, and referring to figures for past management plans. After being checked by managing directors and managing committee members, the draft plan is shown to the middle management such as department heads or division heads, factory managers and sometimes section chiefs. The middle management then work out more detailed plans and send them back to the general staff.

One of the characteristics of the decision-making process of Japanese companies is that it reflects opinions of lower levels of personnels down to section chiefs. It is not merely a bottom-up type of decision-making. Instead, it is a "U" shaped decision-making which starts from the top management and in which views of lower rank employees are absorbed by the top management.

Some 65 to 75 percent of Japanese companies listed in the Tokyo Stock Exchange have a long-range business plan, mostly covering three years. However, only 25 percent have a contingency plan. Companies with a long-range business plan show better business results than others irrespective of external environments. [13]

## 1–8. Management and Control

One of functions of the company president is to carry out business strategy by controlling various activities of the executives in charge. This function includes, planning, organizing and coordinating a business, and motivating and controlling the executives.

Business planning is to draw up business policies and goals along with measures to achieve them, on basis of which the executives in charge perform their functions. Business organizing is designed to assign work to personnel and to identify who has final responsibility and authority. Specifically, it is to have the management direct their respective departments. Coordination of business generally is to unite various business activities through: 1) formal meetings of managing directors, executive directors, management committee members, etc., and 2) breakfast, luncheon and other informal meetings of the top management. It is most important that the company president obtain the consensus of the top executives on these occasions.

Motivating is to provide the executives with what causes them to work hard voluntarily, without forcing them to do so. Important motives for executives include participation in the plans, major delegation of authority, fair personnel management and the president's personal support to them. Controlling a business is not always important if the business planning and motivation of executives are successful. In order to continue for long the above process including business planning and controlling executives, the president needs to evaluate the executives in charge from the long-range viewpoint, taking into consideration the business environment surrounding the company. The

---

(13)   Section 6–4–5.

president with the longr-ange viewpoint may count their ability to educate competent subordinates higher than the ability to increase, for example, sales. The president who is consious of business environments may not evaluate executives by performances alone, because a difference in their performances resulted from a difference in business environments. In this case, even if a better-performing executive may receive a little higher bonus than his fellow executives, but he does not get a higher promotion at all.

## 1-9. Some Characteristics of Top Management's Decision-Making in Japanese Companies

Top management's decision-making in Japanese companies are characterized by: 1) long-range business vision, 2) innovative and prompt strategic decision-making involving many executives, (usually "innovative and prompt decision-making" contradicts "involving many people in decision-making") and 3) management and control through major delegation of president's authority to the executives, the evaluation of whom being made from a long-range viewpoint(see the right side of Figure 1-3).

The long-range business vision results from the Japanese management aiming at long-term survival and growth of the firm itself, rather than at benefiting stockholders; even when there is a drop in profit and stock prices due to a large-scale equipment investment for rationalizing and labor-saving on the long-range viewpoint the top-management are not held responsible for it. Many top managements in Japan cite profits and rate of sales growth as important financial indicators, while less than one percent of Japanese top-management quote stock prices and dividend rate(see Table 1-1 and refer Hypothesis 3-16, 17).

Another aspect concerned with the long-range business vision is the practice of the president nominating his successor. The Japanese Commercial Code stipulates that a president be selected by the company's board of directors. In actual practice, the president nominates his successor. And the nomination is not usually rejected at a general meeting of the company's stockholders. The president-elect is likely to follow the president's business vision.

Some characteristics of the decision-making process of Japanese enterprises are:1) logic of *"Kashi-Kari"* (give and take), 2) *"Nemawashi"* (informal talks behind the scene), and 3) ceremonial decisions made at formal meetings.

A Japanese company president must always do favors to his subordinates and make them have some feeling "in debt" for his favors. The favors include: to help the executives promote or retain their posts, to accept their opinions at official meetings, and to overlook their minor failures related to management. The president even helps the executives to find their daughters' prospective hasbands, or their sons find job. Japanese companies with presidents doing such favors show good business results.[14] Unless executives have feelings "in debt" for the president and they have profound trust between executives and president, vigorious discussion may not result in consentient goals.

Of the four types of Japanese company presidents, the founder, the successor, the company-bred and *Amakudari*, only the first needs not to do his subordinates favors because of his personal charismatic nature, which makes them feel something "in debt" to the president whenever they meet him.

**Table 1-1.** Most Important Financial Indicators

|  | 1978 | '79 | '82 | '85 |
|---|---|---|---|---|
| Rate of sales growth | 9.8% | 10.2% | 12.5% | 16.1% |
| Rate of profit growth | 9.3 | 8.2 | 10.0 | 11.5 |
| Profits | 42.6 | 45.3 | 40.5 | 43.8 |
| Ratio of profits to sales | 22.3 | 21.4 | 17.5 | 18.1 |
| Ratio of profits to equity | 1.1 | 1.3 | 1.3 | 1.0 |
| Ratio of profits to total liabilities and net worth | 11.2 | 9.9 | 13.7 | 6.7 |
| Net worth ratio | 1.7 | 2.6 | 2.5 | 1.0 |
| Receipt and outlay of funds | 1.1 | 0.2 | 1.0 | 0.2 |
| Stock prices | 0 | 0 | 0 | 0 |
| Dividend rate | 0.4 | 0 | 0.4 | 1.0 |
| Others | 0.4 | 0.9 | 0.6 | 0.6 |

Source; Management Ability Indices, 1985, MITI.

---

(14)　Sections 4-3-6 and 5-3-6.

Japanese managers practice *Nemawashi* or informal discussions behind the scene before making decisions. For example, the Japanese company president sometimes proposes a plan on informal occasions such as breakfast and luncheon meetings with the executives. If they disagree with the president, they only harden their faces and ask some questions on the matters, without directly voicing their objections. The president in turn reads their faces and tries to revise his plan if needed. This process is *Nemawashi* of "open type." The other type of *Nemawashi*, that is, "closed type" is that the president entertains personally the executive who is greatly impacted by a new plan, in a Japanese style restaurant, for example, persuade him heartily and get consent from him. These processes of practicing the logic of "*Kashi-Kari* and *Nemawashi*" are sometimes referred to as a political process.

Subjects thus fully discussed informally are approved promptly by the highest decision-making bodies such as the board of managing directors and the board of executive directors. The larger the company, the more democratic the president's decision-making is. A founder-president is more democratic in making decisions, at least in his apparent attitude making his subordinates discuss freely, than other types of president. [15] Because his subordinates knows the founder-president's profound thought well, and they have some feelings "in debt", even if they freely discuss, it result in the same as the president aimes. A son-of-the-founder-president is apt to operate one-man management. Most of the executives around the successor-president are former subordinates of the founder-president and are likely confronted with him. Even if the highest decision-making body of Japanese companies conducts vigorous dialectic discussions like in the West, it makes decisions in a short period of time with its members fully considering their respective positions on subjects given, as there is underlying trust between the president and the other executives.

In many Japanese companies, function of management and control is easy one. Because the highest decision-making body is usually also a highest executive organ, and top managers as a group participate in a strategic decision-making. Substantial delegation of authority from

---

(15)  Hypotheses 3-29, and 3-30 in chapter 3.

the president to the executives in charge easily leads, without particular efforts, to planning, organizing and coordinating a business, and motivating and controlling personnel. For smooth repetition of the process of management and control, the president must evaluate executives' abilities by their capability to educate the middle management and to bring about vitality in workplace as well as their financial performances.

## 1-10. Summary

Top management are highest ranking company executives who think out measures to develop their companies, make strategic decisions for the purpose, and direct and motivate their subordinates to perform better. In many foreign companies, a decision-making body is separated from an executive organ, but in many Japanese businesses, only one body assumes the two functions.

Three main functions of the top management are: 1) To think out future business vision, 2) To make strategic decisions, and 3) To manage and control a business.

(1) The top management draws up future business vision taking into consideration external environments and internal conditions facing the company, and based on their personal business philosophy. The uncertain and discontinuous external circumstances include various factors such as economy, technology, political situation, culture and international relations. Factors which have become increasing important are technology and international relations. Internal conditions refer to strengths and weaknesses of a company. The strengths include conditions that enable the company to cope with discontinuous changes in external environments. Business philosophy is a long-established value system for business operation. The management's philosophy is formulated on the basis of family life in boyhood, school education and experiences in business operation. So, managers with different philosophy hold different future business vision.

(2) The process of a strategic decision-making is made up of two stages: 1) To decide on business policies, and 2) To work out a long-range business plan.

The first stage involves: knowledge of problems and gathering of necessary information, presentation and review of the problems, working out solutions, and decision on business policies. To find problems promptly, the management must constantly be aware of problems affecting future business vision, and contact leaders of various circles in search for vital information. In the ensuring process, they discuss subjects in a logical and scientific manner, but at the same time, they conduct a psychological and political tug-of-war. In the process, the management is required to understand what is really meant in executives' statements and act accordingly. Business policies show the direction a company should take in the future; Japanese enterprises attached importance to share expansion and new product development in a high economic growth period, and cost reduction in a low growth period. In the current stable growth period, new product development is regarded as the most important. Companies actively engaged in developing new products always show good business results irrespective of external economic conditions.

The second stage of a strategic decision-making involves: clarification of business strategy and setting up of a long-range business plan incorporating strategic measures. Business strategy includes measures that enable a company to adjust its main line of business to changing environments according to business policies. It is worked out centering on product strategy. There are two types of business strategy, offensive and defensive. The former includes new product development, business diversification and overseas strategy, while the latter business withdrawal strategy. Amid the current drastic changes in external environments, many Japanese companies are making constant efforts for new product development and business diversification, in addition to conducting overseas strategy. Business withdrawal strategy is necessary to promote the "offensive" business strategy. What is important in abandoning a business is to maintain the trust of the people involved. A long-term business plan is made on the basis of these business strategy and afore-mentioned business policies. Based on a long-term and overall business plan, annual budget and other standards for corporate management and control are worked out. In Japanese companies, a "U"-shaped decision-making is common in which lower rank employees participate in the setting of a long-range business plan.

(3) Management and control of a business is to implement a business strategy which has been decided upon. It includes planning, organizing and coordinating a business, and motivating and controlling the employees. For example, to draw up a profit plan and compile an annual budget, which motivates and controls them.

Some characteristics of the decision-making process of Japanese top management are: 1) long-range business vision resulting from Japanese way of management seeking survival and growth of the firm itself rather than benefitting its stockholders, 2) innovative and prompt decision-making by many executives based on the logic of *"Kashi-Kari"* (give and take), and *"Nemawashi"* (informal discussions behind the scene before making decisions), and ceremonial decision-making at a formal meeting, and 3) delegation of authority and responsibility from the president to the executives in charge of management and control, and the president's evaluation from a long-range viewpoint.

# 2

# The Systematization of Top Management's Abilities in Japanese Firms

## 2-1. Abilities Needed by Japanese Company Presidents

Abilities required for a company head in Japan include the quality to accomplish three managerial functions: 1) Thinking out future business vision, 2) Strategic decision-making and 3) Business management and control. A desirable company president must be able to carry out managerial functions efficiently, adjusting himself to a given environment, and thereby contributing greatly to the growth of his company.

There exist no standard abilities expected in common of company operators, because managerial functions vary with business conditions. In general, successful founder-presidents in Japan are confident of their past decisions who have keen intuition or "sixth sense" concerning management. For example, [1] in the electronics parts manufacturing industry undergoing constant technological innovations, intuition is a quality that is needed by the president. But, such a quality is not always desirable in a stable industry like the "Sake", Japanese rice wine, industry which are conducting no major technological innovations. Instead, the ability in analytical thinking is necessary in order for the president to conduct various management analyses including a market analysis in terms of products and regions, or a sales promotion analysis.

The president of a giant enterprise in Japan does not express his

---

(1) Sections 4-3-4 and 5-3-5.

view in the first place at an executive meeting for fear that his remarks may sound like an absolute order, so discourage free discussions among the executive staff. [2] The president is expected to listen to opinions of his subordinates, rather than be vocal himself. On the other hands, such a passive attitude is undesirable for the successor-president in a medium-large enterprise in Japan, where the executive staff is likely to consist of the right-hand men and co-managers of the founder of the company. If the president of such an enterprise does not take initiative at an executive meeting, chances are that he will follow the company's conventional business strategy centered on old stable products. The successor-president therefore must be able to persuade his subordinates by speaking up himself based on concrete data which support his ideas.

As explained above, there are no such abilities as needed in common by company heads in Japan. The generally-expected abilities of the presidents only refer to individual character or personal traits that facilitate the fulfilment of managerial functions by the presidents. Again, a desirable company operator must be able to adjust himself to a given environment and better contribute to the growth of his company.

## 2-2. Systematization of Abilities Needed by Japanese Company Presidents

In general terms, a Japanese company head with strong entrepreneurship possesses such characteristics as holding beliefs and ability in foresight, while a company head with strong administratorship is featured by respects for human elements in business and scientific thinking. Both types of presidents attach importance to tough body and knowledge on various aspects. Table 2-1 shows abilities needed by Japanese company presidents in relation with three managerial functions. Managerial functions are shown vertically and abilities are horizontally. The table also includes my definition of each ability in business context and my views on how each aspect of abilities are developed. From the table, you can see that an entrepreneur-type president possesses: ambition, sense of duty, philosophy, beliefs, intuition, imagination, insight, determination,

---

(2)    Answer of Hitachi's President in section 3-2-3, and Hypotheses 3-28, 29, 30.

and abilities to take a risk and create discontinuous tension. These factors play a significant role in working out a vision of the future business as well as in making strategic decisions. In contrast, an administrator-type of president has: generosity, fine personality, personal attraction, ethical sense, morality, sense of responsibility, systems approach, effective use of time, quantitative thinking, abilities to endure continuous tension, leadership and readiness to do others a favor. These factors play a big role in strategic decision-making and business management and control. All company heads must possess health and the ability to collect information which take a vital part in all aspects of managerial functions, namely, future business planning, decision-making and corporate management and control.

## 2-3. Ambition, Sense of Duty, Philosophy and Belief

Ambition is a desire that appears beyond one's ability. It is the base for a strong desire to succeed, enthusiasm about the product and business, perseverance, creativity and competitiveness. [3] Ambition is a source of vitality for company presidents; ambitious presidents always enjoy good business performances. [4] Ambition in the top management often stems from an inferiority complex they felt when they were young. A study of Japanese company heads by social and economic conditions shows that those who are from a lower social class family are ambitious, achieving high business results. [5]

The sense of duty refers to a belief that one's job is a task assigned by God. Ambition is not always acceptable to Japanese company employees, rather, it sometimes invite their criticism. The company head in Japan therefore should aim to persuade his employees to do their job not because of his ambition, but because of the sense of duty. In operating a large business in Japan, it is vital to narrow a gap between the purposes of the company and its employees. To include sense of duty in company creeds will help reduce such a gap. An

(3)　Herbert E. Kierulf; *Finding and Keeping Corporate Entrepreneurs,* Business Horizon Vol. 22, No. 1, Feb. 1979.

(4)　Sections 4-3-1 and 5-3-1.

(5)　Hypothesis 3-31 and section 4-2-2.

example of this is Matsushita Electric Industrial Co. Ltd. which has "National service through industrial activities" in its company mottoes. The sense of duty of a company head can be developed by convincing himself everyday that his job is a kind of mission.

Philosophy is a supreme concept that controls individual experiences as a whole. A company head is expected to hold, from his past experiences, knowledge and philosophy, high ideals such as a hope to contribute to the improvement of living standards of all human beings. If his ideals which are compatible with social values are handed down to his successors over an extended period of time, they will become a management philosophy. As individual sense of value changes, so does management philosophy; in a mass society like in Japan, a humanistic and democratic way of thinking is important. The management philosophy is cultivated gradually through efforts to look closely at the social trend and practice soul-searching.

A management-related belief is similar to a religious belief, or something like self-confidence. But for confidence, company head cannot lead his employees. Henry Ford recalls in his autobiography that his belief in automobiles for the masses led him to develop T-model cars. [6] Resembling a religious belief, however, a management belief is likely to result in a failure to meet changing social needs. An example of this is the Ford Motor Co. It suffered a failure because it sticked to T-model cars for too long. A management belief can be constructed as the company head continues to believe in his own management philosophy.

## 2-4. Intuition, Imagination, Insight and Determination

Intuition is the power of mind to understand something without logical reasoning such as judgement and assumption. In philosophical terms, it is an intellectual sympathy. And it can see through the true nature of something. When a company head has a new information, he must be able to grasp it as a whole before thinking about it logic-

---

(6)   Henry Ford; *My Life and Work*, 1922, Entrepreneurship in Britain 1750–1939, pp. 82–87, edited by R. H. Campbell & R. G. Wilson, Adam & Charles Black, London, 1975.

ally. Intuition can be fostered by constant soul-searching and accumulated experiences. Together with analytical thinking, intuition can help the company operator predict a new business condition. Whether his intuition is right or wrong is determined by the actual outcome of his intuition. If the company head repeatedly succeeds in his intuition, he will become confident of himself, which will help him refine his intuition. Likewise, if a new product development which resulted from a president's intuition proves successful, the president will become even more confident with his "sixth sense" becoming keener. In rapidly growing industries like electronics and chain-restaurant industries, [7] the intuition of the presidents is important. This is because in such industries, a business failure caused by an inappropriate dicision can be offset by big profit margins. A quick decision is also vital in these industries so that they can put their products on the market earlier than rival firms.

Imagination is the power of the mind to create a mental image of something. In order to analyse problems identified by his intuition, the company president must first form mental images of the future. I call such images "creative mental images". For having clear creative images, the company head needs strong will and purposes. In other words, the company head must first identify management problems and construct various mental images, from which he must select several effective ones He will then be able to concentrate his thinking on the selected images for solution of problems. What is most important for creating various mental images is to listen to others' opinions constantly, for views that are different from yours help stimulate your imagination. The successful president does not even try to judge on who is right or wrong before he fully understands one's opinions.

Insight is the power to see into things. The true nature of something cannot be seen by analysing related data alone. Instead, a free way of thinking is most important to see through things. The company president must pass a judgement not based on right or wrong, but on natural or unnatural. [8] It is important for a Japanese company operator

---

(7)　Section 4-3-4.

(8)　Rresident Fukujiro Sono of TDK Corporation said in an interview with the author in October, 1981, that he judged something based on whether

to make a constant evaluation of the future business problems of his own company, especially when the management situation is healthy. Many company presidents in Japan cite insight as one of the abilities required for presidency. Those who have insight can afford to roughly understand the other's field of specialization, not fully though they can. Insight is a quality that is beyond knowledge and analytical ability. To cultivate insight, the company head must accumulate experiences in actual business operation and see things, keeping in mind whether they are natural or not.

Determination is the ability to decide on something with confidence and boldness, or even with non-logical thinking if necessary when business situations are uncertain. Determination is indispensable in making a business decision when there is only insufficient information. It is also vital for the company president to select one effective mental image as to uncertain future business situation from among many images, by concentrating his insight. In determining something, the company head must choose one from among the three available alternatives: 1) To go ahead, 2) To cancel and 3) To wait a moment.[9] Determination is increased by experiences and confidence in business operation. If the company head successfully deals with various unstable business situations and gain confidence in his ability, his determination will be further strengthened.

## 2-5.  Entrepreneurship

Entrepreneurship can mean the president's ability in creating for himself discontinuous tension in business context. It also includes the quality to foresee changing environments and decide on a new combination of elements at one's own risk. Entrepreneurship is also a driving force to break off an "inertia" in conventional management

---

it was natural or not. He said, he made a "natural" judgement, not deciding on something based on whether it was good or bad.

(9)  President Katsutaro Kataoka of Alps Electric Co. Ltd., said in an interview with the author in November, 1981, that whenever he faced a decision, he selected one out of three alternatives: to go ahead, to cancel, and to maintain the status quo. Refer sections 4-3-3 and 5-3-3.

practices. The company operator with entrepreneurship participates in the development of new products even when the current method of management centering on stable products can expect a sizable growth of his company. Such a positive attitude comes from his ability in constantly creating new tension in himself. Using this ability, he aims to break the existing framework in pursuit of the optimum. The power to create discontinuous tension is strengthened by past experiences in successful business decision. A company president who had succeeded in his decisions on school selection, getting job, etc. in his private life, and on starting a new project, new product development, etc. in business life, must have gained confidence, becoming optimistic about future success, in addition to enhancing power to create discontinuous tension in himself. Those firms being run by presidents from a lower social class enjoy good busiess performances. Many such presidents and founder-presidents of large enterprises who started their careers from an small business have succeeded in making many critical decisions in the past, so they are confident of their decision-making abilities. Such confidence is a source of power for the company president to create discontinuous tension and entrepreneurship, bringing his company a success.

## 2-6. Generosity, Fine Personality, Ethical Sense and Sense of Responsibility

Generosity is the ability to accept and understand others. It belongs to a broadminded company head who can take others' position into consideration. [10] A generous president allows his executive staff to talk freely without interrupting them. He fully understands what is behind their statements. And he does not begrudge praising them. Where does this generosity come from? The Japanese company head is said to begin showing generosity when he has become free from rivalry against his subordinate executives. In the present-day society in which everything is competition, it is unrealistic to expect in a company president generosity that is similar to a religious mercy. Sense of rival goes out

---

(10)   Section 4-3-5.

and generosity comes on, when the president thinks and believs that his view is more sophysticated and broader than those of his subordinate executives.

Fine personality is a good personal trait. Personal attraction is the power to attract others. Personality is measured not by what one has done, but by what one has not done. Personal attraction comes from being aware of man's weakness or the frailty of human life. An attractive person does his best at work, having the quality of entertaining people around him. An attractive company head with fine personality in Japan does not show off his competence; he must be "somewhat incompetent" in administering his employees. Trust between the company president and his employees is vital for successful personnel management in Japan. Such trust can mean that the company head should sometimes endure incompetent employees, further being "somewhat incompetent" himself. Both fine personality and personal attraction are hard to acquire in a short period of time. A company president, seeking such personal charms, must constantly practice soul-searching and mental training so that he can remove his egotism.

Ethical sense is a respect for morals, while morality is that for socially-accepted rules of behavior. Fairness means one's behavior or judgement is impartial and just. A company operator without ethical and moral senses is feared to make improper decisions, and thereby misleading his company in the long run. If a decision by the president conflicts with social values, it will invite social criticism and endanger his company. Specifically, if the company head is responsible for an environmental pollution problem or involved in an immoral affair with a woman, it will lower his employees' work morale and affect business performances. Fairness of personnel management is essential for business operation. People usually have feeling of fondness or dislike of others. If the company head conducts unfair personnel affairs on his feeling that lacks ethics, he will lose his employees' trust as well as his leadership. Both ethical and moral senses vary with the environment in which one was brought up. An individual from a family in which he was educated in some way about the meaning of human existence or modesty is likely to have acquired ethics and morality.

Sense of responsibility makes someone feel that he is obligated to fulfil a task, and that if he fails to do so, he will be subject to disadvantage or punishment. The company president always feels responsible for developing his company for long and practicing fair distribution of the fruit. He must be ready to resign as president if he becomes unable to continue operating his company for such reasons as a drop in productivity and resultant accumulation of deficits, or frequent labor disputes due to unfair distribution of fruit. An irresponsible company head cannot lead his employees. It is feared that such a president will make a mistake in company management. Sense of responsibility is developed through experiences in doing responsible work at home, in school and in bussiness. Those who have been overprotected by their families are less likely to have strong sense of responsibility.

## 2–7. Systems Approach, Effective Use of Time and Quantitative Thinking

The systems approach concerns the way of viewing a matter as a sub-system of a larger total system. This approach makes possible more scientific and reasonable judgements in business. Suppose a company inquired of several machinery makers about an equipment investment plan for the purpose of labor-saving, and received answers in terms of estimated return on investment. If the highest ROI was ten percent, the sub-optimum will be ten percent even if it is lower than expected. A systems approach will make the company conduct a similar inquiry with other manufactures as well as those in the United States. If all these attempts fail to achieve expected figures, the company must then reconsider the labor-saving plan itself. In this way, the systems approach seeks a total optimum, expanding the scope of one's thinking. It has many advantages such as making it possible to rank several conflicting sub-systems from a broader viewpoint of total system, namely for the purpose of achieving business goals. The systems approach is developed by constant efforts to think of something in a broader framework of space and time. Specifically, the company head must always work out a long-term business plan, in addition to viewing everything from a global point of view.

Effectiveness in using time refers to the ability to handle a matter in a limited time, concentrating mental power, The systems approach helps the company head think of a broader framework in coping with a matter. But, his thinking is limited like others due to the limits of time. He is always faced with limitation of time, so he needs to be constantly aware of important problems so that he can find a solution in a limited time based on a large total system. To achieve this, the president must always aim to identify essential management problems while attending business meetings, reading newspapers or talking with someone, in addition to selecting vital information. Again, for using time effectively, the company operator must always be aware of important problems and continue choosing necessary information.

Quantitative thinking enables the company head to grasp important management aspects through figures. Even if he remembers various financial figures in detail, not knowing important aspects shown in those figures, it does not mean that he is excellent in the ability in quantitative thinking. Important aspects in business operation include the amount of demand for main products, the market share, sales growth rates, sales-profit rates, the break-even point, and financial and personnel expenses, etc.. The knowledge of the break-even point is particularly important to understand the trend of the corporate structure as a whole. In fact, low-growth and smaller firms run by presidents who are exactly aware of their break-even point enjoy good business performances. [11] The quantitative thinking is most used in reading financial indicators. In general terms, the present-day strategic decision-making involves various complex aspects. For passing a comprehensive judgement on such aspects, financial indicators are necessary to integrate complicated figures. For example, various market-related figures such terms as total demand, market share, market prices are reduced to a term of sales by product of the company. To refine the quantitative thinking ability, the top company executive must constantly follow changes in variable and fixed costs, in addition to being aware of the break-even point.

---

(11)  The author has researched into approximately 20,000 small companies jointly with Japan Small Business Corporation several years ago and found that the president being exactly aware of the break-even point of his company made better business performance than those of the others. Also refer section 5-3-5.

## 2-8. Administratorship, Leadership Abilities and Readiness to Do Others a Favor

Administratorship is the ability to efficiently administer his organization as a whole for the purpose of achieving business goals, by enduring continuous tension and keeping in mind such business goals. Administratorship includes strong will, perseverance and calm attitude. These qualities are particularly important to a company operator when he is faced with a serious management crisis. If a technical defect in a new product, which was resulted from the president's decision, caused unrest among the employees, the president must exert his leadership, enduring the situation. Or, if the president is entrusted with a decision on the internal conflict among senior executives over personnel affairs, he must consider alone a possible adjustment of different views. Administratorship alone does not enable innovative management because of its nature of seeking an optimum in a given framework. The ability is useful to the management of the company achieving a stable growth, but is not necessarily useful with the firm requiring innovative management. The ability in enduring continuous tension can be attained more easily by those who have climbed the social ladder, overcoming many difficulties in their youth. Many Japanese company-bred or *Amakudari*-presidents having held various administrative positions have the administratorship quality.

Leadership quality is a combination of various aspects of abilities such as the ability to formulate a long-range management plan, excellent generosity, fine personality, personal attraction, strong confidence, thoughtfulness to others, ethics, fairness and perseverance. The leadership quality cannot function successfully if any of the above abilities is overemphasized. Instead, a balanced use of these abilities is important to the company president. This explains the popular notion in Japan that the leadership means a balanced way of thinking. Leadership can be enhanced by experiences in administering many employees, or serving as division manager or president of an affiliated company.

Readiness to do others a favor includes the practice of trying to understand others' feeling and helping them achieve their hopes. The company president must always know what his executive staff are thinking. [12] For carrying out the logic of *Kashi-Kari* (give and take), the company head must first be aware of the feeling of the executives. If one of the executives has difficulty in getting his daughter married, the president is expected to help her find a prospective husband. Likewise, if another executive has a trouble concerning his work, the president must give him advice. By thus doing favors to his subordinates and obligating them for his favors, the president becomes able to facilitate quick decision in business. The practice of the give-and-take logic is also important in the process of business management and control; the president must constantly offer a helping hand to his employees in anticipation that they will do everything for him when need arises. A truly influential person in Japanese enterprises is one who can afford to constantly do many staffs a favor, and thereby making many persons loyal to him. The readiness to do others a favor can result from constant efforts to please others and know their desires through everyday contacts.

## 2-9.  Health

The health needed by the company president is the state of being tough mentally and physically so that he can work out a long-term vision on the future, make a prompt decision and conduct satisfactory management. Good health is the first and foremost requirement for the company head to demonstrate his abilities. A survey shows that more than 40 percent of company operators in Japan cite health as one of the qualities needed by the presidency. [13] There are no other factors as health that are needed in common by so many company presidents. In smaller enterprises in Japan, physical and mental power of the president serves as a driving force of corporate operation. Health is a necessary condition for the president but is not a sufficient one, although the president who is tough physically and mentally is active in

---

(12)   Sections 4-3-6 and 5-3-6.
(13)   "Toppu Gunzo" (Top Executives), Nippon Keizai Shimbun, Jan. 1979
        ~Aug. 1981.  Refer sections 4-3-8 and 5-3-8.

developing new products or challenging a risk. Some people are born healthy, and other are not, though, the company head can improve his health through such efforts as physical training, leading a steady life, forming good interpersonal relations at work, or substantially delegating his authority. If one remains in the management post for too long, he tends to damage his physical and mental health.

## 2-10. Ability in Collecting Information and Curiosity

The ability to collect information needed by the company head is the ability to collect precise information quickly on ever changing environments both outside and inside the company. [14] The information on outside environments is data for various aspects such as the society, politics, economy, international relations, market, technology, and the present situation and the trend of rival firms. The information on in-house environments refers to the knowledge about such factors as the level of technology, and problems concerning sales, finance and labor management. These information should not be collected at random. Instead, top priority should be given to information on the present and future of the market for a company's main products as well as on technical problems. This is because such a product strategy is a key to successful company operation, being influenced both by ever-changing external environments and the increasing rigidity of in-company conditions. Also important is the knowledge about the relations among informations collected. This means that the company president must have the knowledge on how changing world politics, economy and technology, etc. that look irrelevant to his company, are related to the present and the future of his company's products.

The company president must always make efforts to increase or renew memories built in himself. Not being systematized theoretically, the built-in memories are inscribed in the president's head that come out spontaneously upon receiving a stimulus. These memories, responsive to a new information, are the first criterion for selecting necessary information. If the company head does not renew memories built in

---

(14) Sections 4-3-9, 4-3-10, 5-3-9 and 5-3-10.

himself, he may make an error in selecting information and thus fail in dealing with a new situation. To improve ability to collect information, the company operator must always keep contacts with leaders in various circles in pursuit of new information sources. In addition, he must be always aware of the company's critical problems, integrate the collected information that is directly or indirectly relevant to them and provide his fellows with the newly integrated information.

Curiosity is an interest in novel and unknown things. It is a vital quality for the company head to expand the scope of his knowledge. If he loses interests in things new, his company will stop growing. [15] Business performances of those firms run by executives who are curious about external new things are better than those of others. [16] Management strategy such as new product development and business diversification can result from the curiosity of the company head. Curiosity is not a quality that one has by nature. A company president, who has succeeded in sales of a new product, developed out of his curiosity, will become more active in developing new products, while becoming more curious himself. In fact, many Japanese founder-presidents with rich experiences in new product developments always attach importance to new product development in their business goals.

## 2-11. Summary

Abilities required for a company head in Japan include the quality to accomplish three managerial functions: 1) Thinking out future business visions, 2) Strategic decision-making and 3) Business management and control. A desirable company president must be capable of adjusting himself to a given environment to carry out his managerial duties efficiently, and thereby better contributing to the growth of his company. There exist no standard abilities required in common for company operators.

---

(15)   Edith T. Penrose; *The Theory of the Growth of Firms*, p. 35, Basil Blackwell, 1959.

(16)   Zygmunt A. Piotrowski; *Consistently Successful and Failing Top Business Executives, An Inkblot Test Study* (George Fisk, edited, the Frontiers of Management Psychology p. 26), Harper & Row, 1964.

In our systematization of abilities expected of company heads, such aspects as ambition, sense of duty, philosophy, belief, intuition, imagination, insight, determination and abilities to take a risk and create discontinuous tension play a significant role mainly in thinging out future business vision and strategic decision-making. In contrast, such aspects as generosity, fine personality, personal attraction, ethical sense, morality, sense of responsibility, systems approach, effective use of time, quantitative thinking, abilities to endure continuous tension, leadership and readiness to do others a favor, are useful for strategic decision-making and corporate management and control. Good health and ability in collecting information are vital for the company head to accomplish all of the afore-mentioned three managerial functions.

Finally, I would like to give simple definitions of the above aspects of abilities. Ambition is a desire that appears beyond one's ability. It can contribute greatly to the improvement of business performances. A management-related belief is similar to a religious belief or self-confidence. But for confidence in himself, the company president cannot lead his employees. Intuition is the power of the mind to understand something without logical reasoning. It can be refined by experiences and confidence. Insight is the power to judge something keeping in mind whether it is natural or unnatural. Determination is the ability to decide on something with confidence and boldness, or even with non-logical thinking when necessary. The company president is always required to select one from among three available alternatives: 1) To go ahead, 2) To cancel and 3) To wait a moment. Entrepreneurship refers to the ability in creating tension and challenging new things constantly at one's own risk. Personal attraction comes from efforts to understand man's weakness or the frailty of human life, so do one's best at work and constantly entertain others. The most important aspect of ethics needed by the company head in Japan is fairness of personnel management. The systems approach is the way of viewing a matter as a subsystem of a total system. Effective use of time requires the ability to identify important problems in a limited time. Quantitative thinking by the company operator seeks accurate understanding of the break-even point which shows the situation of a business corporation as a whole. Administratorship is the ability to endure continuous tension. Leadership is a combination of various aspects of abilities such as generosity, personal attraction, confidence, ethical and moral senses. Readiness to do others a favor includes the practice of trying to understand others' feeling as well as pleasing them. Health is a necessary condition, not a sufficient condition to become a desirable company head. In order to improve ability to collect information, the company president must always identify critical problems, while increasing or renewing memories which are built in himself.

# 3

# Interviewing Survey of Presidents in Big Firms

——An Interview Survey of Presidents of 64 Electric Equipment Manufacturing
Firms Listed on Tokyo and Osaka Stock Exchanges——

## 3-1. Introduction

For this interview survey we first prepared preliminary questions,
based on the assumptions about the president's decision-making ability,
decision-making process, etc. as described in Chapter 1, 2. This battery
of questions was revised after a pre-test on 9 presidents in different
sections of Japanese industry. Then we interviewed 64 presidents using
the same list of 42 questions during a nine month period from June
1970 to February 1971. Interviews were conducted with one president
by two or three interviewers with recordings made by all the interviewers to prevent mistakes. On the average an interview lasted one hour
and a half. Since the listed electric equipment manufacturers totaled
130 firms on both the Tokyo and Osaka Stock Exchanges our
interviews covered about one half of all presidents.

## 3-2. Qualitative Analysis of the Behavior and Ways of Thinking of Presidents

In this section we present a qualitative analysis of presidents' daily
lives, forecasts and views on the economy and society, attitudes toward
group administration and human resource development, relations with
other executives, and recognition of the problems and particularities

of their firms—all which affect their decision-making—and from this analysis several hypotheses will be drawn about the behavior and ways of thinking of the presidents of today.

### 3-2-1. The Daily Life of Presidents

From the answers to Q. 2—"What newspaper do you usually read?" —we found that on average an executive subscribes to 3.6 newspapers. The general dailies include the Asahi (36 persons), Mainichi (17), Yomiuri (12), Sankei (6), Nikkan Sports (4), Tokyo (3), Akahata (2), Hōchi (1) and local papers (4) and the business newspapers include the Nihon Keizai (50), Nikkan Kōgyō(34), Nihon Kōgyō (22), Dempa (12), Denki (3), Kabushiki (2) and other (1). In total, 58 persons responded and the number of papers amounted to 209. From this we could have a working hypothesis as following:
*Hypothesis 3-1* : The concern of presidents is in the ratio of 3 (economics) to 2 (general news).

Ten presidents took neither the Asahi nor the Mainichi—the most popular among the general dailies—, of whom eight were founder or successor presidents. It may be said by this that owner presidents have a stronger interest in economic affairs than in general news in comparison with other types of presidents. Fourteen read at least two papers from among the Asahi, Mainichi, Yomiuri and Sankei (general papers), of whom twelve were very talkative taking more than one hour and a half for the interview. Hence we felt that those presidents who absorb a large volume of information are inclined to express more.

Previously we had thought that the presidents of top-class firms read foreign papers such as the Wall Street Journal, Die Zeit or L'Express, but unexpectedly the papers they read were mainly Japanese dailies. However, their managerial targets were quite different, as will be explained later. In particular the presidents of medium-large firms have unique targets. This may be because, though having the same information, they grasp problems in a different way. Thus we could have:
*Hypothesis 3-2* : Corporate presidents in Japan today, though receiving the same information, have individual abilities for making different and unique decisions based on information stored in their memories and

on different ways of thinking.

For Q. 17—"What periodical do you read regularly?"—economics-related magazines were overwhelmingly numerous and few answered literary and general news magazines. Academic journals of a techno-logical nature were quite numerous. The economic magazines included: the Diamond (16 persons), Tōyō Keizai (16), President (8), Economist (7), Nikkei Business (2), Management (2) and others; literary and general news magazines: Bungei Shunjū (14), Chuō Kōron (7) and others; academic journals: the Electronics, Denki Tsūshin Gakukaishi, Denki Gakukaishi and Telephone Daily read by a total of 8 persons. Thus their interest in economic and technological periodicals seems to be three times larger than general news magazines. From this result and the answers to Q. 2 we can say that the presidents in this industry have a great interest in economic and technological information, but are little interested in changes in society or in social thoughts.

To Q. 3—"How many times were you the go-between for marriages last year?"—the answers were: none (16 persons), once (10), twice (11), three times (9), four (2), five (2) and six or more (4). And to the question "were you willing to play that role" 20 presidents answered "I refuse in principle," 16 "I actively do so," and 16 "I do not always refuse if requested." The reasons for refusal were "recog-nition of particular individuals is undesirable," "doing something out of self-interest is not right," etc., while the reasons for positive behavior were "loyalty to the firm is increased," "it's a joy to see employees' growth," etc.

Judging from these answers there appear to be two types of presidents: those who seek active contact with their employees to create better relations, and those who diminish personal contact to maintain impar-tiality. In the case of owner presidents the former type is more numerous (12 out of the 16 who actively served as go-betweens were owner presidents), while among company-bred and *Amakudari* presidents the latter type is more common (11 out of the 20 who were against acting as go-betweens were company-bred or *Amakudari* presidents). These attitudes towards the role as a go-between correspond with attitudes toward home life. When asked about how they spent Sundays

(Q.4), 14 persons of the 16 presidents of the first type answered something other than golf, while 12 of the 20 presidents of the second type mentioned golf.

To Q.4—"How do you spend Sundays?: golf, fishing, spending time with the family (dining, theatre), doing company business, attending various ceremonies and celebrations, gardening or, other?"—the answers were golf (55), gardening (15), spending time with the family (13), doing company business (10), reading and writing (7), resting (6), fishing (2), listening to music (2), playing *Igo* (1), drawing (1), *Nagauta* song (1), tennnis (1), and hiking (1). The reasons given for playing golf, which received the highest number of answers, were to keep healthly and for change of atmosphere. Those who took work to home totaled 10 persons or 15% of the total, while 6 persons (less than 10%) mentioned inactive recreation—gardening, being with family, resting. Thus we could say presidents utilize their leisure time very effectively.

To Q.5—"Are you a member of a rotary club, lions club or some similar organization? And if Yes, please select one of the reasons given below: a) many friends are members, b) I can meet many friends, c) social service, d) much information is available."—twenty-two presidents answered Yes, about one-third of a total of 64 persons, and the reasons given were: a)–3 persons, b)–6, c)–3 and d)–9. Since the reasons "to obtain information" and "to see many friends" were numerous, this suggests that business is always an important consideration in joining a club. Furthermore this is supported by the fact that a number of the presidents replied that growth of their business was itself a social service.

To Q.6—"If you are invited by a presidents group of which you are a members to travel abroad for a general "observation tour" would you go?"—50 persons answered No. Some presidents replied that they had participated in such aimless trips before they took office. This also shows that, after becoming president, they focus on their goals and avoid rambling acts. Thus from Qs. 4, 5 and 6 we have:

*Hypothesis 3–3*: The daily life of presidents in present Japan is of a positive and goal-directed nature, rather than being filled with inactive rest and an enjoyment of leisure itself.

To Q. 12—"Which type of high school teacher do you think is preferable?: teacher A instructs low-achievement students with perseverance and force; B instructs them by finding one's personality and fostering it."—53 persons chose B and 6 said both A and B are necessary. Thus almost all supported teacher B. However, not a few persons wished for some degree of directed instruction while agreeing in general with the practices prevalent today. For example typical responses of this type were: "This type B represents the common idea of implying negation of the past and hope in the future, but the Spartan type of education should also be taken into account" (president of Origin-Denki, maker of semiconductor) and "Teacher B type is desirable but leadership power is also necessary as a whip spurring students toward making efforts." (Toyo Communication, maker of communication equipment). The reason for choosing type A is that directed education is necessary because personality is not yet fully developed in high school students.

To Q. 13—"Choose one person you think most suitable as an executive from among a) Iyeyasu, b) Nobunaga, c) Shingen and d) Kenshin" (these four are very famous warrior statesmen in Japanese history; Iyeyasu was known for his perseverance, Nobunaga for his decisiveness, Shingen for his mightiness and Kenshin for his preciseness)—Iyeyasu was mentioned by an overwhelmingly large number (46 persons), followed by Nobunaga (8), Kenshin (6), Shingen (2) and uncertain (2). This question was devised to distinguish between the importance placed on stability and that on growth assuming that Iyeyasu and Kenshin would fall into one group and Nobunaga and Shingen into another, but this result did not occur. An interesting point is that 6 out of the 8 presidents choosing Nobunaga were owner presidents.

To Q. 15—"What do you think about religion: a) earnest, b) not so earnest, c) indifferent and d) unnessary?"—the answers showed 37 persons "not so earnest," 17 "indifferent," 9 "earnest" and 1 "unnecessary." Even among those answering "not so earnest" there were many who said having a sense of humility is necessary. "A religious mind is necessary as humility is necessary because we are but one link in a long chain of humanity" (Weston Onki, audio parts). Also those presidents answering "earnest" asserted that religion even if not directly related to business helps develop a sense of modesty. "A religious mind prevents haughtiness and so I would like to be serious about my religion" (Nippon Elect., leading communication equipment maker).

### 3-2-2. Forecasts and Attitudes toward Socio-Economic-Changes

Here we shall examine what predictions the presidents made concerning changes in the social economy and what plans they were considering in relation to these predictions.

To Q. 20—"Speaking generally, without reference to your own firm, do you think such ultra-radical actions which disregard the existing rules of labor unions and the such will arise within enterprises?"—52 presidents answered "will not" and 10 "will." The reasons for "will not" were: workers must earn a living unlike college students; their standand of living is improving; they are conscious of being responsible citizens; they feel they belong to the middle class; stockholding employees are numerous; there are many opportunities to eliminate dissatisfaction; radicals will be assimilated in the seniority order system. On the other hand the reasons cited for "will arise" were: enterprisers are concerned only about efficiency and results; new ideas from educational circles are beginning to have an effect; employees are self-confident about finding jobs elsewhere. Rebellious actions include quitting in groups, slow downs, etc. Thus we have:

*Hypothesis 3-4*: Most executives of today feel that ultra-radical moves that may destroy a firm will not occur because employees regard the enterprises in which they work as part of their lives.

To Q. 18—"What will be the state of Japanese-Chinese trade five years from now; a) remarkably improved, b) improved, c) unchanged, d) uncertain?"—44 persons among 66 answered "improved," followed by "unchanged" (10), "remarkably improved" (5) and "uncertain." The major reasons for "improved" were the views that "the force of natural development toward a global economy will break artificial, political or ideological walls" (Kokusai Elect., radio communication equipment) and "the economic conditions in China working to raise the standard of living and the attractiveness of China as a market for Japanese goods will work to change the political climate" (Shiba

Elect., broadcasting equipment). Another common answer was that "relations between the same oriental peoples will develop" (Oki Elect., leading communication equipment maker). It is interesting that these views were held by presidents who had resided in China before or after World War II.

Next, reasons given for "unchanged" were: "the present state will not change as long as the restoration of diplomatic ties is a precondition and political restrictions exist" (Hitachi Ltd., all-round maker of electric equipment) and "Mao Tsu-tung emphasizes self development and has no wish for rapid industrialization" (Sanken Elect.). These opinions were given by many who were engaged in trade with China directly or indirectly.

To Q. 19—"Do you think revaluation of the yen will take place in three years: Yes, No or uncertain?"—a substantial number, 28 out of 64 respondents, said Yes, 22 No and 14 "uncertain." A typical reason for Yes was "our balance of payments will continue to be in the black on account of the vitality of the Japanese, and the yen revaluation will become inevitable after the foreseen fourth stage of liberalization" (Tokyo Elect., medium-large maker of office machines). Similarly, "our surplus may reach 7 or 8 billion dollars because of our superior vitality, deligence and knowledge" (Alps Elect., leading maker of electronic parts, esp. tuners). Most of the presidents predicting a revaluation were those engaged in active export trade. On the other hand reasons given for "No" included: "Japans's economic power will not become very strong; her growth will not be as it has been to date because of rising wages, worsening labor-management relations and stagnation of exports" (Meisei Elect., medium-large maker of communication equipment). The presidents who answered No and "uncertain" were mostly those in large firms or medium-large firms with few exports. A view interesting to note is "executives of large enterprises have thorough knowledge of accounting within business but little knowledge of national finance or international finance" (Tokyo Elect.).

From the above Questions 18 and 19 (which were asked before the "Nixon Shock" in August 1971 and the establishment of ties with China in September 1972 by the Tanaka cabinet), we have:

*Hypothesis 3-5*: Generally, presidents of Japanese firms have comprehensive forecasts about the future and especially good insight on matters relevant to present business operations. Insight for decision-making can be highly developed only through actual experience in business.

Q. 23—"In marketing a new product, do you consider using additional channels?"—Yes was given by 47 presidents, No by 11 and "it depends on the case" by the rest. Most of the presidents who answered Yes contemplated new channels after considering whether or not existing channels were sufficient. Manufacturers of household electric appliances seemed most active in developing new channels.

Most of the presidents who answered No were parts manufactures, including manufacturers of communication equipment parts delivered to the Telegraph & Telephone Public Corporation(Nippon Telegraph and Telephone, now) However, most manufacturers of parts related to household appliances and small electric calculators answered Yes.

To explain this point in greater detail, "We have always developed new channels, for example, bicycle shops to handle batteries, electric service shops to sell radios, heating equipment shops for oil stoves and office machine shops for calculators" (Sanyo Elect., a leading household appliances maker); "To market new products we consider banks, insurance companies, souvenir shops, and book stores" (Crown Radio, medium-large household appliance maker); "We actively consider development of new channels for new products, either as an addition to those already existing or as a different type of channel" (Matsushita Elect., largest household appliance maker).

On the other hand reasons given for "No" answers were: Development of new channels is difficult because our products are mainly communication-related and of a technological nature, 50% for T & T and 50% for personal use; in fact new dealers handling our automatic vending machines for milks were unsuccessful (Oki Elect.); "Other routes are impossible because our products are parts" (Sanken Elect.); "We don't consider developing new channels because our goods are delivered directly to T & T"(Meisei Elect.). Thus we have:

*Hypothesis 3-6*: New marketing routes are generally considered in conjunction with new product development and the firms most actively developing new routes manufacture household electric appliances, followed by parts manufacturers, while least active are makers of communication equipment and parts.

Q. 25—"When or if you introduce a new computer, do you select it mainly on the basis of economic considerations or in terms of its future possibilities?"— 32 presidents choose future possibilities, 19 economic considerations and 13 "depends on the case." Generally speaking, the reasons given for "economic considerations" were clearer than those given for "future possibilities." Answers given for "future possibilities" included: "Greater efficiency or reduction in costs is unsupportable at present, so considering a computer's future potentialities it was introduced" (Fuji Electrochemical, electronic parts manufacturer); "We wish to produce control systems using computers based not on economic considerations but on future growth" (Origin Elect.). Reasons given for economic considerations included: "We introduce a new computer after considering efficiency of inventory control, process control or the handling of changes of delivery date" (Meisei Elect.). A "depends upon the case" answer was: Economic calculations of cost accounting, and future possibilities for technical use" (Nippon Elect.).

Q. 27—"Have you any system to delegate your responsibilities over an extended period of time, e.g. when you go abroad or if you become ill?"—Yes (49) and No (18). An interesting answer was "I am always thinking of how to train the next president; I'm always saying that a president should train the next president, a department-chief the next department-chief, and a section-chief the next section-chief, otherwise he himself cannot be a good leader" (Sanyo Elect., leading household appliance and calculator manufacturer).

In connection with this we asked "What type of person do you think desirable for your successor?" Answers varied but can be divided into personality-related and ability-related. Among the personality traits mentioned were: moral repute, tolerance, generosity and trust. Ability-related traits included: decisiveness, insight, ability to maintain an overall balanced outlook, the ability to recognize the actual state of things, the ability to take action, and good health. Among these features decisiveness and insight were cited most frequently.

Interesting statements included: "A president must be able to under-

stand the specialities of others, not only one's own" (Sanyo Elect.);
"Generosity and persuasiveness are necessary and therefore one must
not express all that he wishes to say" (Clarion Co., audio equipment);
"Generous accepting persons are more important than clever persons
because clever persons can be used as a president's subordinates" (Casio
Computer, manufacturer specialzing in small calculators); "Persons
capable of team work, especially those who can lead the specialists"
(Tensho Elect., manufacturer of moulding parts). Interesting to note,
is that all the presidents holding these views were founder or owner
presidents. From these answers we have:

*Hypothesis 3–7*: The ideal president is one who is generous and accepting of others, has deep insight, and is decisive in handling matters.

Next, to study the attitudes about the overseas advancement of
Japanese firms, we asked, "What do you think about the issues in
international relations connected with the overseas activities of Japanese
firms?" A forward-looking opinion was that firms in foreign countries
must be managed on the premise that eventually they will become local
firms. The most common response was that advance into developing
countries should involve give and take where Japanese firms first offer
technical assistance to raise the level of the host country and later
receive the profits on the invested capital. The view that Japanese
firms must advance into developing countries because of low wages was
rarely expressed.

"Being prepared to become a company of the host country is important,
and technology which is in the national interest of the host country
should be transferred to it. The entrance of American businesses entailed
outflows of capital but the firms remained American and hence failed"
(Nippon Elect.). "Whether it be a joint venture or a 100 percent
controlled firm, realization that it is a firm of the country in which
it is, is necessary. We do not discriminate against the citizens of a
country whether it be for a management post or for regular employment"
(Matsushita Elect.). "Management that gains the respect of the local
citizens is necessary. Profits gained in a region should be reinvested
there, and not be be brought back to Japan, because gaining trust is of
greater concern than making profits" (Nippon Columbia Co., general

audio equipment). These are examples of the most progressive opinions.

Next, representative arguments for giving technological assistance were: "In advancing into southeast Asia we form joint ventures and teach techniques;an attitude of gaining from the beginning is unsuitable; in the United States, however, we aim for profits from the start" (Iwatsu Elect., medium-large manufacturer of telephones and other communications equipment); "In developed nations we seek technical cooperation in terms of an international division of labor; in developing countries we give technical aid." (Yushin Co., electric auto motive parts); "Firms should be set up through mergers to decrease resistance and low level technology should be transferred" (Ushio Elect., lighting fixture manufacturers).

Even those presidents who did mention "low wages" added that this merit was losing importance due to excess competition and the resultant rises in wages. An interesting fact here was that progressive ideas were mainly seen in presidents of large firms, while desire for immediate profits was seen among medium-large firms, notably with a founder president. Thus we have:

*Hypothesis* 3-8: The idea held by most presidents concerning the establishment of firms in developing countries is to first provide technological aid and then profit on invested capital, based on the idea of give and take.

## 3-2-3. Attitudes of Presidents toward Group Management and Human Resource Development

Let's examine presidential decision-making in detail.

Q.24—"When a plan you think necessary, e. g. equipment expansion to increase competitiveness, is opposed by the majority of the managing directors, do you force your idea through or do you postpone making a decision in order to persuade them and make a final decision with less opposition?"—9 presidents mentioned forced decision, persuasion was cited by 36 and 19 said it depends on the situation.

10 presidents said that such opposition by a majority of directors did not occur. The reasons for this were: 1) informal discussions prior to the meeting were conducted by the president; 2) proposals were made by the executives themselves; and 3) such opposition just never occurred.

Examples of the first case are: "I have talks prior to the meeting so as to prevent opposition; executives do not oppose unless there is fear of something." (Takamizawa Elect., communication equipment, esp. relays): "Prior consultations are always made" (Aiwa Co., household appliances, and Origin Elect.); "A directors' meeting is held to propose what has already been agreed upon prior to the meeting" (Toyo Communiction).

As for the second reason: "In order to prevent opposition I first draw out proposals from the executives, having noted their personality traits, and generally, matters go as I intend" (Teikoku Tsushin Kogyo, electronic parts); "In decision-making my vice-president becomes the chairman and while I observe, the *other members* first express their opinions" (Omron Tateishi Elect., electronic control systems).

The third reason is as follows. "No direct opposition exists because capital investment is one link in a long-range plan which is prepared by the staff"—an organization reason—(Hitachi Ltd.); "Because there are few executives, opinions converge with certain boundaries" (Tokyo Elect., medium-large office machine manufacturer); "Since I am the founder, communicattion with executives is always perfect and therefore little opposition arises" (Denki Kogyo Co., communication parts); "There is harmony and respect and hence such opposition seldom occurs" (Sharp Corp., household appliance and calculator manufacturer); "Communication between the president and the executives prevents opposition; in fact an investment plan involving 2 billion yen was carried out in only four months" (Sanken Elect.); "I am always desirous of greater opposition to my views; a feeling of separation according to divisions is strong among the directors, and opinions on matters outside their divisions are few by reason of uncertainty" (Aiden Co., lighting apparatus manufacturer). Thus lack of opposition is attributed to the structural organization in which the executives find themselves.

There were 36 presidents out of the 64 who used persuasion, the reason being to have executives take responsibility for carrying out the decisions. "Decisions are made by the group in order to avoid possible errors" (Oki Elect.); "Loyal cooperation is impossible to expect under conditions of forced decisions, and executives will not take responsibility in the event of bad results" (Meisei Elect.); "Majority rule does not apply to business but I make efforts to avoid forcing through my own decisions; I entrust decision-making to the others to make them responsible" (Nippon Elect.).

Then, for how long a period are decisions postponed? The length of time used for persuasion varied. "I try to use persuasion right then and there on each occasion because our growth depends on mobility" (Sanyo Elect.); "One day at the longest, so decisions are almost forced through in reality" (Nippon Koden Kogyo Co., medical instruments); "Formerly I pushed through my decisions but recently I postpone them for two or three days, maybe because of my age; and recently, I appointed the person who gave the strongest opposition as manager of a plant construction project" (Clarion Co.); "In introducing IC's, talks continued half a year" (Sanken Elect.); "My mottto is to attain a goal step by step and so I spend much time reaching a conclusion" (Iwasaki Elect., lighting fixtures); "Friction resulting from coercion is a waste; so I make decisions gradually, although I am always thinking about speeding matters up" (Fujitsu Ltd., largest computer manufacturer).

There were no reasons given that mentioned benefits to be gained from forced decision-making. "The results of forced decisions are doubtful, yet there is no need to follow majority opinion since complete unanimity cannot lead to something new" (Shiba Elect.). Thus the rule of majority decision is opposed. "Even after a forced decision is made, strong leadership that can make people follow is necessary; yet actually persuasion is used" (Yokoo Mfg. Co., communication parts).

From the above, we could have:

*Hypothesis 3-9*: The reason a president permits group management is to make the executives responsible for the decision, and not for the sake of developing their abilities.

To Q.26—"When a seminar of a technological nature is held, do you send personnel in charge of accounting of sales to attend it?" —27 presidents responded Yes, 17 answered No, and 20 said "it depends." This question was based on our idea that for human resource development specialists of the future need competence in two or more quite different fields, for example electric engineering plus accounting. Therefore presidents answering Yes were perhaps more interested in human resource development.

Among the reasons given for sending personnel to attend these seminars was that in these times of rapid innovation, an understanding of technology by administrators is indispensable. "Techno-economists who can understand both technology and economics are necessary; in fact in our firm technological forecasts are made by personnel from non-engineering backgrounds" (Hitachi Ltd.); "Generally the separation of engineers and managers creates an unfavorable business environment. The higher the post, the better one must understand one's co-workers. Therefore I send personnel to the seminars" (Shiba Elect.); "I would send them to suminar; at present accountants and other personnel are alway sent to factories so that they can learn about the technology that is being employed" (Meisei Elect.); "Generally speaking knowledge should be absorbed from sources outside the firm, and in our firm managers are sent abroad to study technological advances" (Tamura Seisakusho Co., manufacturer of transformers); "I want to send personnel because in our firm technical education is also given to general-affairs personnel" (Nippon Signal Co., manufacturer of signals); "Specialized education in universities is of little use; we send our personnel to such a seminar which is more useful." (Ando Elect., manufacturer of measuring equipment); "We send staff because our firm operates in all phases of development, manufacturing and sales" (Iwatsu Elect.); "Our personnel attend because the marketing division includes export, domestic sales, design and research sections" (Foster Elect., audio parts such as speakers); "An adequate estimation of orders is impossible unless accountants can understand engineering" (Tensho Elect.). Thus, the general view is that technological knowledge is indispensable for management personnel.

On the other hand, the presidents answering No did not appear to give constructive enterprising reasons. "I think it is easier for engineers to learn management skills than it is for managers to learn technological skills" (Omron Tateishi Elect.); "Sending engineers holds top priority, followed by managers who can understand technology" (Hitachi Koki Co., motor tool); "Only engineers are sent because they must make forecasts regarding future technology" (Nippon Columbia Co.). Thus for the priority of sending engineers any constructive reason is not given. The last two firms are Hitachi-affiliated. Generally, Hitachi-line firms value technology. Thus we have:

*Hypothesis 3-10*: In this age of rapid technological innovations, many presidents want management to be able to understand engineering concepts and are desirous of having management be considered as a total system that includes both technology and economic.

Q.28—"Suppose that a section chief submitted a proposal to his department chief and the latter, though not without a fear of the risks involved, agreed to give it as a try in terms of its being a learning experience, but the project resulted in failure. Do you approve of the department chief's decision?"—Through this question we wanted to know a president's attitude toward the human resource development of subordinates. 36 said they would "approve," 12 said it would "depend on the situation," and 16 said they would "disapprove." Thus, there was an appreciable number of presidents who regarded developing abilities as important.

The answers giving the strongest support were: "Trial and error is better than non-action; trial brings about results other than the original aims; shrewd men hesitate to take action out of fear of failure but this is wrong" (Sanken Elect.); "I always advise staff to go forward without fear of failure, especially in research work" (Shindengen Elect.). Most of the presidents answering "it depends" overlooked small mistakes by a department-chief if the failures don't bring great damage to the firm. "Approval and disapproval depends on the degree of the mistake: if small it can be chalked off as a learning experience"(Hoshiden Elect., electronic parts); "I approve if the matter does not affect the firm's business results" (Iwasaki Elect.); "I approve unless it affects the whole company even if I have not been notified beforehand" (Nihon Kohden Kogyo Co.); "Small mistakes are permissible but large ones are not" (Ando Elet.); "Where the damage is great, I can't approve; if trifle, I approve for learning purposes (Casio Computer).

Other "it depends" answers were: "I will not assign responsibility but hope for better results in the future" (Toa Elect., measuring equipment); "Approvable, but a department chief should advise a section chief on such an occasion" (Tensho Elect.); "I always tell a department chief or upper level staff to have their own philosophy; if they judge and agree to the proposals of their subordinates based on this philosophy and give advice later, I give my approval" (Alps Elect.); "l will overlook it but make sure the department chief has the section chief find out the cause of failure and not to repeat it" (Iwatsu Elect.); "Approvable if the said risk contributes to cost-reduction, community development, etc.; but the basis for such decisions should be indicated by the president" (Takamizawa Elect.). Thus an active attitude of the department chief is a major precondition.

The "disapprove" presidents gave the reason that in enterprises the mere aim of training does not render failures permissible. "Enterprises do not exist to train; it is wrong to use business for such a purpose" (Omron Tateishi Elect.); "Education teaches the avoidance of risks; small firms such as our's are always operating at a risk and cannot afford to engage in this type of education" (Shibaura Engineering Works, motor parts); "It is nonsense to seek an educational experience through that for which a risk is foreseen; education involves things that are certain" (Toyo Communication); "Learning takes place even without experiencing a failure; a big failure might be serious" (Meisei Elect.). Thus we have:

*Hypothesis 3-11*: Most presidents will overlook small business mistakes by subordinates and consider them a learning experience unless the firm suffers a great loss.

To Q. 29—"which type of president do you think is better?: President A who avoids making proposals as much as possible, and draws out ideas from others, judges their reasonableness and carries them out, or B who thinks that the president should make proposals on important matters, prepare concrete plans and carry them out forcefully"—A was chosen by 19 persons, B by 21 and "it depends on the situation" by 24. The situations mentioned were broadly divided into 1) discrepancy between the ideal and reality, 2) size of the business and 3) the subject being considered. In other words, 1) A is better but actually B must be taken, 2) A is more common in large firms and B in small firms, and 3) A for daily decision-making and B for emergencies.

The answer "ideally A, actually B" was given by the presidents of the following 10 companies: Denki Kogyo Co., Sanken Elect., Nohmi Bosai Kogyo Co. (accident prevention equipment), Yokoo Mfg. Co., Shindengen Elect., Fuji Electrochemical, Aiden Co., Nippon Columbia Co., Teikoku Tsushin Kogyo Co. and Kyoei Sangyo Co. (moulded parts, esp. printed circuit).

The presidents who replied "A for large firms, B for small" were the presidens of Nippon Electric Ind. (medium-large manufacturer of heavy equipment), Oki Elect., Kokusai Elect., Teac Corp. (audio products) and Takamizawa Elect.

The presidents who mentioned "the subject being considered" said: "Generally A but in cases where a decision must be made between two choices, B; but B's attitude does not encourage the development of the potential of the staff if always taken" (Sanyo Elect.); "My own proposals pertain to such matters as equipment, organization, morale, atmosphere, ideology or discipline; other matters are presented by others" (Mitsumi Elect., leading electronic parts manufacturer); "I myself make proposals regarding management and organization" (Aiden Co.); "A for that which is incomprehensible and B for what is understandable" (Alps Elect.); "A for daily matters and B for vital matters" (Nihon Koden Kogyo Co.); "A for smaller problems and B for serious ones, because for the latter I take the risks" (Nippon Elect.); "A for matters such as product standards" (Toyo Dry Battery, dry battery); "A in cases where a learning experience is desirable, and B when a mistake must be avoided" (Weston Onki); "A for general matters and B when a division of opinions is foreseeable" (Iwasaki Elect.).

Beside these, interesting remarks included "It depends on the environment, especially the composition of top management—that is, A when many of the executives are progressive thinkers and B when such persons are absent" (Yushin Co.); "A for firms during a stable period and B for unstable times" (Meisei Elect.).

Next, the reasons for choosing A were: "In such a large organization as ours my proposals are taken as orders and so I usually say nothing, but I take care so that the many proposals do not result in maintaining the status quo" (Hitachi Ltd,); "one cannot understand proposals from others unless he has the ability to make proposals himself, but in my firm the proposals of the staff generally reflect my views because my way of thinking influences the staff" (JEOL Ltd., scientific instruments such as electronic microscopes).

The reasons given for choosing B were: "Type B is inevitable in our small-scale firm because the products are diversified and competition is severe" (Shibaura Engineering Works); "I will first present my views as a basis for discussion and revisions; it is unwise to only wait for opinion" (Tamura Seisakusho Co.); "I make proposals myself and see what happens; opposition may arise" (Pioneer Elect. Corp., audio products such as stereos). From the answers to Q. 29 we have:

*Hypothesis 3-12*: Most presidents believe in group management and human resource development as an ideal, but actually take cotrol. This is especially true in small firms or when emergency decision-making is required.

And the result of this Question 29 agree with Hypothesis 3-28— drawn from a quantitative analysis to be explained later—"the larger the scale, the more the president is inclined toward group management and human resource development."

To Q. 38—"Do you remove from his post a sales manager who has failed to attain sales targets for two successive years, or let him try once more after advising him?"—21 presidents answered "let him try again," 18 "remove him" and 25 "it depends on the situation."

Among those answering "it depends on the situation," the reason given most frequently was that a sales manager could remain in his position if the failure resulted from a product's relation to its markets, but he would be removed if his performance was the cause. Examples are: "He will be discharged if he lacks capability in terms of handling the products or the social situation" (Toyo Communication); "Of course I will remove him if he lacks ability, although the economic situation will be taken into account" (Kokusai Elect.); "He shall not be transferred if the cause lies in market trends or if he has leadership ability with the sales personnel" (Mitsumi Elect.); "In our firm the performance of the sales department depends on the quality of affiliated sales outlets and so a failure in reaching goals alone will not necessarily result in a transfer to a lower post" (Toa Elect.); "Factors such as a recession or local condition shall be considered, and if inability is the cause he will be removed" (Anritsu Elect., communication equipment such as phones); "Changes of posts are not determined solely by target attainment because our firm depends on customers; in our firm market shares are the standards for appraisal" (Teikoku Tsushin Kogyo). Two other presidents expressed similar views, making a total of 8 persons.

Again many expressed the opinion that a failure in fulfilling a goal was the responsibility of top management. "If the reason for the inefficiency is evident, the president is responsible, but if a failure has occurred despite favorable conditions, the sales manager shall be removed" (Tokyo Cosmos Elect., manufacturer of electronic parts such as small variable condensers); "If lack of ability is the cause I criticize myself for my mistake in placing this person and I will not blame the manager, but will transfer him" (Tensho Elect.); "The president must discover the cause, or else others will repeat the same mistake" (Yokoo Mfg. Co.); "The president is responsible if the goal was too high" (Sanyo Elect., medium-large manufacturer of motors); "Top management should also take some measures, for example, visit customers with him; if this is still fruitless, he should be removed" (Takamizawa Elect.); "We send staff members from the home office to help offices with poor sales performances" (Clarion Co.). These opinions recognize the importance of the responsibility of the president and top management.

Other unique ideas among the "it depends on the situation" answers were: "It is better not to transfer persons where a firm is highly specialized; our firm deals with government agencies, handles old products and new products, so that appraisal is made according to improvements in sales growth and contribution to profits, etc." (Anritsu Elect.); "For a person in a new post, attainment of targets is difficult for two years; where there is failure in an old post the sales manager will be removed; a new target that takes into account past performance is given to a new manager of an office with a poor performance record" (Sanyo Elect.); "Our firm respects quality control, and thus if there is a problem concerning this, advice is given; otherwise the sales manager will be transferred" (Toko Elect. Corp., transformer manufacturer).

Among the presidents who said they would not remove the sales manager, 3 persons mentioned "a shortage of capable personnel" and 3 others that "goal attainment is not the sole measure." A interesting response was: "Sales managers are not dealt with in terms of red-ink figures alone; often a manager is not responsible for failures; our policy is rather to praise successful managers" (Nippon Elect.).

Notable reasons given for "remove him" were: "We don't let an unsuccessful manager try again; but managers with performance records beyond set targets will be transferrd, too" (Teac Corp.); "The manager will be transferred but care is taken so as not to prevent hurt feelings or a sense of isolation; we give advice on the presnt post and transfer him after he becomes able to attain our target" (Nohmi Bosai Kogyo Co.). And 3 presidents replied that transfers would take place but the housing situation would be taken into consideration. Thus we have:

*Hypothesis 3-13*: Presidents of today are very careful in their treatment of managers of business offices. When a target is unmet they see whether they are responsible and whether the cause lies with top management, and even when the responsibility does rest there, they do not transfer personnel for the sole reason of failure to attain a target.

To Q.39—"Which do you appreciate more: the attainment of a target by a veteran department chief or a failure by a new department chief after great efforts?"—22 presidents chose the veteran deprtment chief, 18 the new department chief and 24 persons answered, "it depends on the situation."

First many of the presidents answering, "it depends on the situation" replied that appraisals of department chiefs are not simply made according to the extent of target attainment. For example: "An appraisal of performance is not done in terms of target figures alone; attitudes, ability and willingness are also taken into account" (Yushin Co.); "We seek the reasons behind everything; targets are a artificial yard-sticks; we do not evaluate highly the achievement of a 100 million yen sales by someone who does so without making an effort" (Toyo Dry Battery); "Mere achievement does not exactly reflect the abilities of a middle manager; many other considerations are made" (Fuji

Electrochemicals); "I do not think it appropriate to relate targets with numerical values alone; other unquantifiable targets should be considered" (Hitachi Ltd.). Other noteworthy reasons given for "it depends on the situation," were: "I appraise a new head in terms of targets set by top management and the veteran in terms of goals set by himself" (Aiwa Co., audio equipment such as microphones); "I evaluate the new chief as to whether his future is promising or not, and the veteran in terms of the short run" (Anritsu Elect.); "I appreciate the new chief if the next term is promising, but I generally value high performance" (Iwatsu Elect.); "I don't appreciate either; attainment of targets is to be expected" (Teac Corp.); "I make appraisals on the basis of giving minus points for performance both over- and below-target; achievements of as high as 120% or 140% mean an incorrect setting of targets" (Takamizawa Elect.).

Among those chosing the veteran interesting reasons were "appraisal is impossible for an unreached target; it depends on results" (Ando Elect.); "Appreciation depends on the degree of difficulty overcome; for the same level of difficulty it depends on the results" (Nihon Koden Kogyo Co.); "So long as matters of the enterprise are concerned, success should be appreciated" (Kokusai Elect.).

Among those who said they would appreciate the new chief, many said they would provide support: "If it is a slight failure I myself will go and encourage the new chief and give moral support" (Denki Kogyo Co.); "As for new chiefs support should be given by the entire firm" (Origin Elect.); "We appreciate faithful employees irrespective of failure, and help them change their ideas so as to find good customers" (Makita Elect.); "Large differences between target and performance do not emerge in our firm because studies are made every month, and if a performance is unfavorable support is given by the home office" (Sanyo Elect.).

Beside these, there were these interesting views: "New chiefs who have made efforts should be highly valued, but the type of effort must also be considered" (Weston Onki Co.; JOEL Ltd.); "Training new middle managers is the responsibility of top management" (Alps Elect.); "We expect new staff members to motivate themselves; this is especially true in research establishments" (Toa Elect.). Thus from Q. 39 we have:

*Hypothesis 3-14*: Most presidents of today do not make evaluations of department heads solely according to the degree of attainment of targets. However, greater weight is placed on the extent of goal attainment rather than on the amount of effort expended.

### 3-2-4. Relation of President to the Other Top Managers

The composition and functions of top management vary from firm to firm and so generalizations are difficult. In our survey, the highest decision-making body took three forms—a board of directors, managing director's board and a meeting of the department chiefs. Some firms have all three and others, one or two. However, existence and actual functioning are different matters. In not a few cases board of directors is held once a business term. In our survey, generally a board of the directors was held at least once a month, and that of the managing directors once a week.

Where board of the executives or managing director's board is functioning well, good communication is maintained between the president and other executives, resulting in mutual understanding. To illustrate examples: "In our firm the chairman of the board of directors, the president and the vice-presidents have their desks in the same room, and so an executives' meeting is easily held whenever necessary" (Toko Elect. Corp., transformers); "Board of directors are held occasionally at the president's request" (Nippon Elect. Ind.); "Department chiefs are in charge of production, sales, etc. and participate in managing director's board which is held every week; at this time the president receives various information" (Foster Elect.); "a meeting of the managing directors, which also includes other directors, is held regularly twice a week on Mondays and Thursdays" (Origin Elect.). These examples reflect a high degree of cohesiveness.

By what factors is such closeness maintained? Of course in the case of founder or successor presidents, family-like relationships may be usual. However, by observing the actual situation in Japan, we thought that the homogeneity of the president and executives—with their similar educational backgrounds in non-engineering or engineering (or in science or literature)—might be working as a factor. So we investigated the backgrounds of the presidents and executives through the official financial statements submitted to the stock exchange authorities as well as other materials and classified them according to the divisions mentioned above. This classification was generally possible by examining which university they had graduated from and when necessary we used Question 40 about the major field of the president.

Please see Figure 3-1. On the horizontal axis the president's background is divided into that of engineering and non-engineering, and on the vertical axis the percentage of executives (excluding the president) with engineering background, is marked for each firm. For example, for Hitachi Ltd. the president has an engineering background and of the 13 executives (managing director or above) 10 have engineering backgrounds and 3 have non-engineering backgrounds (77%). As seen in the figure, the average percentage of executives with an engineering

**Figure 3-1.**   Backgrounds of Presidents and Other Executives

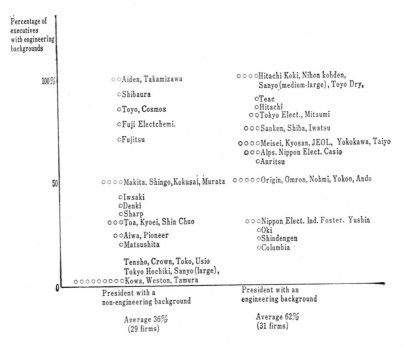

background in firms with a president having a non-engineering back-ground is 36%, much lower than the 62% in firms with a president with an engineering background. This difference is statistically significant. Thus, it can be seen that presidents are inclined to introduce persons having the same training into the decision-making body.

This indicates that in Japan the content of a science education and that of a non-science education differ to the extent that the graduates of these respective courses cannot communicate completely, make mutual appraisals or establish trust.

However, for modern enterprises both types of ways of thinking are necessary—knowledge of economics, markets and human relations on the one hand and that of R & D, new techniques and production on the other. Accordingly as a way of making adjustments, presidents with engineering degrees have a number of executives with non-engineering backgrounds, and vice versa where the president has a non-engineering background. From the above analysis we have:

*Hypothesis 3-15*: Where the background of the president is non-engineering, on average two-thirds of top managemnt have similar back-grounds, and in the case of presidents with engineering backgrounds, two-thirds of the top managers also have engineering backgrounds.

## 3-2-5. Business Goals Held by Presidents and the Characteristics of Firms

If an enterprise is to survive and grow in a rapidly changing environ-ment various business goals must be fulfilled. In our survey, focus was placed on two items among the many goals, namely the potential for profits and growth, which are the basis of competitive power. Our Quesion 34 was "Among the following essential indicators of business, please indicate the three items you think most important: a) the growth rate of sales, b) market shares, c) the ratio of exports to sales volume, d) profits, e) capital structure, f) the ratio of new product sales to total sales volume and g) dividend rates." We assumed that a) sales growth, c) exports and f) new products indicate a firm's potential for growth, that d) profits, e) capital structure and g) dividends relate to profits, and that b) market share is neutral.

Firms are classified according to three business goals in Table 3-1, and from this table we drew Figure 3-2. On the horizontal axis, for example, "1 profits and 2 growth" means that of the three selected items 1 profits and 2 growth of items were included. The values in the figure are skewed to the right, indicating that in the electric equipment industry growth potential is more highly valued than profits. This is understandable in view of the many technological innovations in this industry. Yet, no firm chose three growth indicators, whereas one firm chose three profits indicators. This indicates that even such firms that stress growth cannot ignore profits.

According to Table 3-1 the most important indicators were the growth rate of sales (50 firms) and profits (49), then market shares, (30) and new-product ratio (30), followed by capital structure (16), dividends (12) and export ratio (5). Such an emphasis on market shares and profits is in agreement with common sense. And the large numbers choosing market shares in comparison to those choosing export ratio seem to mean that in Japan's electric equipment industry domestic markets are still the mainstay.

Further analysis of Table 3-1 suggests the following. Firms with presidents who emphasize dividends or capital structure are family corporations or else firms affiliated with the Nippon Electric Co. Included in the family corporations are: Koa Elect., Yokoo Mfg. Co., Nikko Elect., Crown Radio, Origin Elect., Shin Chuo Kogyo, Alps Elect., Pioneer Elect., Foster Elect., Sanyo Elect. (medium-large), Teikoku Tsushin Kogyo, Weston Onki, Makita Elect., and Taiyo Yuden. The Nippon Electric Co. line firms include: Nippon Elect., Meisei Elect., Tokyo Communication Equip., Denki Kogyo, Nippon Elect. Ind. Co., and Anritsu Elect. These firms aside, only two other firms mentioned dividends or capital formation—Kyosan Elect. Mfg. and Nippon Signal.

The reason for the heavy weight given to dividends among the family corporations may be that the presidents themselves and family members hold a large percentage of the shares, and the concern for capital formation is supposedly from a fear that outsiders might seize control of the management.

The similar emphasis on dividends and capital structure by the Nippon Elect.-affiliated firms appears to reflect the fact that their

**Table 3-1.**   Business Goals Selected by Presidents

| | |
|---|---|
| Growth rate, Profits, New product ratio (adf) | Tokyo Elect., Oki, Sanken, Hochiki, Mitsumi, Cosmos, Shindengen, Toko, Fuji Electrochemi., Aiden, Teac, Iwatsu, Yokogawa, Kyoei (14 firms) |
| Growth rate, Market share, Profits (abd) | Hitachi, Hitachi Koki, Shibaura, Nohmi Bosai, Sharp, Sanyo (large), Shiba, Clarion, Iwasaki, Murata, Ando, Toyo Dry, Takamizawa (13 firms) |
| Growth rate, Market share, New product ratio (abf) | Kokusai, Hosiden, Toa, Nihon Kohden, Matsushita (5 firms) |
| Growth rate, Profits, Dividend rate (adg) | Origin, Toyo Communication, Meisei, Nipppon Elect., Shin Chin (5 firms) |
| Growth rate, Profits, Capital structure (ade) | Nippon Signal, Foster, Sanyo (medium-large), Teikoku Tsushin (4 firms) |
| Market share, Profits, Capital structure (bde) | Aiwa, Alps, Pioneer, Fujitsu (4 firms) |
| Market share, Profits, New product ratio (bdf) | Tamura, Ushio, Columbia (3 firms) |
| Growth rate, Export ratio, Profits (acd) | Omron, JEOL (2 firms) |
| Growth rate, Capital structure, New product ratio (aef) | Weston Onki, Yushin (2 firms) |
| Profits, New product ratio, Dividend rate (dfg) | Kowa, Taiyo (2 firms) |
| Growth rate, Market share, Capital structure (abf) | Makita (1 firm) |
| Growth rate, Market share, Dividend rate (abg) | Denki Kogyo (1 firm) |
| Growth rate, Export ratio, Dividend rate (acg) | Kyosan (1 firm) |
| Growth rate, New product ratio, Dividend rate (afg) | Nikko (1 firm) |
| Growth rate, Capital structure, Dividend rate (aeg) | Crown (1 firm) |
| Market share, Export ratio, Capital structure (bce) | Nippon Elect. Ind. (1 firm) |
| Market share, Capital structure, New product ratio (bef) | Anritsu (1 firm) |
| Market share, Export ratio, New product ratio (bcf) | Casio (1 firm) |
| Profits, Capital structure, New product ratio (def) | Tensho (1 firm) |
| Profits, Capital structure, Dividend rate (deg) | Yokoo (1firm) |

**Figure 3-2.** Profit-Orientation and Growth-Orientation of Firms

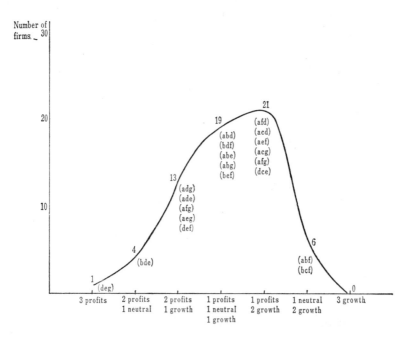

products are delivered mainly to Nippon Telephone and Telegraph (NTT) so that marketing is not of great importance. Furthermore, the policies of the Sumitomo Bank, through which all the firms handle their transactions, are followed by the presidents.

It seems that the presidents of the Hitachi-affiliated firms regard market shares and profits as their main goals. Hitachi Ltd., Hitachi Koki, Shiba Elect. and Nippon Columbia are among such firms. Market shares are emphasized because of steady management which places emphasis on technology, and especially because these firms manufacture finished goods.

Firms with presidens stressing unusual goals—that is goals that were selected by only one or two firms—were nearly all small-scale, family corporations. These companies were: Omron Tateishi, JOEL, Weston Onki, Kowa Elect., Taiyo Yuden, Makita Elect., Denki Kogyo,

Nikko Elect., Crown Radio, Casio Computer, Tensho Elect., and Yokoo Mfg. Perhaps the unusual attitudes of these founder presidents provided the very basis for growth or, alternatively, unusual policies are impractical for large-scale firms.

70% of the firms with a president valuing market shares were manufacturers of finished goods. Among the firms producing durable consumer goods, only two Nippon Elect. and Tokyo Elect. did not emphasize market shares. Similarly, 70% of the firms emphasizing the new product ratio were parts manufacturers. This is shown in Table 3-1 and Figure 3-2. Thus we have:

*Hypothesis 3-16*: The presidents of firms in the Japanese electric equipment industry emphasize growth potential rather than potential for profits.

*Hypothesis 3-17*: Firms with family ownership place value on financial indicators such as dividend rates and capital structure.

*Hypothesis 3-18*: Firms with presidents having less commonly mentioned goals are found in medium-large, family-type corporations.

*Hypothesis 3-19*: The presidents of firms affiliated with Nippon Elect. are finance-oriented and respect dividend and capital structure.

*Hypothesis 3-20*: The presidents of firms affiliated with Hitachi are product-market-oriented, depend on technology and respect market shares and profits.

*Hypothesis 3-21*: Presidents of firms manufacturing durable consumer goods value market shares, while those manufacturing parts respect new product ratios.

## 3-2-6. Recognition of Problems and Features of Today's Firms

Although the president surveyed held the outlooks and ways of thinking described above, what did they regardas immediate management problems? In response to Question 42, "what are the the present management problems? the most common answers were: markets, shortage of managers, technological innovations and rising labor costs. Only a few presidents referred to lack of funds and difficulties in recruiting personnel which were topics widely discussed by the general public.

In particular, we obtained the following responses: market matters

(22 presidents), shortage of managers (19), technological innovations (19), rising labor costs (12), shortage of labor (1) and lack of funds (0). Thus we have:

*Hypothesis 3–22*: In the electric equipment industry of 1970, important concerns were: strategy, including market matters and innovations, as well as human resource problems which included shortages of managers and rising labor costs. Scarcity of funds was of little concern.

Speaking broadly, the manner of pointing out problems was abstract and indirect by the presidents of large firms, while concrete and direct by those of medium-large firms. Let's consider this in greater detail.

In regard to technololgical innovations, for large firms the focus was on how to handle technological advances, while for medium-large firms it was on the ability of the engineers to keep up with the rapid changes. This supports the fact that new products of large firms are innovational while those of medium-large firms are products that have been improved upon.

One president said: "The problem is how to cope with technological innovations from abroad; up to date we have followed them but now we must go ahead" (Oki Elect.); another, "In order to keep up with rapid innovations in this era of rapid international communication, firms must perform their own basic research, and build up a techno-structure to produce commodities for markets" (Hitachi Ltd).

On the other hand, presidents of medium-large firms pointed out the difficulties in keeping an engineer's ability up-to-date. "An Engineer's knowledge becomes obsolete in five years; a research management system is soon disturbed because innovation renders appraisal impossible, leaving no other choice than to have researchers set their own goals" (Ushio Elect., lighting apparatus such as mercury lamps); "Our techniques have become worthless because of the change from mechanical to electronic signals" (Nippon Signal); "I am recommending all employees to acquire a liberal education in order to maintain flexibility; in particular, efforts are being made to train specialists in mathematics and creativity; for technological development we follow the practice of relying on a few personnel in whom we instill a sense of duty" (Casio Computer); "Our principle has been to do what others do not do, but now increasing the numbers of engineering personnel is most important due to the greater numbers of innovations recently" (Crown Radio).

And because of such difficulties with the advances in technological know-how, parts manufacturers have tended to make composite parts with the levels of ability at hand. "We are always searching for ways to develop new products, and now through project teams efforts are being directed to the integration of parts" (Mitsumi Elect.); "Our strength is our high level technology, and we are shifting from a mere parts manufacturer to producing integrated parts" (Tamura Seisakusho); "Overly rapid innovations are making the life cycles of products shorter, which is quite painful for us; we are always searching for new products that make possible effective utilization of our large facilities which are designed for integrated work without subcontracting" (Alps Elect.). Thus we have:

*Hypothesis 3-23*: As for technological innovations, the problem for large firms is how to foster innovations, and for medium-large firms the problem is how to keep up with the rapid advances.

Regarding markets, medium-large firms are concerned about their over-dependence on particular large firms. First domestically, "Since our dependence on Tokyo Shibaura Electric is great, technological developments are few and sales do not increase as expected because of negative thinking" (S. W.); "At present exports make up 40% of sales; this is due to the technological superiority of our firm and that of Nippon Electric; but we wish to become independent of Nippon Electric by developing our own products" (N. I.); "Our dependency on the National Railways and other railways is large and since both are unfavorable performance, our sales growth rate is stagnant" (K. E.); "Since our products have no brand names and are delivered to such large firms as Hitachi, Sony, Philco and General Electric, sales are apt to be affected by their policies, and improving the reputation of our firm is difficult; we wish to develop products with our own name" (F. E.); "Our policy has been to stress unique technology, but since deliveries are confined to specified large firms our marketing capacity and notably our ability for planning has weakened" (Sanyo Elect., motor maker); "Formerly we depended on electric power companies and the National Railways but henceforth we will advance into general markets; our problem is how to free ourselves from specified customers" (Toko Elect.); "Our products are varied and of small-volume production and at present our customers are mostly public agencies, large firms and research departments of universities; we wish to enter new markets" (Ando Elect.); "Our dependency on the car manufacturer Toyo Kogyo is very great—70% of our sales; we wish to consider other fields, for example, data writers for computer systems or exports of tachographs to the United States" (Y.C.). All these firms were considering the gradual breaking away from large firms. This may be because medium-large firms have now grown and are changing from small-volume production of many items to mass production and sales. Thus we have: *Hypothesis 3-24*: Since most medium-large firms in this industry deal with a few large firms, they perform as subcontractors. Consequently their marketing power is weak and extricating themselves from this situation is a common problem.

Next, the instability of exports to the U.S. was mentioned as a problem. This was especially true for parts manufacturers. "Recently exports to the U.S. have become remarkably stagnant, greatly affecting sales." (Tamura Seisakusho, Alps Elect. and Koa Denko); "Due to declining exports of TV sets to the U.S. sales of our parts are decreasing" (Teikoku Tsushin Kogyo); "We should like to extend our sales network, which has been focused on the U.S., to other parts of the world" (Weston Onki).

A shortage of managers was a problem appearing among rapidly growing medium-large firms. "The abilities and personalities of managers cannot keep up with a firm's growth; ability denotes selecting that which contributes to a firm, and personality is that which does not limit the development of one's potential." (Nihon Koden Kogyo); "Due to rapid growth there are not enough middle managers so they are being trained in a 250 days program" (Alps Elect.); "Managers cannot keep up with growth; so we are educating them by having them attend seminars given by outside lecturers as well as participate in discussions and on-the-job training programs" (Kyoei Sangyo); "Managers are in short supply" (JOEL, Mitsumi Elect., Teac Corp., Casio Computer,

Pioneer Elect., Tokyo Cosmos, Sanken Elect., Kokusai Elect. and Denki Kogyo). Firms mentioning a shortage of managers were those that had attained speedy growth. Again, a president of large firm commented, "managers, both for top and middle management positions, must be increased by about 30% a year; to do this it is necessary to transfer responsibility to lower levels and allow the managers to work without constraints; especially important is on-the-job training for new product development because this promotes the development of managerial abilities, thus providing a simultaneous solution to the problems of product innovation and lack of capable managers" (Nippon Elect.). However, the following answer was given: "To cut down on labor, first the number of managers will be reduced" (Sanyo Flect., large manufacture of household appliances). This indicates that the shortage of managers was not such an acute problem among large firms, even after rapid growth, since they were able to hire skilled personnel because of their good reputations, Thus we have:

*Hypothesis 3-25*: For rapidly growing medium-large firms the size of the managerial staff does not keep pace with the rapid expansion of the organization, and human resource development presents a problem.

To Q. 42—"What are your present problems?"—12 persons said rising labor costs. As for the methods to handle this, new product development, rationalization, labor-saving, mass production and human resource development were mentioned.

Here new product development includes improved products that allow price increases, or those for which cost reduction is possible by improvements production processes. Rationalization means the elimination of of inefficiency through good management of office work and production; labor-saving can be accomplished through mechanization, mass production through standardization, and human resource development attempts to raise productivity more than wage increases. The numbers of answers were new products (21), rationalization (13), labor-saving (12), mass production (8), and human resource development (6). The employment of female workers and a sliding wage scale system were mentioned by only 2 and 3 persons respectively.

Let's observe these in greater detail. First, let us consider new product development and rationalization. It seems that rationalization can cover an annual rise in labor costs of up to 7–10%, but beyond this product development is relied upon. "We cover half a rise by rationalization (10%) and the other half by improved products at higher prices (10%)" (Ushio Elect.); "Annual rises in labor costs of up to 7% can be covered by rationalization and improved skills, with rises above this percentage covered by the development of new products" (Anritsu Elect.). "Abstractly, new products are those having larger value added content, but more concretely, they are new products with new circuit designs" (Casio Computer), "products of the technology-intensive type, not labor-intensive" (Sanyo Elect., motor), or "products relevant to information which we had not previously known about" (Nippon Elect. Ind.).

Rationalization is related to office management. "To cope with rising labor costs we first will consider simplifying the bill collection system and the the structure of the organization, and lastly introduce MIS" (Yokogawa Elect., measuring apparatus). "We will cope with rising labor costs by rationalizing office manangement" (Toyo Communication, Nippon Elect., and Iwatsu).

Labor-saving is the switch from human to mechanical power. "We will introduce a machine costing 2 million yen if it can do the work of one person" (Sharp, Tensho Elect.); Automatization and mechanization will be applied at least to standardized products, if only partially" (Takamizawa Elect.); "Standardization, mechanization and automatization will be used as much as possible, by which surplus labor power of housewives living on farms may be utilized" (Nippon Columbia, Sanyo Elect. motor). The target for labor-saving appears to be 2 million yen per capita and the method is a shift to simple labor through standardization.

The reason for choosing mass production and selling as a countermeasure lies in cost reductions. And the reason for human resource development is to raise levels of ability above wage raises. "Training will be given to raise productivity more than the increases in wages" (Teac Corp.). "We will not employ graduates of famous universities to whom a high salary must be paid but hire others at a lower salary and conduct in-company training" (Denki Kogyo). Thus we have:

*Hypothesis 3-26*: As countermeasures to meet rising labor costs, new product development, rationalization, labor-saving, mass prodution and human resource development are the main measures being considered.

As can be seen by the above, there is some agreement among the presidents concerning the problems or demerits they recognize in their own firms, the patterns of recognition and the methods of solution. On the contrary, there is no agreement concerning the characteristics or merits of a firm. That is, to Question 41—"In what aspects is the management of your firm notably superior to that of others?"—the answers varied widely. While "technology and research and development" was mentioned by 16 presidents, "a set clientele" was chosen by 6, and "young employees or the active use of young people" by 5. Thus commonly-accepted opinions were few. Other items were "favorable labor-management relations" (3), "sound finance" (3), "precise planning" (2), and "profit sharing system" (2). Except for these choices, no other commonly-held opinions. In comparison to the answers to the other questions, this lack of agreement seems to indicate that firms employ a *unique* strategy to achieve growth depending upon their environment. Thus we have:

*Hypothesis 3-27*: Among the successful firms of today, a president's strategy sets the particular characteristic of each firm, so that general agreement is rare even among firms in the same field.

Interesting answers to Question 41, beside the above-mentioned included: "Trust is our motto and complaints are handled regardless of profit or loss and I myself visit customers to solve the problems" (Denki Kogyo); "I tell others to copy the good things done by others and not to worry about being copied, for imitation serves as advertising and increases the originator's profits" (Sharp Corp.); "We always investigate the firms in the same field and improve our plans" (Sanyo Elect., leading manufacturer of household appliances); "I stress the idea that contributing to social welfare is a duty of enterprises" (Matsushita Elect.). "Training specialists in man-machine interference" (Nihon Koden Kogyo). "Reinforcement of the sales network is always kept in mind; now we have 21 branches or business offices and 34 representative offices, and are engaged in transactions with 400 wholesalers dealing in electric materials and with the same number of secondary wholesalers" (Iwasaki Elect.). "Close trade with foreign countries" (Mitsumi Elect.). "We have set up trade and manufacturing divisions to promote stable growth" (Kyoei Sangyo). Thus the business goals and policies are very diversified and illustrate the characteristic of each firm.

## 3–3. Quantitative Analysis of the Contribution of a President's Behavior and Way of Thinking on Business Results

In this section, firstly we quantified a president's behavior and way of thinking and then discussed how these quantified factors correlate and contribute to business results.

### 3–3–1. Quantification of the President's Attitudes toward Group Management and Human Resource Development

We think that decision-making by a firm's top management is not done by the president alone but is a result of a group decision. This is because of the assumption that group decision-making is superior, and in almost all firms in Japan decisions by top management are of a collective nature.

In this process of group decision-making, the presidents take leadership. Good leadership may differ according to a firm's external situation, the thoughts and experience of the president and his relative power over the other executives. However, one common finding is that improvement of leadership can be attained not by isolating the leader from the group but by adjusting the relations between the leader and the other members. [1] Accordingly as a general theory, the relations with other executives must be improved if there is to be better leadership by a president. So we shall consider the patterns of a president's decision-making by taking account of past experiences and

---

(1) Robert L. Kahn & Daniel Katz, *Leadership Practices in Relation to Productivity and Morale, in Group Dynamics Research and Theory*, ed. by D. Cartwrite & A. Zander, 1957, pp. 489–92.

relations with other executives.

Let's first explain the method to exhibit quantitatively to what extent the president's way of decision-making in business reflects group management and human resource development. For this we used Qs. 24, 26, 28, 29, 38 and 39.

For Q. 24 "When a plan you think necessary, e. g. equipment expansion to increase competitiveness, is opposed by the majority of the managing directors, do you force your idea through or do you postpone making a decision in order to persuade them and make a final decision with less opposition?" We gave 1 point to presidents answering Yes to the latter because it implies consideration for group decision-making. A 0 was given to those who chose the former, and 0.5 to those who replied Uncertain or gave a conditional Yes to either of the two attitudes.

For Q. 26 "When some seminar on technological nature is held, do you send personnel in charge of accounting or operations to attend it?" 1 point was given to presidents answering Yes because this expresses support for developing abilities; answer No was given 0 and Uncertain or conditional, 0.5.

Q. 28 "Suppose that a section chief made a proposal to his department chief and the latter, though not without a fear of the risk involved, agreed to give it a try in terms of its being a learning experience, but the project resulted in failure. Do you approve of the department chief's decision?" This involves the willingness to develop the ability of subordinates through trial-and-error, training-on-the-job. 1 point was given for Yes, 0 for No, and 0.5 for Uncertain or conditional.

For Q. 29 "Which type of president do you think is better?: President A who avoids making proposals as much as possible, and draws out ideas from others, judges their reasonableness and carries them out; or B who thinks that the president should make proposals on important matters, prepare concrete plans and carry them out forcefully," 1 point was given to those who answered type A because of the group management attitude; 0 to the latter and 0.5 for Uncertain or conditional.

For Q. 38 "Do you remove from his post a sales manager who has failed to attain targets for two successive years, or let him try once more after advising him?" We gave 1 point to presidents who replied "let him try again" because the reply implies a willingness to develop abilities; 0 for "remove" and 0.5 for a conditional answer such as "it depends on the case."

For Q.39 "Which do you appreciate more: the attainment of a target by a veteran department chief or a failure by a new manager after great efforts?". Presidents who chose the latter were given 1 point for supporting the development of subordinates, while those who chose the former received a 0, and conditional answers, 0.5.

As can be seen from the above questions, we wanted to look at a president's attitudes and ways of thinking from a broad viewpoint.

Assuming that the questions are equally weighted, the scores, representing presidents' attitudes toward group management and human resource development, ranged in value from 0 to 6. These values are depicted by firms in Figure 3-3. The horizontal axis represents degrees of group managemnt and support of human resource development while the vertical axis represents firm scale. The symbols next to a firm's mark denote the background of the president—that is, A founder, B successor, C company-bred, and D *Amakudari.*

The second set of symbols, L and M, indicate the educational background of the presidents: L for non-engineering and M for engineering. Where educational background was uncertain answers to Q.40 (president's strong points) were used. The symbols, P, Q, and R represent the major products of the firm: P final consumer goods, Q finished producer's goods and R intermediate goods.

The results of the scoring are summarized in Table 3-2. From the averages by business scale we obtained:

*Hypothesis 3-28:* The larger the scale of a firm, the greater the tendency for group management and human resource development to appear in a president's decision-making behavior.

This seems to derive from the fact that larger scale involves more complicated decision-making where the president does not have enough information nor insight and hence the opinions of many persons are valuable. And furthermore since the execution of such decisions must be entrusted to many executives, it becomes necessary to invite these

**Figure 3-3.**  Presidents' Attitudes toward Group Management and Human Resource Development

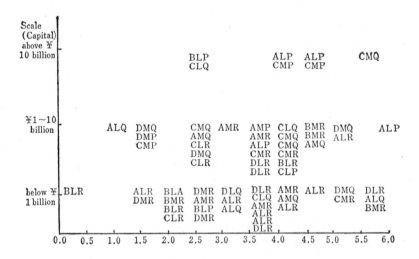

**Table 3-2.**  Presidents' Attitudes toward Group Management and Human Resource Development in Decision-Making

|  |  | Score | Firms |
|---|---|---|---|
| Average of all |  | 3.40 | 64 |
| Average by scales | Capital above ¥10 billion | 3.93 | 7 |
|  | 〃　　¥ 1 to 10 billion | 3.41 | 28 |
|  | 〃　　¥ below 1 billion | 3.24 | 29 |
| Average by type of president |  |  |  |
|  | A.  Founder | 3.63 | 23 |
|  | B.  Succesor | 2.95 | 10 |
|  | C.  Company-bred | 3.50 | 17 |
|  | D.  *Amakudari* | 3.17 | 14 |
| Average by president's educational background |  |  |  |
|  | L.  non-engineering | 3.30 | 33 |
|  | M.  engineering | 3.49 | 31 |
| Average by product | P.  final consumer goods | 3.46 | 11 |
|  | Q.  finished producer's goods | 3.58 | 19 |
|  | R.  intermediate goods | 3.27 | 34 |

executives to participate in the decision-making process and make them responsible for carrying out these decisions.

On the average:

*Hypothesis 3–29*: Founder presidents are more group management-oriented and willing to foster human resource development in decision-making than comany-bred or *Amakudari* presidents.

This contradicts the general view that the former are more directive than the other types. We suppose that our result derives from the fact that in firms with a founder president there is good communication, since there are few top executives and most have been assistants to the president since the company's establishment and hence their viws do not differ greatly.

Next, we have:

*Hypothesis 3–30*: Successor presidents are more directive than founder, company-bred, or *Amakudari* presidents.

Most of the firms with successor presidents surveyed in this study were facing a turning point in their business. Founder presidents had had their executives' assistance since the start of the company during which time the executives were able to develop their abilities and display their capabilities. However, the firms had grown remarkably larger by the time the successor presidents arrived with new ways of thinking, and this thinking conflicted with that of the surrounding executives who had been close to the founders. In such cases, in general, many of the executives continue to hold strong production-centered thinking prevalent during the Second World War and cannot keep up with scientific management concepts centering on marketing. For this reason young successor presidents do not heed the advice of older executives, and hence one-man decisions result.

Considering hypotheses 3–28, 3–29, and 3–30, the group management attitude held by founder presidents and presidents of large scale firms indicates that they display their leadership fully in decision-making.

From the average scores of the presidents' educational backgrounds, we have: "The tendency toward incorporating group management and human resource development in decision-making is clearer in engineer-

ing-type presidents than in those with non-engineering backgrounds."
This hypothesis, however, does not seem so significant.

As seen from the above, most presidents are favorably disposed
towards human resource development. They also are pro-group management, although more out of a desire to place responsibility for the
results of decision-making with the executives rather than for the purpose
of developing ability.

In any event, most presidents hold human resource development and
group management as an ideal but in actuality they have to be directive-
type presients. This is especially true where the firm is of small scale
or when decision-making is of an urgent nature.

### 3-3-2. Simple Correlation Analysis Involving a Time Lag

From the end of the 1960s to the 1970's the Japanese economy began
to show remarkable distortions, and accompanying the high growth
rate, caused social criticisms of such an intensity that companies were
forced to make big changes in their managerial policies. Therefore, at
the time this analysis was started—three years after the interview survey
of 1970—we decided to consider how the factors studied in the foregoing
sections had affected subsequent business performance and other matters.

We used the following ten variables: [Vari. 1] Regarding the business
goals explained in 3-2-5, a 1 was given to indicators of growth potential
(such as the growth rate of sales), a zero was given to indicators of
profits potential, and a 0.5 to neutral indicators (market shares),
and from the sum of the assigned values for the three business goals
selected in 3-2-5 the variable, growth strategy, was formed. [Vari.
2] Values were given to the growth rate of sales from the 2nd half
of '65 to the 1st half of '70 (a zero was given for an average semi-
annual rate under 8%, a 0.5 to 8.1%–18.1%, and a 1 to 18.1% and
over, and the scores in the ten periods were totaled). [Vari. 3] Values
were given to the growth rate of net profits for the same period (a
zero was assigned for an average semi-annual rate under 13.3%, a 0.5
for 13.4%–23.%, and a 1 for 23.3% and over, and the ten scores of
the ten periods were totaled) [Vari. 4] Combined performances of the
above (refer. business results in 4-2). [Vari. 5] Values for the growth
rate of sales for eight terms from the 1st half of '70 to the 2nd half

of '73 (a zero for an average semi-annual rate under 0.8%, a 0.5 for 0.8 %–10.8%, and a 1 for 10.8% and over, and the scores in the eight periods were totaled). [Vari. 6] Value were given to the growth rate of net profits for the same period (a 0 for less than −1.4%, a 0.5 for −1.4−8.6%, and a 1 mark for 8.6% and over; and the scores were totaled). [Vari. 7] Combined performances of the above. [Vari. 8] An attitude supporting group decision-making in business. [Vari. 9] Democratic decision-making at home (refer. note of this chapter); [Vari. 10] Social status scores of 3, 2 and 1 were given according to upper, middle and lower class of the president's parents in his boyhood. Using these the variables we composed a simple correlation matrix, Table 3-3.

From this matrix we see that the variable, social status [10] correlates negatively with all of the achievement variables for '65–'70 [2, 3 and 4] and those for '70–'73 [5, 6 and 7]. This shows that firms with presidents from lower social classes show better performance records during both favorable and fluctuating periods. Supposedly these presidents are filled with the entrepreneurial spirit—the capacity to endure continuous tension and take risks—because they have been able to overcome many difficulties in the past. Thus we have:

*Hypothesis 3-31*: Presidents who have grown up in lower social classes are full of the entrepreneurial spirit and have superior performance records in both favorable and fluctuating periods.

The variable, decision-making attitude in business [8], shows little correlation with the achievement variables associated with the high growth priod of the economy [2, 3 and 4] but correlates negatively with the same variables during periods of fluctuating conditions [5, 6 and 7]. This indicates that in favorable periods it is uncertain whether a president should be mere democratic or authoritarian in decision-making, but at least during fluctuating periods a group-management attitude by president has a negative effect on results, because this method is apt to result in opinions of a mediocre nature and decision-making is slower. Thus we have:

*Hypothesis 3-32*: Group management decision-making and a democratic attitude on the part of presidents has harmful effects on a firm's

**Talbe 3-3.**   Simple Correlation Matrix Involving Time Lag

| | | [1] | [2] | [3] | [4] | [5] |
|---|---|---|---|---|---|---|
| Growth strategy | [1] | 1.0000 | −0.1094 | −0.0335 | −0.6275 | 0.0149 |
| Growth rate of sales '65-'70 | [2] | | 1.0000 | 0.4550 | 0.8602 | 0.1885 |
| Growth rate of net profit '65-'70 | [3] | | | 1.0000 | 0.8306 | 0.0902 |
| Combined performances '70 | [4] | | | | 1.0000 | 0.1850 |
| Growth rate of sales '70-'73 | [5] | | | | | 1.0000 |
| Growth rate of net profits '70-'73 | [6] | | | | | |
| Combined performances '73 | [7] | | | | | |
| Group decision-making in business | [8] | | | | | |
| Democratic decision-making at home | [9] | | | | | |
| Social status | [10] | | | | | |

| | | [6] | [7] | [8] | [9] | [10] |
|---|---|---|---|---|---|---|
| Growth strategy | [1] | −0.2093 | −0.1266 | 0.0629 | 0.0744 | −0.1496 |
| Growth rate of sales '65-'70 | [2] | 0.0466 | 0.1249 | 0.0611 | 0.2313 | −0.1819 |
| Growth rate of net profit '65-'70 | [3] | −0.0552 | 0.0135 | 0.0339 | 0.2675 | −0.0448 |
| Combined performances '70 | [4] | 0.0103 | 0.1022 | 0.0679 | 0.2868 | −0.1633 |
| Growth rate of sales '70-'73 | [5] | 0.4296 | 0.7961 | −0.0794 | 0.0580 | −0.1297 |
| Growth rate of net profits '70-'73 | [6] | 1.0000 | 0.8771 | −0.1792 | −0.1458 | −0.1102 |
| Combined performances '73 | [7] | | 1.0000 | −0.1996 | −0.0620 | −0.1404 |
| Group decision-making in business | [8] | | | 1.0000 | 0.1901 | 0.0249 |
| Democratic decision-making at home | [9] | | | | 1.0000 | −0.1119 |
| Social status | [10] | | | | | 1.0000 |

performance in periods of fluctuation.

Lastly, growth strategy [1] is negatively correlated to the sales growth rate for '65–'70 [2], but is positively correlated (though only slightly) to that for '70–'73 [5]. This may indicate that the presidents of those firms showing small growth potential at the time of the interviews in 1970, later intensified their growth strategy so that effects after a three year lag were noticeable. Thus we have:

*Hypothesis 3–33*: The change of strategy of firms gradually changes its performance, although with 3 year's time lag.

**Notes:**

To find a presidents attitude toward ability-development in the home, the answers to Qs. 9, 10 and 11 were used.

In Q. 9. "A son who has graduated college, wishes to get a job in a firm to be independent, while another son intends to study at a graduate school in the U. S. to broaden his outlook and receives financial support from his parents. Which do you think is more desirable?", the answer "depends on his ability" or take into account his outlook and ability" was given 1 point, "studying is desirable" 0.5, and "independence is desirable" 0 point. Consideration for ability and respect for his wishes is considered as an ability-development attitude. In future society a wide range of knowledge is required, and in this sense study abroad in a graduate school is useful for developing abilities in the long run.

As to Q. 10. "Suppose your daughter is learning English in preparation for study in the U. S., but marriage has been proposed which is suitable to the conditions she has laid down and also appears favorable to you. She prefers study to marriage. She is twenty three years old. Do you approve of her studying abroad?" "Depends her ability" was given 1 point, "approve studying abroad, if this will make her happy or on the condition that she will get engaged first" 0.5, and an unconditional "No, " 0. We placed emphasis on the president's attitude toward ability in regards to the daughter.

For the above two questions we assigned scores of 0, 0.5 and 1, but for an answer between 0 and 0.5 we gave 0.25.

In Q. 11. "When your daughter's clothes go against your taste; do you (1) say nothing, (2) express your opposition, (3) express your preferences? the answer "express your preferences" was given a 1, "say nothing, " 0.5, and "express your opposition" 0. We thought one-sided opposition was not an ability-development attitude. Saying nothing was considered a midway attitude.

We constructed the variable "democratic decision-making at home" by totaling the above three scores.

# 4

## An Empirical Research on Top Management's Abilities

——Through a Field Research on 79 Companies in the Electronics and Chain Restaurant Industries——

## 4-1. Introduction

The abilities required for the top management include the quality to accomplish managerial functions in a given environment, which are roughly classified into three: thinking out future business visions, decision-making and business management and control. By demonstrating this quality, the top management can better contribute to the company's growth, successfully adjusting to the business circumstances in which he is placed. Desirable top management's abilities vary with the environment, however, it is generally agreed that the top management should have a character or personality which makes it easy for him to fulfill above functions. [1]

This chapter is designed to study the abilities necessary for company head from various viewpoints. First, I will discuss objective attributes of the top management, such as family origin, business career and age. Described next will be my research and analysis on president's abilities, including ambition, determination, intuition and persuasion, which I consider requisite to the top management. As a method of research, I refrained from directly asking company heads about their abilities. Instead, I asked them about their views on business life and behavioral pattern, as surrogates for abilities expected of them. A set

[1] Chapter 2.

of abilities referred to in this paper is based on the past work of the author. [2] Thirdly, I will examine top management's set patterns of decision-making and management concept. Finally I will study the consequences of the decisions made by the comany head in terms of ratios of new products, new equipment and new stores.

This chapter is characterized in that it not only studies top management's attributes, abilities and decision-making patterns, but also discusses them in relation with respective business results and employees' morale, along with the integrated business results. For excellent employees' morale is essential for the company to become vital and continue to develop for long.

This chapter is an attempt to examine how company head's comprehensive abilities help enhance employees' morale and business performances, analyzing the electronics industry undergoing rapid technological innovation and the chain restaurant industry where consumption structure is drastically changing.

As to the method of research, I sent a questionnaire to nearly 100 companies in each of the two industries. Of these, 47 in the electronics industry and 32 in the chain restaurant industry gave effective answers. In addition, I interviewed the presidents of six electronics companies and four chain restaurant firms. These works were conducted with the staff of the Nikkei Business in autumn of 1981. The combined method of observation of large numbers and interviews with the top management is used to make my analysis and interpretation of the subject matters objective and appropriate. In analyzing the result of questionnaire survy, I used the method of QAQF, Quantitative Analysis for Qualitative Factors, [3] which the author and his group have developed.

The results of analysis are all hypothetic because the number of samples used is comparatively small. If future surveys result in similar hypotheses, they will be theorized.

---

(2)  *op. cit.*

(3)  Ryūei Shumizu, *Growth of Firms in Japan*, Keio-Tsushin 1980, pp. 207~221.

# 4-2.   Attributes of President

## 4-2-1.   Type of President

When presidents are classified into four types of: founder of the company, successor, company-bred and *Amakudari* (retired high ranking bureaucrat), the number of company-breds is the largest in the electronics industry, while the founder-president is dominant in the chain restaurant industry. This is probably because the former industry has a relatively long history, compared with the latter.

Table 4-1 shows the relation between president's type and business results. The underlined figures show the maximum number in each category and those with * are statistically significant at a level of 5 percent. From Table 4-1, the following hypothesis can be drawn:

*Hypothesis 4-1*: In the four-type classification of presidents, the firms whose presidents are their founders have the best business results.

*Explanation*: the founder-president has strong entrepreneurship and

**Table 4-1.**   President's Type and Business Results

| Industry | President's type | Percentage | Employees' [4] morale | Business [5] results | Integrated business results |
|---|---|---|---|---|---|
| Electronics | Founder | 14.9% | 4.00 | 5.74 | 9.74 |
| | Successor | 19.2 | 3.44 | 4.25 | 7.69 |
| | Company-bred | 34.0 | 4.00 | 4.92 | 8.92 |
| | Amakudari | 31.9 | 3.60 | 5.13 | 8.73 |
| Chain restaurant | Founder | 59.4 | 3.90 | 5.31* | 9.21* |
| | Successor · | 28.1 | 4.11* | .4.87 | 8.98 |
| | Company-bred, Amakudari | 12.5 | . 3.25 | 3.52 | 6.77 |

---

(4)   Calculation of "employee's morale".

We have used a SD method to calculate "employee's morale". Namely, we have used the sentence as follows. What is the level of morale of your employees compared with other firms in the same field? Please select from the below for both "college graduate employee" and "junior & high school graduate employee".

1) Lower, 2) Slightly lower, 3) Almost equal, 4) Slightly higher, 5) Much higher.

Then we can devise employee's morale of a firm as follows.

excellent planning ability. In the electronics industry, he is actively engaged in research and development of new products, and in the chain restaurant industry, he is desperate in establishing additional stores, working on new service systems. But, the founder-president sometimes discourages employees' morale due to his too strong personality.

## 4-2-2. Family Origin

In order to verify a general notion that the company head is required to have a so-called "hungry spirit", I raised the following question to the presidents: "How do you rate the standard of living of your family

---

"Employee's morale" $=\frac{1}{2}$ (morale score of college graduate employee+ morale score of junior & high school graduate).

(5)  Calculation of "business results".

First of all, a distribution curve of growth rates was drawn and the average value calculated, but interval of $\pm 2.5\sigma$ was taken. All firms below $-2.5\sigma$ were given 0 and those above $+2.5\sigma$ a 5. Growth rates lying between $-2.5\sigma$ and $+2.5\sigma$ were assigned $Z=\dfrac{x-\bar{x}}{\sigma}+2.5$ (See Figure).

Using the same method scores for profitability were also calculated.

By means of such standardization, distortions by abnormal values were prevented, and the effects of external factors such as the growth rates of each industrial sector or of the national economy were eliminated.

Next, from the growth and profit ability scores the composite index "business results" was devised simply as follows. Business result=growth score+profit score. Also "integrated business result" was calculated as follows. Integrated business result=employee's morale+business result.

**Figure** Assignment of Scores to Growth Rates

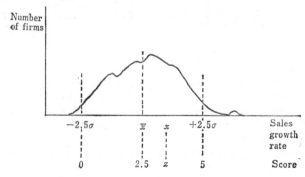

when you were aged between ten and 15? Please choose one out of the nine social classes of: "uppermost, middle upper, lower upper, upper middle, middle, lower middle, upper low, low, and lowest".

President Katsutarō Kataoka of the Alps Electronic Co., chose "middle". He recalls: "My father was once a joiner with about 25 employees, and ran a transport company using some 50 buses and automobiles. Having failed in both businesses later, he sold his big house. I felt sad that I was sent to usurer to pay loan interests every month." President Tadao Kashio of Casio Computer Co., answered "lower middle," saying that he was born in a farming household, and graduated from a night school, called Waseda Koshu School. "In those days, a salaried worker could not expect a position higher than section chief unless he finished higher education, so I became self-employed," says Kashio. President Satoshi Sakurada of Mos Food Service Inc., selected "lower upper". He says, "I was born as the tenth and youngest son of a relatively big Japanese restaurant in Iwate, northern Japan." "Since my parents regarded higher education as an asset they could give to their children, I was allowed to come up to Tokyo to attend a high school and then university," Sakurada says. President Shohei Tomita of Kentucky Fried Chicken Japan Ltd., replied, "middle". Born in Tokyo, he was a student of Tokyo Prefectural Middle School II when he was 15 years old. Later, after graduate from university he entered Mitsubishi Corporation: in 1968, he was transferred to the food division after returning from overseas assignment. He joined Kentucky in 1969 when foreign capital investment was liberalized in Japan. President Yōzō Ishizuka of Pioneer Electronic Corporation picked up "upper middle". "My father was a school principal," says Ishizuka, "When I was graduating from university, I had a vague idea of my future course. Out of romanticist and humanitarian feeling at the time, I sought career in the labor management field." President Den Fujita of McDonald's Co., answered "middle". He was a student of Kitano Middle School in Osaka when he was aged 15. He established a shop when he was a law student of University of Tokyo. "Japan was defeated by the U.S. in the Second World War due to money power of the U.S.," says Fujita, "So, I always thought of beating her on the strength of money." President of Aiwa Co. Ltd., Yūsuke Sanbe came from an uppermost class family, but he insists on the need of "hungry spirit" for business management. He says, "Those who experienced athletic activities in their school days, should be able to show off fighting spirit at work." President Fukujirō Sono of TDK Electronics Co., chose "middle". He recalls: "My parents inspired me with a spirit of self-reliance, so I dreamed of becoming independent as early as possible when I was young." "As a graduate of an Ikuei Commercial School, my educational background is poor, however, I used to read Marx's *The Capital* and consider how to realize better society," says Sono.

Table 4-2 shows the result of an observation of large numbers. Please note that "upper class" in the table includes uppermost, middle upper, lower upper and upper middle classes, and the "lower class" does lower middle, upper low, low and lowest classes. "middle class" equals middle. From Table 4-2 and above remarks of presidents, the following hypothesis is available.

**Table 4-2.**    President's Family Origin and Business Results

| Industry | Presidnet's family origin | Percentage | Employees' morale | Business results | Integrated Business results |
|---|---|---|---|---|---|
| | Upper class | 57.5% | 3.59 | 4.55 | 8.14 |
| Electronics | Middle class | 27.7 | 4.00 | 4.79 | 8.79 |
| | Lower class | 14.9 | 4.00 | 7.01* | 11.03* |
| Chain restaurant | Upper class | 43.7 | 3.86 | 4.95 | 8.80 |
| | Middle class | 31.3 | 4.00 | 4.51 | 8.51 |
| | Lower class | 25.0 | 3.75 | 5.56 | 9.31 |

*Hypothesis*: *4-2*: The firms whose presidents were brought up in the lower social class enjoy better business results.

*Explanation*: The company heads, coming from the lower class, have a "hungry spirit". They are confident of their own thought and manners as they won the current positions by managing many critical decisions. Their innovative and prompt decision-making and entrepreneurship daring displayed in every situation have brought about high business performance.

## 4-2-3.  Age, Period of Presidency and Field of Specialization

The average age of presidents in large manufacturing firms as a whole is between 62 and 63, and 60 to 61 in medium large companies. [6] The average age of the presidents surveyed is 59.2 for the electronics industry, and 52.1 in the chain restaurant industry. The difference between the two industries may be attributed to the fact that the latter is comparatively young itself.

The average period of presidency on the whole is seven to eight years in large manufacturers, compared with eight to ten years in medium large manufacturers. [7] In contrast, the figure for those surveyed is 9.2 years in the electronics industry, and 13.7 years in the chain restaurant industry. The difference between the two industries may reflect that in many of the latter industry, the presidency has been held by the founders. No significant relations were observed between president's age and period of presidency, and business results.

A classification of presidents by field of specialization shows that engineering and production ranks first in the electronics industry, while sales and trades is the most dominant in the chain restaurant industry. Only an insignificant relation was seen between president's speciality and business performances. This is probably because most of the presidents have already become generalists as well.

## 4-3. Abilities of President

In order to find out what abilities are required for the top management, I drew up a questionnaire which asks them about views on business life and management concept. The quesitionnaire consists of ten alternative questions. An example goes like this: "Suppose you drink and eat out with your familiar friend, who will pay the expenese? Answer A: We usually split the account. Answer B: I usually pick up the bill. Please encircle one of the following four sub-answers: 1. Answer A, 2. Answer A, more or less, 3. Answer B, more or less, and 4. Answer B".

Following are the results of the questionnaire survey on ten items and the interviews with the top management.

---

(6)  Ryūei Shimizu, *Growth of Firms in Japan*, Keio-Tsushin 1980, p. 48.
(7)  *Ibid.*

## 4-3-1.  Ambition

*Question*: "How do you make your future business vision?" Answer A: A future business vision is made based on the result of a detailed analysis of the present strengths and weaknesses of the firm. Answer B: A future business vision is made with ambition to, for example, become No. 1 within the industry ten years after.

President Yutaka Oyamada of Clarion Co., says, "I always consider the ambitious business condition which will enable us to win a runaway victory over all other firms in terms of productivity, quality and cost reduction. In particular, it is vital to take an unquestionable lead in the overseas business strategies." Mr. Oyamada thus attached a great importance to ambition. McDonald's Fujita places emphasis on a "simplified" ambition, saying that Answer A refers to tactics, and Answer B does strategies. He says, "The ambition-oriented strategy must be as simpe as possible." Pioneer's Ishizuka is also in favor of ambition. He insists that without ambition, vitality which is indispensable to win a business war, will not come out. On the other hand, Alps Electric's Kataoka refers to the necessity of considering the strengths and weaknesses of his own company first. He explains: "It's impossible for us to produce a competitive video tape recorder, because our rival firms, Hitachi and Toshiba have engineering abilities ten times better than ours. Furthermore, they have a number of research facilities, such as production research institute and industrial material laboratory."

Table 4-3 shows the result of an observation of large numbers concerning the relation between ambition and business results.

From table 4-3 and above remarks of the top management, the following hypothesis is possible.

*Hypothesis 4-3*: The firms whose presidents stress the need of a simple ambition in future planning, enjoy high employees' morale and business performances, compared with those whose presidents give priority to their strenghts and weaknesses.

*Explanation*: Company heads need to have a tremendous ambition which will make it possible for them to lead the employees, make a business reform and thus improve employees' morale as well as business results.

**Table 4-3.** Ambition and Business Results

| Industry | Thinking out future business concept | Percentage | Employees' morale | Business results | Integrated business results |
|---|---|---|---|---|---|
| Electronics | Based on strength and weakness | 46.8% | 3.50 | 4.66 | 8.16 |
| | Based on ambition | 53.2 | 4.00* | 5.26 | 9.26 |
| Chain restaurant | Based on strength and weakness | 56.3 | 3.78 | 4.78 | 8.55 |
| | Based on ambition | 43.7 | 4.00 | 5.20 | 9.20 |

## 4-3-2. Ability in Coping with a New Situation

*Question*: "If the information comes in that a new material has been developed, what will you do?" Answer A: If it appears to have no direct bearing on my company, I will wait for further information. Answer B: Although it appears to have no direct bearing on my company, I will actively consider how to use it.

Alps' Kataoka is for Answer B. He says, "I am very much interested in industrial raw materials, such as ceramics, ferrite and insulators, on which research is undertaken at the company's Central Research Institute. I will work on a possible use of any new raw materials." Mos Food's Sakurada also mentions the importance of a deep insight into and quick response to a new business environment. He says, "I, as president, always set to work on a new product. For instance, once I was informed of the popularity of pizza and chicken in the United States, I started its research, and set lead time for actual production. Such efforts resulted in hamburger with calcium." Kentucky's Tomita selected Answer B, too. He says that the bio-technology will have a large impact on the food industry, by substituting a decomposition by ferment for heating. It is possible, he notes, a substitute item now will become a main item in the future. "If we wait for further information, taking no actions, the rival firms will take initiative," says Tomita.

Table 4-4 shows the result of an observation of large numbers as to the relation between president's ability in coping with a new situation and business results.

From Table 4-4 and above remarks of the presidents, the following

**Table 4-4.**    Ability in Coping with New Situation and Business Results

| Industry | Reaction to new situation | Percentage | Employees' morale | Business results | Integrated business results |
|---|---|---|---|---|---|
| Electronics | Wait for more information | 23.4% | 3.55 | 4.69 | 8.24 |
|  | Consider how to use it | 76.6 | 3.83 | 5.07 | 8.90 |
| Chain restaurant | Wait for more information | 25.0 | 3.50 | 4.36 | 7.86 |
|  | Consider how to use it | 75.0 | 4.00 | 5.16 | 9.16 |

hypothesis is possible.

*Hypothesis 4-4:* The firms whose presidents are quick to respond to a new situation, enjoy better employees' morale and business results, compared with those where presidents take a wait-and-see attitude.

*Explanation:* The top management need to have a deep insight into and a long-term prospect for a changing business environment. But for such an ability, they will be unable to lead the employees, and therefore fail to improve business performance.

## 4-3-3.  Determination

*Question:* "If sales of main products or main projects, you are in charge of, decline for three years, what will you do? Answer A: I will continue the production and sale of them as long as they are profitable. Answer B: I will completely withdraw.

Alps' Kataoka stresses the importance of clear determination. He says, "When you face a decision on an on-going project, all you can do is to select one out of three alternatives; to further promote the project, to cancel it and to continue it as it is now. In my case, I have boldly discontinued a joint venture with Motorola three years after the establishment due to a difference of business principles." He cites another example: "In September last year, company withdrew from the video camera field, because our potential ability was insufficient to manufacture the systems product." He insists that a determination should be based on the analysis of merits and demerits of the company. Pioneer's Ishizuka explains an example of determination he showed in cancelling production of loud speakers: "Pioneer was once manufacturing speakers in a relatively low wage area in Yamagata, northern Japan, as a subsidiary of a large company. But as wage levels went up there, we transfered the job to a factory in Taiwan later. When we faced a determination on whether we should continue the production or not, many workers of Pioneer sticked to the long-time main product, although it was a near break-even item. After several years of discussion, however, we gradually discontinued it in an effort to allocate business resources to items of high investment efficiency. Ishizuka thus points out that investment efficiency is a decisive factor for a delicate decision of withdrawal. Likewise, president Tasuku Chino of Restaurant Skylark Co., asserts that giving up a thing is sometimes necessary. He says that determination results from breaking off "an inertia of feeling" in management practices.

Table 4-5 shows the result of an observation of large numbers concerning the relation between president's determination and business results.

From Table 4-5 and above remarks of presidents, the following hypothesis is available.

**Table 4-5.** Determination and Business Results

| Industry | Determination | Percentage | Employees' morale | Business results | Integrated business results |
|---|---|---|---|---|---|
| Electronics | Continue production | 59.6% | 3.57 | 4.84 | 8.41 |
|  | Discontinue production | 40.4 | 4.05* | 5.19 | 9.24 |
| Chain restaurant | Continue production | 25.0 | 3.75 | 5.11 | 8.86 |
|  | Discontinue production | 75.0 | 3.92 | 4.91 | 8.83 |

*Hypothesis 4-5:* In the electronics industry which has ample opportunity for developing new products, the firms whose presidents have a determination to give up a declining product enjoy better employees' morale and business results. In this case, the president is expected to fully consider the strengths and weaknesses of the company, and the return on investment. However, this hypothesis is not true in the chain restaurant industry where chances of product development are slim.

*Explanation*: Although the top management must gather as much information as possible under uncertain business environment, he should be able to make a bold and even non-logical decision should the need arise. In other words, if he waits until the situation becomes certain, his company will lag behind other firms and no management reform will be expected.

### 4-3-4.  Intuition

*Question*: "On what basis will you estimate the total sales for five years after? Answer A: related figures and information in stead of my intuition. Answer B: my intuition rather than related figures and information.

Aiwa's Sanbe insists on the importance of intuition. "People of slow perception are useless. I've been urging the middle management to train their intuition," Sanbe says. "In order to refine intution, you should constantly try to foresee a change in business situation through experience. Persons with excellent intuition are likely to have a good luck." Many other presidents note the need to use intution backed by objective information, however. For instance, Skylark's Chino says, "I would value my intuition highly, but I base it on relevant figures and information." Mos Food Service's Sakurada is proud that he bears in mind more figures and information than anyone else, based on which he uses perception. "Errors of my profit estimates have been about ten percent. You can train intuition if you challenge with enthusiasm and curiosity," he says. Clarion's Oyamada warns that perception will become dull unless you think of the background of available figures and information. "Persons of slow perception are no good. The president has better perception than his subordinate executives because he has constantly made critical decisions," he says. McDonald's Fujita refers to the necessity of intuition plus objective information in making a decision. He says, "Figures alone are insufficient. In 1978 when a new shop was planned for Enoshima, a summer resort near Tokyo, the research section estimated an annual sales of the shop at 10 million yen in view of the relatively small number of pedestrians and little possibility of the frequent fast drivers dropping in at the shop." "But, I launched it, following my intuition that it would attract the speeders.

It recorded an annual sales of 80 million yen," says Fujita. "On the contrary, my intuition was a failure in the case of a shop in Kurosaki, southern Japan. The existence of a supermarket near the planned site for the shop made me overestimate the local effective demand. But, the reality was that the distance between a near-by train station and the shop served as a negative factor," he recalls. Alps' Kataoka is among those who stress the necessity of objective data only. He says, "Now that the company's production size has become large, I rely on objective information, rather than my intuition when I make sales estimate." Pioneer's Ishizuka is confident that he has successfully made sales projections on the basis of figures for the past ten years. Kentucky's Tomita also values objective data highly. He says, "In working out a long-range business plan covering five years, we make it a rule to follow a sales forecast based on objective data." "Annual budget plan has been formulated tightly as well," he adds.

Table 4–6 shows the result of an observation of large numbers concerning the relation between intuition and business results.

The following hypothesis has been induced from it.

*Hypothesis 4–6*: In the rapidly growing industry, the firms whose presidents value intuition, backed by their past experiences, in making a sales estimate, enjoy better business performances.

*Explanation*: In the rapidly growing industry, it is rather easy to foresee a desirable course of business strategies, and a failure can be recovered by implementing alternative projects. Starting action following such a course faster than rival companies is more important than making a detailed analysis. Thus intuition takes precedence over objective data.

**Table 4–6.** Intuition and Business Results

| Industry | Sales estimate | Percentage | Employees' morale | Business results | Integrated business results |
|----------|----------------|------------|-------------------|------------------|-----------------------------|
| Electronics | Based on data | 70.2% | 3.79 | 4.92 | 8.71 |
| | Based on intuition | 29.8 | 3.71 | 5.12 | 8.83 |
| Chain Restaurant | Based on data | 62.5 | 3.75 | 4.89 | 8.64 |
| | Based on intuition | 37.5 | 4.08 | 5.09 | 9.17 |

## 4-3-5.  Respecting Others

*Question*: "Suppose you made a reasonable decision on personnel management involving an executive, but you still feel somewhat sorry for him, what will you do?" Answer A: I will convince myself that presidency is a lonely job. Answer B: I will think of better alternatives.

Aiwa's Sanbe rejects the possibility of the question itself, saying that he would conduct personnel management in a way which wouldn't cause such a feeling.  One of the company heads surveyed reveals that he will dismiss an executive if he fails to rectify his attitude after he receives a warning on two occasions. He says, "the president is exclusively responsible for personnel issues involving executives. Suppose I often hear a bad rumor about an executive, I will confirm whether it is true or not, in addition to questioning him. If necessary, I will reprimand him and eventually discharge him in a way which will not disgrace him." From above episodes, we understand how careful company heads are in handling personnel matters involving executives.

Table 4-7 shows the result of an observation of large numbers concerning the relation between president's concern for others and business results.  As in the table, the two industries produced opposite results. This is probably because in the chain restaurant industry, president's attitude to respect others improves employee's morale and improved morale further leads to better business results, whereas in the electronics industry, undergoing a drastic technical innovation, business performance is influenced by the enhancement of product functions.

From Table 4-7 and above interviews with the presidents, the following hypothesis can be induced.

*Hypothesis 4-7*: In the restaurant chain industry, where improved

**Table 4-7.**  President's Respect for Others and Business Results

| Industry | President's attitude | Percentage | Employees' morale | Business results | Integrated business results |
|---|---|---|---|---|---|
| Electronics | Impersonal, rational | 63.8% | 3.80 | 5.06 | 8.86 |
| | Human feelings-oriented | 36.2 | 3.71 | 4.83 | 8.54 |
| Chain restaurant | Impersonal, rational | 65.6 | 3.81 | 4.90 | 8.71 |
| | Human feelings-oriented | 34.4 | 4.00 | 5.08 | 9.08 |

morale of workers is especially important to obtain better business results, the firms whose presidents have a warm personality and attitude to respect others, enjoy higher business performances. However, this is not always true in the electronics industry, going through a major technological innovation, where product performance directly affects the business results.

### 4-3-6. Willingness to Do Others a Favor

*Question*: "Suppose you drink and eat out with your familiar friend, who will pay the expense?" Answer A: We usually split the account. Answer B: I usually pick up the bill.

I drew up this question in an attempt to verify my assumption that the president should constantly obligate his subordinate executives for his favors to facilitate a decision-making. This is called as a "logic of *Kashi-Kari*" which is one of the characteristics of Japanese management. [8]

Casio's Kashio says that he has a few intimate friends, and that it is always his treat when he asks his colleagues or the employees for a company. McDonald's Fujita is also in favor of treating. He says, "I cannot drink as much as I like when I know others will pick up the bill. I think I am the only president to pay for drinks using pocket money in Ginza, Tokyo's popular spot, among expense-account spenders." All other presidents interviewed gave similar answers, but with a different nuance: Alps Electric's Kataoka says, "We don't go Dutch. Suppose I pay for someone one time, he will treat me to drinks next time. In the long run, it becomes Dutch account as a result." Pioneer's Ishizuka insists that the *"Kashi-Kari"* (give and take) approach is essential to maintain good human relations with his colleagues. He says, "I pay for my colleagues usually."

Table 4-8 shows the result of an observation of large numbers as to the relation between president's willingness to do his colleagues favors and business results.

The following hypothesis is possible from the table.

*Hypothesis 4-8*: The firms whose heads always obligate his colleagues

---

(8) *ibid.* pp. 36~39, and 1-9 of this book.

**Table 4-8.**    Willingness to Do Others a Favor and Business Results

| Industry | President's attitude | Percentage | Employees' morale | Business results | Integrated business results |
|---|---|---|---|---|---|
| Electronics | Split the expense | 21.3% | 3.70 | 4.69 | 8.39 |
| | Pick up the bill | 78.7 | 3.78 | 5.06 | 8.84 |
| Chain restaurant | Split the expense | 21.9 | 3.86 | 4.69 | 8.55 |
| | Pick up the bill | 78.1 | 3.88 | 5.74 | 8.92 |

and subordinates for their favors, such as treating them to drinks, enjoy better employees' morale and business results.

*Explanation*: In order to expedite a decision-making by the highest decision-making body, it is vital for the president to constantly obligate his subordinate executives by making *Kashi* or doing a favor for them and to lay a sufficient groundwork for obtaining their approval.


## 4-3-7.  Persuasion

*Question*: "If an executive opposes your new product strategy, what will you do?" Answer A: I will shelve up my plan temporarily,  and try to persuade him through occasional contacts with him. Answer B: I will try to persuade him persistently on the basis of objective data.

Alps' Kataoka denies the possibility of this question,  saying that he will inform fellow executives of a new project well before it is launched, and that he has been faced with few objections from others. However, he stresses the necessity of objective data in laying a groundwork. He says, "I won't jump to a conclusion on a critical issue." Some of the presidents interviewed explain how they successfully persuaded colleagues. For example, Mos Food's Sakurada says, "When I planned to include sandwiches in the list of our service items, I faced an objection which sticked to the existing items,  profitable hamburgers." "I could persuade the opposer, however,  by explainning consumers' need for sandwiches,  using related data, " says Sakurada. Pioneer's Ishizuka cites a similar example: "When voices for video tape recorders prevailed within the company,  I was persistent in starting video disk by referring to its high sound quality, compared with tape recorders." Fujita of McDonald's goes further to speak on the positive aspect of objection.

He says that he will welcome an objection which clarifies a problem area involved in a new project. "We can take a precautionary step against it in the process of materializing the project," Fujita says. He continues: "A unanimous consent is not always desirable."

Table 4-9 shows the result of an observation of large numbers concerning the relation between president's persuasion and business results.

From Table 4-9 and presidents' remarks above, the following hypothesis can be induced.

*Hypothesis 4-9*: The firms whose presidents are able to persuade fellow executives, opposing their business strategies, enjoy better employees' morale and business results, compared with those whose presidents freeze the strategies temporarily.

*Explanation*: The top management is required to have a clear understanding of his own idea. It must be presented as a material for discussion with other executives. Without a firm belief in his thinking, he will be unable to persuade them to conduct a new project.

**Table 4-9.** Persuasion and Business Results

| Industry | President's attitude | Percentage | Employees' morale | Business results | Integrated business results |
|---|---|---|---|---|---|
| Electronics | Shelve up temporarily | 19.2% | 3.56 | 4.77 | 8.33 |
| | Persuade persistently | 80.8 | 3.82 | 5.03 | 8.84 |
| Chain restaurant | Shelve up temporarily | 12.5 | 3.50 | 4.05 | 7.55 |
| | Persuade persistently | 87.5 | 3.93 | 5.09 | 9.02 |

## 4-3-8. Health

In an attempt to examine president's views on health, which is considered to be one of requisites to presidency, I have asked them whether they are taking good care of their health while engaging in duties, or they are giving top priority to the duties. Answer A: I work within the limit of my physical power. Answer B: I give top priority to my duties, irrespective of my health.

The company heads surveyed appear to be blessed with health mostly.

Aiwa's Sanbe says that he has never felt tired as he has a strong constitution. Fujita of McDonald's is proud that hes hasn't stayed away from office for the past 30 years. "If the president takes a day leave, the company will lag behind rival firms by 30 days," Fujita says. "Likewise, a misjudgement made by him one day can be corrected on the following day if he appears at the office every day," he adds, "People become sick when they are careless about health." Mos Food's Sakurada holds a similar view, "I haven't suffered any diseases. Every meals taste good. I think people catch cold because of lack of mental concentration." Alps' Kataoka also insists that priority should be given to duties. He explains: "I work to the very limit of my physical strength if necessary. When I feel like eating *"zenzai"* (sweet adzuki bean soup), it's a danger signal for my health. I can recover from fatigue by taking a two-day leave." Clarion's Oyamada is also confident of health. He says, "My view on health care has changed as I grew older. I worked like a dog in my forties, but I came to take some care of my health after I became 50 years old." Being very healthy, however, they still are taking various ways to maintain health. Mos Food's Sakurada eats nothing after 9:00 p.m. He goes to bed before 12 midnight and gets up at 6:00 a.m. He eats brown rice and plays golf once a week. Likewise, TDK's Sono takes a cold bath every day. Of those interviewed, Casio's Kashio is the only president who is unhealthy. He says, As I have intestinal difficulties, I refrain from drinking and eating too much. I have undergone periodical physical check-up." But, he is confident that he has a strong determination

**Table 4-10.** Health and Business Results

| Industry | President's attitude | Percentage | Employees' morale | Business results | Integrated business results |
|---|---|---|---|---|---|
| Electronics | Health-conscious approach to work | 61.7% | 3.79 | 4.90 | 8.69 |
| | Give top priority to work | 38.3 | 3.72 | 5.12 | 8.84 |
| Chain restaurant | Health-conscious approach to work | 53.1 | 3.59 | 4.96 | 8.55 |
| | Give top priority to work | 46.9 | 4.20 | 4.96 | 9.16 |

trained in adversity, and is ready to work hard.

Table 4-10 shows the result of an observation of large numbers concerning the relation between president's health and business results.

The following hypothesis is available from Table 4-10 and above remarks of presidents.

*Hypothesis 4-10*: The firms whose presidents give preference to their duties, irrespective of health, enjoy better business results, compared with those where the heads are health-conscious while engaging duties.
*Explanation*: The top management needs goods health so that he can survive a hard work. Daily self-control and health care are essential for this purpose.

## 4-3-9. Ability in Gathering Information

I have drawn up the following question on the assumption that it is necessary for the top management to collect information in consideration of its possible effect on the products of the company, rather than to do so at random.

*Question*: "What do you think of gathering product-related information?" Answer A: I constantly collect as much information as possible. Answer B: I collect information, considering its possible effects on the products of the company.

Alps' Kataoka chose Answer A. He explains: "Our sources of information are large manufacturers, SRI, and speech meetings sponsored by the Japan Productivity Center, and through U.S. tours. In addition, through various informal contacts with others comes information." Thus he indicates that he is active in gathering information through many channels. Mos Food's Sakurada also insists on the positive attitude, saying that he always props an antenna for information gathering, and that he sees both sides of the information coming in. "I obtain microscopic information through each store, and macroscopic one from my fellow experts," he says. Skylark's Chino choses Answer B.

Table 4-11 shows the result of an observation of large numbers as to the relation between president's ability in gathering information and business results.

The following hypothesis has been induced from Table 4-11 and above statements of presidents.

**Table 4-11.** Information Gathering and Business Results

| Industry | President's attitude | Percentage | Employees' morale | Business results | Integrated business results |
|---|---|---|---|---|---|
| Electronics | Gather as much as possible | 89.4% | 3.86 | 5.01 | 8.86 |
| | Gather select information | 10.6 | 3.00 | 4.77 | 7.77 |
| Chain restaurant | Gather as much as possible | 78.1 | 3.92 | 5.17 | 9.09 |
| | Gather select information | 21.9 | 3.71 | 4.21 | 7.92 |

*Hypothesis 4-11*: The firms whose presidents gather as much information as possible constantly, enjoy better employees' morale and business results, compared with those whose presidents engage in information gathering, considering its influence on the company's products.

*Explanation*: Japanese firms are facing cross-industrial competitions both in the domestic and overseas markets. Thus, changes in international politics, social situations as well as consumption structure, or technological innovations, which are apparently irrelevant to the company, are organically related to its management. In this light, the top management should gather as much information as possible, rather than valuable information alone.

## 4-3-10. Ability in Gathering Indirect Information

In an effort to verify my assumption that a top management needs a broad range of knowledge in order to think out future business visions and make related decisions, I drew up the following question. "Do you often read newspaper articles on politics, international relations, literature and other matters which appear to have no direct bearing on the company management?" Answer A: No. Answer B: Yes.

Pioneer's Ishizuka says, "Business management cannot be separated from political, economic and international affairs. Speaking of literature, I can understand the life style of young employees by reading, for example, a best-seller novel for youngsters, *"Nanto-naku Kuristal"* (*Somewhat Chrystal*). I read it earlier than some of my employees." Kentucky's Tomita says, "As for domestic articles, I only read captions, but I follow overseas news in detail." He adds that he is subscribing to a small daily paper, "Nikkan Gendai" (Contemporary Daily) as well as leading papers, because the latter carry only "formal" articles. Fujita of McDonald's also seeks overseas information: "I usually read the front page and a literary column, and review them in a world-wide framework."

Table 4–12 shows the result of an observation of large numbers concerning the relation between indirect information gathering and business results.

The following hypothesis is available from Table 4–12 and above remarks of the presidents.

*Hypothesis 4–12*: In the electronics industry where internationalization of business is in progress, the firms whose presidents often read articles on international affairs and literature as well, enjoy better employees' morale and business results, compared with those whose heads only read professional articles. This is not the case with the chain restaurant industry where management has not been internationalized.

*Explanation*: It is necessary for the top management, who is interested in entering the international market, to obtain information on overseas affairs, and review domestic news from an international standpoint.

**Table 4–12.** Gathering Indirect Information and Business Results

| Industry | President's attitude | Percentage | Employees' morale | Business results | Integrated business results |
|---|---|---|---|---|---|
| Electronics | Don't read newspaper articles extensively | 23.4% | 3.55 | 4.83 | 8.38 |
| | Read the above often | 76.6 | 3.83 | 5.02 | 8.86 |
| Chain restaurant | Don't read newspaper articles extensively | 18.8 | 3.83 | 5.61 | 9.44 |
| | Read the above often | 81.2 | 3.89 | 4.82 | 8.70 |

## 4–3–11. Requirements for President

The abilities necessary for the top management differ depending on the business environment under which he is placed, and on the functions he is assigned. Then what are the general qualities requisite to presidents in the two industries surveyed? I had the respondents choose the first three requisites to the top management from among those I

listed up below, considering my past works on presidential qualities. [9]
*Direction*: "Please select the first requisite (put a double circle), and
two second requisites (put a circle each) from among the following
qualities."
*Qualities*: 1. ambition, 2. sense of duty, 3. philosophy, 4. belief,
5. intuition, 6. imagination, 7. insight, 8. determination, 9. boldness
to run a risk, 10. broad-mindness, 11. personal attractiveness, 12.
ethics, 13. systematic thinking, 14. effective use of time, 15. quantitative thinking, 16. leadership, 17. sense of responsibility, 18. health,
19. general knowledge, 20. knowledge of other executives' thinking,
21. curiousity, 22. others

Table 4-13 shows the frequency of each quality, as cited by the
respondents.

**Table 4-13.**    Requisite Qualities for President

| | Frequency of Qualities (%) | | | | | | | |
|---|---|---|---|---|---|---|---|---|
| | Quality 1 | 2 | 3 | 4 | 5 | 6 | 7 | 8 |
| Electronics | 0% | 21.3 | 6.4 | 14.9 | 2.1 | 2.1 | 27.7 | 46.8 |
| Chain restaurant | 3.1% | 37.5 | 18.8 | 21.9 | 12.5 | 6.3 | 15.6 | 28.1 |
| | Quality 9 | 10 | 11 | 12 | 13 | 14 | 15 | 16 |
| Electronics | 0% | 8.5 | 25.1 | 2.1 | 0 | 0 | 4.3 | 53.2 |
| Chain restaurant | 3.1% | 6.3 | 31.3 | 0 | 6.3 | 0 | 15.6 | 25.0 |
| | Quality 17 | 18 | 19 | 20 | 21 | 22 | | |
| Electronics | 17.0% | 46.8 | 0 | 0 | 0 | 21.3 | | |
| Chain restaurant | 15.6% | 28.3 | 0 | 0 | 3.1 | 2.9 | | |

The following hypothesis is possible from the table.
*Hypothesis 4-13*: Health tops the list of qualities which modern
Japanese top managements think the first requisite to presidency.
Following health are leadership and personal attractiveness in the
administratorship category, and insight, determination, sense of duty
and conviction in the entrepreneurship category.

Among those who cite personal attractiveness is McDonald's Fujita.
He explains: "Personal attractiveness is a combined quality of intuition,
imagination, insight, determination, broad-mindness as well as sense

_____
(9)    Chapter 2.

of ethics. Without it, the president cannot lead the employees." Pioneer's Ishizuka says that the top management is not gifted with all the necessary qualities, he need expert's assistance in business operation. "To attract bright experts who want to demonstrate their abilities he must have strong personal attractiveness which can be trained through efforts," Ishizuka says. Alps's Kataoka also stresses that personal attractiveness is an indispensable requisite for the company head to lead young employees. He says, "The up-to-date electronics industry requires the contribution of young workers. Those aged below 40, especially between 27 and 37, are the main work force in the industry." "The company head should have a fine personality, among other abilities, to lead the young work force, since they don't follow him only because he is a senior," Kataoka says. Mos Food's Sakurada is among those who highly value sense of duty and conviction. "I have a feeling of duty toward my own tasks. I have instructed the employees and franchisees to work with the feeling. But for it, you can't expect a vital work", he says. Similarly, Fujita of McDonald's regards sence of duty as a driving force of active management. He says that without the sense, one can't engage in business in an aggressive manner. As to conviction, he points to the need for the top executive, as a weak human being, to have a firm belief in operating the company, which requires a high level of mental action. Kentucky's Tomita holds a similar view on conviction. "Unless I have an indomitable determination to operate the company, the workers won't follow me. I have kept my firm belief by constantly encouraging myself," he says. TDK's Sono considers deep insight and determination necessary for the president. He says, "Insight is a quality which enables you to make a "natural" decision, namely, whether it is natural or not? I can't decide when I try to judge something on the basis of whether it is goot or bad." On determination, Alps's Kataoka expresses the view that it is displayed when the president decides on whether to further promote a plan, to cancel it, or continue it as it is.

The next topic is whether the above qualities have actually contributed to the betterment of business results or not. Let's look at the relation between the requisite qualities for the top management and business performance by classifying the qualities into three categories:

1. entrepreneurship: qualities numbered 1 (ambition) through 9 (boldness to run a risk), 2. administratorship: qualities numbered 10 (broadmindness) through 17 (sense of responsibility), and 3. health (quality number 18). Other qualities have been excluded as no presidents selected them.

Table 4-14 shows the result of an observation of large numbers based on the three-category classification.

**Table 4-14.**  Requirements for Presidents and Business Results

| Industry | Requirements | Percentage | Employees' morale | Business results | Integrated business results |
|---|---|---|---|---|---|
| Electronics | Entrepreneurship | 51.1% | 3.71 | 4.86 | 8.57 |
| | Administratorship | 31.9 | 4.00 | 5.37 | 9.37 |
| | Health | 17.0 | 3.50 | 4.62 | 8.12 |
| Chain restaurant | Enterpreneurship | 62.5 | 3.90 | 5.24 | 9.14 |
| | Administratorship | 25.0 | 4.00 | 4.54 | 8.54 |
| | Health | 12.5 | 3.50 | 4.39 | 7.89 |

The following two hypothesis are possible from the table.

*Hypothesis 4-14*: In the electronics industry, the firms whose presidents have vigorous administratorship, rather than entrepreneurship, achieve better business performances. In the chain restaurant industry, the result was opposite.

*Explanation*: In the rising electronics industry, where R & D and new product development are comparatively easy due to technological innovation, the president is required to have a moderate thinking which enables sound business management and harmonious human relations. This has been proved in the related data prepared by the Ministry of International Trade and Industry for the past seven years. On the other hand, in the chain restaurant industry, the products and services do not vary greatly with the company. So, in order to take lead over a rival firm, the president must have entrepreneurship qualities, such as insight into a change, even a slight one, in consumers' need, and the ability to cope with it.

*Hypothesis 4-15*: Health is a necessary condition, but not a sufficient one for the president.

*Explanation*: The president will be unable to make a long-term and innovative decision unless he is healthy. But, without entrepreneurship abilities, including firm conviction and insight, as well as administratorship qualities such as leadership and personal magnetism, he will fail to lead his employees and to achieve continued growth of the company.

## 4-4. Decision-Making in Business

### 4-4-1. The Strengths of Firms Cited by President

The growth of a firm is largely affected by what its president considers to be the strengths of the firm, and by how he can make use of it.

Casio's Kashio cites as the strengths of the company the excellent executive staffs and their strong unity. "They are in concert in never giving up a project halfway. They are always attentive to musical instruments, computer and ECR technology," he says. McDonald's Fujita regards the firm's popularity and brand as merits of the firm. He says that the company totally relies its product and technical development, such as chicken sandwiches and speed meat roaster on the parent company in the U.S. Fujita thus stresses the U.S. excellence in developing ability, which underlies the strong brand. TDK's Sono refers to the stable sales markets: "The primary clients of TDK include most of the Japanese large electric companies including Matsushita Electric Corporation and Hitachi Limited. Most of these firms hold our stocks. There are no major differences in sales of our products among our clients." He thus notes the company's close ties with clients.

The result of an observation of large numbers is shown in Table 4-15.

The following hypothesis can be induced from Table 4-15 and above remarks of the presidents.

*Hypothesis 4-16*: In the electronics industry, the firms whose presidents consider ability in product development to be a strength of the company enjoy best business performances, while those whose heads cite tradition, popularity and brand name have bad business results. A similar tendency was observed in the chain restaurant industry, but no clear conclusion as reached.

*Explanation*: It is the most essential of the electronics industry to develop new products, coping with technological progress. If they

**Table 4-15.**  Firm's Strengths and Business Results

| Industry | Firm's strength | Percentage | Employees' morale | Business results | Integrated business results |
|---|---|---|---|---|---|
| Electronics | Tradition, popularity, brand | 14.9% | 3.57 | 3.97 | 7.54 |
| | Characteristics of product | 21.9 | 3.67 | 4.46 | 8.12 |
| | Product development | 57.7 | 4.23* | 5.60* | 10.22* |
| | Excellent subcontractors, stable clients | 17.0 | 3.38 | 5.08 | 8.46 |
| | Executive staff, contents of assets | 8.5 | 3.75 | 5.23 | 8.98 |
| Chain restaurant | Tradition, popularity, brand | 34.4 | 3.82 | 4.83 | 8.65 |
| | Executive staff, employees' quality | 12.5 | 4.00 | 4.14 | 8.14 |
| | Stable clients | 31.3 | 3.70 | 5.36 | 9.06 |
| | Product development | 21.8 | 4.14 | 5.07 | 9.21 |

depend on stable products with popular brand, they will be unable to deal with the changing business situation. In contrast, it is presumably necessary for the chain restaurant industry to obtain regular customers, and develop new products according to their tastes.

## 4-4-2.  Setting Business Goals

Business goals set by the company head determine whether the company operation will become offensive or defensive.

Casio's Kashio attaches importance to development of new products. He says, "Our company has technology which can make various human dreams come true. I believe the company can make whatever people want to have, and there will be no end to technical advancement." Skylark's Chino also notes the need of developing new products, using the strengths of the company. He explains: "Since a project lasts only ten years here in my company, we work on a more-profitable project about five years after one project started. In this process, a total of 300 stores nationwide play an important role." Kentucky's Tomita, on the other hand, sets a market share expansion target. He says that the company is serving improved food, such as smoked chicken, in order to maintain and expand the share of its main products. Clarion's Oyamada says that the company can expand its market share by developing new products and reducing costs, and thus equally rates the importance of these business goals.

Table 4-16 shows the result of an observation of large numbers concerning the relation between president's business goals and business results.

**Table 4-16.** Business Goal and Business Results

| Industry | Business goal | Percentage | Employees' morale | Business results | Integrated business results |
|---|---|---|---|---|---|
| Electronics | New-product development | 66.0% | 3.90 | 5.11 | 9.02 |
| | Share expansion | 23.4 | 3.45 | 4.84 | 8.29 |
| | Cost reduction | 10.6 | 3.60 | 4.46 | 8.06 |
| Chain restaurant | New-product development | 31.3 | 4.20 | 4.91 | 9.11 |
| | Share expansion | '56.2 | 3.78 | 5.01 | 8.79 |
| | Cost reduction | 12.5 | 3.50 | 4.87 | 8.37 |

*Hypothesis 4-17*: In the electronics industry, the firms whose presidents set new-product development as a business goal achieve best business results. In the chain restaurant industry, those whose heads aim at expanding market share have the best ones. In both industries, those whose heads value cost reduction suffer the poorest business performances.

*Explanation*: In the electronics industry, development of a new-product encourages that of human resources, and vice versa. Such reciprocal process helps the company revitalize, bringing better business results. In the chain restaurant industry, where technological innovation is not so active as in the electronics industry, it is essential to expand a market share by increasing the number of chain stores. If the company continues to stick to cost reduction as a way to improve the poor business performance, it will maintain the status quo and lose organizational vigor, eventually resulting in poorer business performances.

## 4-4-3. Decision-Making Pattern

I presented the following three methods of decision-making to the presidents surveyed for their choice: 1. decision-making according to the president's viewpoint, 2. decision by the president upon consultation with executives, 3. decision according to executives' views.

Pioneer's Ishizuka is for the decision-making by the president. He says, "Discussing everything is time-wasting. 18 years ago when pioneer was a small firm, each employee spoke up too freely, which disturbed the order of the company. Now that we have grown to a large enterprise, I, as president, make business decisions, consulting the executive." TDK's Sono takes the same stance as Ishizuka. He says that the president naturally takes initiative in making a decision, which is his responsibility. "There are few arguments among the subordinate executives as to my decision," says Sono. Alps's Kataoka says that he announces a new project two years before it is started out in order to lay a sufficient groundwork for obtaining agreement of the individuals concerned. He thus insists on the decision-making according to the president's view, but with a special concern for unofficial talks behind the scene. In comparison, Mos Food's Sakurada makes a decision after discussing with the executives on an equal footing. He says, "I raise an objection to the executive's opinion, in an attempt to encourage further discussions." McDonald's Fujita points to the necessity of discussion: "A founder-president is in danger of receiving the only information which is likely to please him, so he should discuss with the executives to work out constructive ideas." Lastly, Kentucky's Tomita speaks for the decision-making, respecting opinions of the executives. He explains: "Before a plan is submitted to the board of executives, consisted of department heads and myself, for approval, it has already been agreed on by managers and other lower ranking employees."

Table 4-17 shows the result of an observation of large numbers concerning the relation between president's decision-making pattern and business results.

*Hypothesis 4-18*: In the electronics industry, the firms where the president is a main decision-maker, enjoy better business results, compared with those where the president gives priority to executives' opinions, or consults them on an equal footing. In the chain restaurant industry, the firms, where decision is made upon discussion between the president and his subordinate executives on an equal basis, have better business results.

**Table 4-17.**   Decision-Making Pattern and Business Results

| Industry | Decision-making | Percentage | Employees' morale | Business results | Integrated business results |
|---|---|---|---|---|---|
| Electronics | According to president's view | 25.5% | 3.92 | 5.83* | 9.75* |
| | Upon discussions with executives | 63.8 | 3.70 | 4.69 | 8.39 |
| | According to executives' view | 10.6 | 3.80 | 4.67 | 8.47 |
| Chain restaurant | According to president's view | 28.1 | 3.56 | 4.83 | 8.38 |
| | Upon discussions with executives | 59.4 | 4.05 | 5.22 | 9.27 |
| | According to executives' view | 12.5 | 3.75 | 4.06 | 7.81 |

*Explanation*: In the electronics industry, the firms, with the president being a main decision-maker, can expect a prompt and progressive decision, being quick to cope with changing business environment. However, to give the executives too big a say will lead to a time-consuming and mediocre decision. In the chain restaurant industry, where competitions are underway over similar products and services, better business results are achieved by those firms, with the president absorbing opinions of the executives in decision-making, and holding them responsible for administrating a decision made.

## 4-4-4.  Motivation of Employees

How the president's way of thinking about motivation of the employees influences their morale? I studied which one of the following factors the top management considers important as a motivating force: 1. pay/wages, working conditions, 2. human relations, 3. status/promotion, 4. job satisfaction.

McDonald's Fujita says that to provide the highest wages in Japan is our company principle. "The employees who are aged 27.8 on the average receive an annual salary of four million yen. No enterprises have ever gone bankrupt for reasons of high wages," says Fujita. Alps's Kataoka also notes the importance of high wages which, he says, help improve the workers' standard of living. "Only forcing moral factors is improper," he says. Aiwa's Sanbe holds a similar view. He says a survey conducted by the company on the former employees shows that dissatisfaction with low wages and bad relation with superiors top the list of reasons for their resignation. In contrast, Kentucky Fried Chicken's Tomita says, "Now that the Japanese economy has grown to a satisfactory extent, it's my job to prepare the working condition under which the employees can display their abilities." Skylark's Chino emphasizes job improvement, calling for agreement on company philosophy by all the employees. He says he wants them to share common "romanticism" at work.

The result of an observation of large numbers concerning the relation between the way of thinking about motivation for employees and business results is shown in Table 4-18.

**Table 4-18.**   Motivation of Employees and Business Results

| Industry | Motivation | Percentage | Employees' morale | Business result | Integrated business results |
|---|---|---|---|---|---|
| Electronics | Pay/wages, working condition | 21.3% | 3.50 | 3.92 | 7.42 |
| | Human relation | 34.0 | 3.94 | 5.15 | 9.09 |
| | Status/promotion | 14.9 | 4.00 | 6.43* | 10.41* |
| | Job satisfaction | 29.8 | 3.64 | 4.82 | 8.46 |
| Chain restaurant | Pay/wages, working condition | 40.6 | 3.84 | 5.29 | 9.14 |
| | Human relation | 28.1 | 3.44 | 4.21 | 7.65 |
| | Status/promotion | 15.6 | 4.00 | 4.22 | 8.22 |
| | Job satisfaction | 15.6 | 4.60 | 6.21* | 10.81* |

*Hypothesis 4-19*: In the electronics industry, the firms whose presidents emphasize promotion of the employees as a motivating force, achieve best business results, whereas those whose heads stress wages and working conditions suffer the worst ones. In the chain restaurant industry, the companies whose heads place priority on job satisfaction, wages and working conditions achieve better business performances than others.

*Explanation*: In the electronics industry, the employees are more or less controlled in a relatively large operation system, and enjoy high standard of living. Thus, they are greatly concerned about promotion leading to higher status within the company. In the chain restaurant industry, where part-time employees are the main work force, and a regular staff member, fresh from college, is likely to become a store manager in a short period of service, job satisfaction, higher wages as well as better working conditions may take precedence over other factors.

### 4-4-5. Attitude toward R & D

Whether the company will be able to develop a new product or not is determined by the president's attitude toward R & D. I have presented three alternative attitudes to the company heads surveyed for their choice: 1. active participation in R & D, 2. exerting leadership to some extent, 3. delegation of authority to experts.

Aiwa's Sanbe says that essentially, R & D requires boldness to run a risk. He says, "As technical department manager tends to be afraid of a failure, I initiate R & D." TDK's Sono is also an active R & D planner. He says, "I can predict, by intuition, a future course of industrial materials, which are an object of R & D in the company. I inquire what I don't understand with the engineers. They always only fulfill technical duties which they understand." Clarion's Oyamada insists on the positive commitment of the president in setting R & D targets. "I hold a meeting with the employees responsible for technical development almost bi-monthly, where I have them explain delicate technical issues, such as the difference between new and old elements, from a marketing viewpoint." In contrast, Casio's Kashio indicates that R & D has been entrusted to experts. "I approve of a budget plan for R & D as requested, but I check the final for myself," he says. Likewise, Kentucky's Tomita leaves R & D to the technical staff within the company, with vice president taking part in. "I don't hand it out to outsiders," Tomita says. McDonald's Fujita relies the company's R & D on the U.S. parent firm. "I know limitations of my abilities; I have excellent driving force, but lack boldness to take a risk. I know I am poor in R & D, so I leave everything about new product development to the U.S. headquarters."

Table 4-19 shows the relation between R & D-consciousness of the president and business results, as a result of an observation of large numbers.

From the table 4-19, the following hypothesis is available.

*Hypothesis 4-20*: In the electronics industry, the firms whose presidents are active in setting an R & D goal, demonstrating a pioneer

**Table 4-19.** President's Attitude toward R & D and Business Results

| Industry | President's attitude | Percentage | Employees' morale | Business results | Integrated business results |
|---|---|---|---|---|---|
| Electronics | Active role in setting R & D goal | 14.9% | 3.57 | 5.75* | 9.32 |
| | Exert leadership | 68.1 | 3.94* | 4.87 | 8.80 |
| | Delegation of authority to experts | 17.0 | 3.25 | 4.76 | 8.01 |
| Chain restaurant | Active role in setting R & D goal | 56.3 | 4.00 | 4.86 | 8.86 |
| | Exert leadership | 28.1 | 3.78 | 4.35 | 8.13 |
| | Delegation of authority to experts | 15.6 | 3.60 | 6.43* | 10.03 |

spirit, have better business results than those whose heads transfer the responsibility to other experts. The situation in the chain restaurant industry is opposite.

*Explanation*: In many of the electronics companies, where the president has a long experience of product development, it is possible to work on R & D with a due consideration of technical, marketing and financial aspects. In addition, substantial risk-bearing is possible for progressive research. In the chain restaurant industry, however, it is safer to delegate R & D-related responsibility to experts, because the president hasn't a long experience with food production and service fields.

## 4-4-6.  The Criteria for Promotion to Department Head Cited by President

How the president considers criteria for promotion of the employees to department head affects the company morale, and eventually the company growth? I have presented the following criteria for the promotion to the presidents surveyed: service period, educational background, professional qualifications, ability and performance.

Casio's Kashio says, "We check a department head candidate according to the company's qualification system first, and then review how he has contributed to business results. For instance, among the criteria for being sales department manager are an outstanding job in increasing sales and enticing agents from other companies." Similarly,

TDK's Sono rates highly the candidate's contribution to business performances. "I measure his achievement by how efficiently he educated his subordinates. To educate them, to level up harmony in the section, headed by him," says Sono. Kentucky's Tomita also takes the performance-oriented stance. He says that he values the employee, in the accounting section, for example, who made a system improvement or reduced work load. Mos Food Service's Sakurada, on the other hand, puts emphasis on abilities in planning and materializing a project, as well as leadership quality, which he says, will encourage others to participate in a project. "It is not desirable for superiors to do everything on their own," says Sakurada. Clarion's Oyamada explains that the employees are promoted based on a three-grouped qualification system. "They are placed in one of the three groups after three years of service. The first one is the most promising, having a special promotion plan, and two other groups have not such a special promotion plan, but they have a few *"return-match* opportunity." Oyamada says.

The result of an observation of large numbers concerning the above question indicates that most of the respondents cited the employee's over-all abilities and achievements as criteria for promotion, but no clear correlations between them and business results.

## 4-5. Consequences of Decision-Making, Ratios of New-Products, New-Equipment and New-Stores

The growth of a company is boosted in the process in which a new-product development encourages a human ability development, and vice versa. Other factors for the company growth include introduction of new equipment, which will bring about better quality and cost reduction of products. Futhermore, opening a new store has the same impact as the new-product development. In this section, I have studied the ratios of products developed, new and powerful equipment introduced, and stores opened, for the past three years respectively.

Table 4-20 through 4-22 show the results of the large number observations on the relation between each factor and business results. *Hypothesis 4-21*: In the electronics industry, the firms, whose sales

**Table 4-20.**    New-Product Ratio and Business Results

| Industry | Ratio of New product sales | Percentage | Employees' morale | Business results | Integrated business results |
|---|---|---|---|---|---|
| Electronics | below 10% | 12.8% | 3.33 | 4.35 | 7.68 |
| | 10 to 19% | 27.7 | 3.69 | 4.40 | 8.09 |
| | 20 to 29% | 23.4 | 3.73 | 5.11 | 8.84 |
| | 30% and above | 36.2 | 4.00 | 5.57 | 9.57* |

**Table 4-21.**    New-Equipment Ratio and Business Results

| Industry | Ratio | Percentage | Employees' morale | Business results | Integrated business results |
|---|---|---|---|---|---|
| Electronics | below 20% | 10.6% | 3.60 | 4.48 | 8.08 |
| | 20 to 29% | 23.4 | 3.73 | 4.47 | 8.20 |
| | 30 to 39% | 25.5 | 3.75 | 4.84 | 8.59 |
| | 40% and above | 40.5 | 3.84 | 5.49 | 9.33 |

**Table 4-22.**    New-Store Ratio and Business Results

| Industry | Ratio | Percentage | Employees' morale | Business results | Integrated business results |
|---|---|---|---|---|---|
| Chain restaurant | below 20% | 31.3% | 3.70 | 4.17 | 7.87 |
| | 20 to 39% | 25.0 | 4.00 | 4.64 | 8.64 |
| | 40% and above | 43.7 | 3.93 | 5.71* | 9.64* |

of the products newly developed in the last three years, account for more than 30 percent of the total, achieve high employees' morale and business performances, while those with such ratio being below 10 percent are low in both factors.

*Hypothesis 4-22*: In the electronics industry, the firms whose new equipment introduced in the past three years account for more than 40 percent of the total equipment, have high employees' morale and business performances, whereas those with such ratio being below 20 percent are poor in both factors.

*Explanation*: When a firm's main product reaches a stable stage in its life cycle, the firm invests in the rationalization of production facilities, aimed at cost reduction and quality improvement, and in labor-saving efforts, which is necessary to win competitions with other companies. Such a positive attitude of the top management helps enhance financial results of the company.

*Hypothesis 4-23*: In the chain restaurant industry, the firms whose new shops opened for the past three years account for more than 40 percent of the total, have high business performances, while those with such ratio being less than 20 percent are low in business performances. *Explanation*: Opening a new store steps up the growth rate and profitability of the company through increased total sales and lowered cost of mass-produced products.

## 4-6. Summary

I have compiled in Table 4-23 the factors expected of the top management, which reflected in the company's business results. Some are common in the two industries surveyed, and other factors not. There are a few other factors which have no relations with business results.

In terms of objective attribute of top management, a most desirable president common in both industries is the one who is a founder of the company, coming from a low social class. Other factors such as age, the period of presidency and field of specialization are insignificant in determining a good president.

Seen from a viewpoint of abilities, the desirable president has the following abilities in common; bold ambition, quick response to cope with a new situation, keen intuition, willingness to do colleagues or subordinates favors, persistence in persuasion, superb health and ability in collecting a wide range of information. Other abilities, such as determination and respect for others are not among decisive factors for a good company head. When presidents' abilities are divided into two categories, i.e., the entrepreneurship and administratorship, the latter is expected in the electronics industry, and the former in the chain restaurant industry.

On the management concept and decision-making pattern, the desirable factors vary with the industry. As to the strengths of the company, for the electronics industry presidents, to cite new product development is desirable, while for the chain restaurant heads, to cite a stable demand from regular customers is desirable.

On management goal, for the electronics industry attaching importance to product development is desirable, whereas that market share expansion is given a top priority is desirable in the chain restaurant industry.

**Table 4-23.**   Factors Expected of Top Management

| Factor | Desirability in the two industries | Most Desirable Factor | |
|---|---|---|---|
| | | Electronics Ind. | Chain Restauraunt Id. |
| **Attribute** | | | |
| Type of president | Same | Founder | Founder |
| Family origin | Same | Lower social class | Lower social class |
| Age | ⎫ No significant relations observed | | |
| Presidency | ⎬ | | |
| Specialization | ⎭ | | |
| **Ability** | | | |
| Ambition | Same | Great ambition | Great ambition |
| Coping with new situation | Same | Quick response | Quick response |
| Determination | Different | Bold determination | Unknown |
| Intuition | Same | Intuition | Intuition |
| Respecting others | Different | Impersonal | Human feelings-orientation |
| Willingness to do other favors | Same | Always willing | Always willing |
| Persuasion | Same | Persistent persuasion | Persistent persuasion |
| Health | Same | Superb health | Superb health |
| Gathering information | Same | As much information as possible | As much information as possible |
| Entrepreneurship, administratorship | Different | Administratorship | Entrepreneurship |
| **Management Concept, Decision-Making Pattern** | | | |
| Strengths and weaknesses | Different | Product development capacity | Stable clients |
| Business goal | Different | New product development | Market share expansion |
| Decision-making pattern | Different | President's initiative | Upon discussions with executives |
| Motivation of employees | Different | Status, promotion | Worthwhile job |
| Attitude toward R & D | Different | Active participation | Delegation of authority to experts |
| Criteria for promotion to department head | Unknown | | |
| **Consequences of Decision Making** | | | |
| New product ratio | —— | above 30% | —— |
| New equipment ratio | —— | above 40% | —— |
| New store ratio | —— | —— | above 40% |

Concerning decision-making pattern, the firm whose president is the main decision-maker achieves a good business performance in the electronics industry, while the firm whose president consults his subordinate executives before he makes a final decision makes a good business performance in the chain restaurant industry.

In the electronics industry, status promotion is the most important motivation of the employees, while in the chain restaurant industry, worthwhile job is the leading driving force.

On the research and development, active participation is desirable for the president in the electronics industry, and it is desirable for the company head in the chain restaurant industy to entrust R & D to the experts.

In terms of sequencescon of decision-making, positive business management is desirable in both industries: in the electronics industry, the firms with the ratios of new products and new equipment being above 30 percent and 40 percent respectively, are desirable, while in the chain restaurant industry, those with the ratio of new stores being over 40 percent are expected.

As noted above, the objective and specific factors determining the desirable president, including attributes and consequences of president's decision, do not vary with the industry. For the abilities of the president, the situation is similar with a few exceptions. However, other factors for a successful president, such as management concept and decision-making pattern, differ depending on the industry. This is probably because these factors are greatly influenced by business environment surrounding the president.

# 5

# An Empirical Research on Top Management Abilities in the Sake Brewing Industry

## 5-1. Introduction

The top management generally contribute to better business performance by displaying their abilities in three functional processes: thinking out future business visions, strategic decision-making, and business management and control. More specifically, the top management contribute to the improvement in financial performance through devising and implementing product strategies. To evaluate abilities of the chief executives, it is necessary to make an analysis of the relationship among factors related to them such as required abilities, product strategies, and corporate performance. This chapter examines the relationship between top management's abilities and business results in the Sake brewing industry where products are relatively stable.

An attempt is also made to investigate the relationship between business performance and the pattern of decision-making concerning product strategy, as well as the result of management and control of a decision made. This chapter also discusses desirable top management abilities, and the decision-making process by which such abilities contribute to excellent corporate performance. In addition, an analysis is made on the influence of external environment and attributes of the top management on the formation of their desired abilities. In other words, this chapter deals with following factors related to chief executives: external environment, abilities and attributes of the top management, decision-making, consequences of decision-making, and business performance.

The framework and methodology of analysis, and surrogates used in this chapter are the same as those adopted in Chapter 4. The present discussion is based on the result of a questionnaire survey conducted jointly by the author and the Sake Section of the National Tax Agency in October, 1981, which covered 800 Sake brewing companies across the country. In the survey, a total of 749 companies gave effective answers. To help make an accurate analysis of the survey result, the author interviewed the chief executives of 29 companies from among those surveyed.

## 5-2. History of the Sake Brewing Industry and Attributes of Chief Executives

Objective factors related to attributes of the president such as historical environment, family origin and up-bringing substantially influence his way of thinking, behavior pattern and decision-making practices. The characteristic environment surrounding presidents of Sake brewing companies are the long history and high social status of the industry, and a very intense market competition inside the industry.

The afore-mentioned survey shows that about 80 percent of Sake manufacturing firms were founded in and before the *Meiji* Era (1868–1912); 35.6 percent in the *Edo* Era (1603–1867), 43.0 percent in the *Meiji* Era, 11.6 percent in the *Taisho* Era (1912–1926) and 9.7 percent in the *Showa* Era (1926–present). The presidents in the Sake brewing industry enjoy high social status in their home-grounds, assuming many posts in public offices and various other organizations. As to profitability, however, only 25.2 percent are not red figures or profitable, and the rest of others are either not on a paying basis or barely retain the break even point. Despite the difficult situation faced by the industry, 88 percent of the presidents have their successors appointed. This is attributed to the high social status of the industry, rather than to economic factors. While a total demand for Sake has been levelling off, 2,700 smaller Sake brewing companies nationwide are engaged in keen competitions with one another in the production and sales of products of similar kinds.

As described above, the presidents in the Sake brewing industry with a long history have been faced with difficult management situations.

Concerning the type of presidents, an overwhelming number of presidents—74.8 percent—are sons or grandsons of their predecessors; 6.7 percent are sons-in-law, 4.4 percent are spouses and 4.3 percent are relatives. Looking at the relationship between the type of the president and business performance, the company headed by an offspring of its former president shows a lower degree of business results; its average value is 4.99, which is compared with 5.14[1] for the other companies. This is probably due to such president's lack of flexibility and failure in vitalizing his company and its products.

The chief executives of Sake brewing firms are unexpectedly young; their average age is 56.5. Companies with younger presidents achieve excellent business performance apparently because of their ability in bringing about vitality; the relative value of business performance is 5.12 for firms with presidents aged 49 and younger; 5.11 for those headed by presidents aged between 50 and 59; 4.85 for those with presidents aged between 60 and 69; and 5.00 for those with presidents aged 70 and older. Overall, companies with presidents aged 59 and younger enjoy a high level of business performance.

The period of presidency in the Sake brewing industry is generally long—19.3 years on the average. Companies whose presidents remain in office for a relatively short period show excellent performance; its relative value being 5.11 for firms with presidents serving for less than ten years; 5.09 for those between eleven and 25 years; and 4.88 for those more than 26 years. This can be attributed to the long-serving presidents' lack of flexibility and failure in vitalizing their companies and products.

By major field of presidents, those who received non-technical education, such as economics and science of commerce, outnumbers those who have technical backgrounds including agricultural chemistry and science of brewing. No significant relationship exists between chief executives' major fields and their business performances.

---

(1)   The underlined figures show maximum values.

## 5-3. Abilities of President

Most of the Sake brewing firms are small in scale, and their products are not largely different with each other, so managerial abilities of the chief executives have direct effects on corporate results. In order to identify their desired abilities, the presidents in the Sake brewing industry were asked to fill in a questionnaire consisting of ten questions. One of the questions was, for example, : "Suppose you drink and eat out with your familiar friends, who will pay the expense?" Answer A: We usually split the account. Answer B: I usually pick up the bill. Please encircle one of the four sub-answers: 1. Answer A; 2. Answer A, more or less; 3. Answer B, more or less; and 4. Answer B. By this SD(Semantic Differential)method, the president's willingness to do others a favor was quantified

### 5-3-1. Ambitions

Concerning ambitions which are considered as a driving force of an entrepreneur, the chief executives were asked to choose from these two possibilities: A: A future business vision is made based on the result of a detailed analysis of the present strengths and weaknesses of the company. B: A future business vision is made with ambitions, for example, of becoming No. 1 within the industry ten years after.

A correlation analysis of president's ambition and the other attributes shows that president's ambitions aren't markedly related with his attributes, but that the president of a profitable firm tends to become ambitious (correlation coefficient between company's profitability and the president's ambition is 0.103*).[2] This is probably because soundness of the company helps the president increase his confidence.

Further Table 5-1 shows the relationship between president's attitude toward ambitions and business performance. Thus we have: *Hypothesis 5-1*: Regardless of business scale, companies whose presidents think out a future business vision with a clear ambition show better business results than those headed by the presidents who emphasize corporate strengths and weaknesses.

---

(2)  Figures with a *mark show statistical significance (5 percent level).

**Table 5-1.** Ambition and Business Results

| President's attitude | Whole Sake brewing industry | | Companies producing less than 200kl of Sake a year | | Companies producing 200 to 2000kl | | Companies producing more than 2000kl | |
|---|---|---|---|---|---|---|---|---|
| | Percentage | Bus. Results | Percentage | Bus. Results | Percentage | Bus. Results | Percentage | Bus. Results |
| Based on strength and weakness | 87. 4% | 4. 97 | 89. 7% | 4. 72 | 86. 1% | 5. 22 | 71. 4% | 5. 75 |
| Based on ambition | 12. 6 | 5. 44* | 10. 3 | 5. 23* | 13. 9 | .5. 40 | 28. 6 | 6. 74* |

The top management are required to possess ambitions; ambitious presidents can conduct an innovative management, and thereby improving corporate performance. Larger companies tend to have more ambitious presidents than smaller businesses. The president of a small company is unlikely to become ambitious because of the management difficulty faced by him.

## 5-3-2. Ability in Coping with a New Situation

President's ability to foresee a changing environment and to deal with it quickly is indispensable for corporate growth.

*Question*: "If the information comes in that a new brewing technique has been developed, what will you do?" Answer A: If it appears to have no direct bearing on my company, I will wait for further information. Answer B: Although it appears to have no direct bearing on my company, I will actively consider how to use it.

A correlation analysis indicates that ability in coping with a new situation is generally demonstrated by the presidents who received technical education (correlation coefficient: 0. 158*), actively participate in seminars (0. 176*) and give top priority their self-studies in daily life (0. 119*). This provides us with the following hypothesis:

*Hypothesis 5-2*: A chief executive with technical education, vigorous health and enthusiasm toward self-study has an excellent ability in

**Table 5-2.** Ability in Coping with New Situation and Business Results

| President's attitude | Whole Sake | | <200kl | | 200~2000kl | | 2000kl≦ | |
|---|---|---|---|---|---|---|---|---|
| | Percentage | Bus. Results | Percentage | Bus. Results | Percentage | Bus. Results | Percentage | Bus. Results |
| Wait for more information | 70. 5% | 4. 98 | 76. 4% | 4. 75 | 65. 0% | 5. 21 | 50. 0% | 6. 41 |
| Consider how to use | 29. 5 | 5. 14 | 23. 6 | 4. 85 | 35. 0 | 5. 32 | 50. 0 | 5. 66 |

coping with changing environments.

Table 5-2 shows the relationship between the chief executive's ability in coping with a new situation and business performance.

*Hypothesis 5-3*: Those Sake brewing firms headed by presidents who can quickly cope with a change in environment by using new information achieve high level of corporate performance.

A more detailed analysis shows that although the above hypothesis holds with smaller companies with annual Sake production amount of less than 2,000 kilolitters, it doesn't do so with larger businesses. This can be attributed to a lower degree of necessity of the ability in quick response to changing environment in larger companies which have a stable market for their stable products.

## 5-3-3. Determination

In an uncertain business situation, the chief executives are often required to make a "non-logical" decision.

*Question*: "If sales of main products you are in charge of decline for three consecutive years, what will you do?" Answer A: I will continue the production and sales of the products as long as they are profitable. Answer B: I will completely withdraw them.

The determination of the president has few relationships with the environment surrounding him and his attributes, although younger presidents seem to have determination (correlation coefficient: $-0.081$). The president's willingness to respect others is negatively related with determination $(-0.155^*)$.

Table 5-3 shows the relationship between president's determination and business results. As seen in the table, there are few differences

**Table 5-3.**  Determination and Business Results

| President's attitude | Whole Sake | | <200kl | | 200~2000kl | | 2000kl≦ | |
|---|---|---|---|---|---|---|---|---|
| | Percent-age | Bus. Results | Percent-age | Bus. Results | Percent-age | Bus. Results | Percent-age | Bus. Results |
| Continue production | 72.4% | 5.03 | 72.9% | 4.81 | 71.8% | 5.21 | 71.4% | 6.04 |
| Discontinue production | 27.6 | 5.02 | 27.1 | 4.69 | 28.2 | 5.34 | 28.6 | 6.02 |

in business results between companies with the two categories of presidents. It can be said that in the Sake brewing industry as a whole, the president's bold determination doesn't have large effects on business performance. A more important factor is quantitative thinking as will be discussed later.

## 5-3-4. Respecting Others

To become a successful corporate leader, the chief executive must have a respect for his subordinates

*Question*: "Suppose you think you have made a reasonable decision on personnel management involving an executive, but you still feel somewhat sorry for him, what will you do?" Answer A: I will convince myself that presidency is a lonely job, and do nothing about it. Answer B: I will think out better alternatives.

A correlation study shows that elderly presidents have more respects for others than young ones (0.105*).

*Hypothesis 5-4*: The older the president, the more respects he shows for others.

Table 5-4 shows the relationship between president's respects for others and corporate performance.

*Hypothesis 5-5*: In small-sized businesses, like Sake brewing companies, presidents' attitude of respecting others helps improve corporate performances.

**Table 5-4.** President's Respect for Others and Business Results

| President's attitude | Whole Sake | | <200kl | | 200~2000kl | | 2000kl≦ | |
|---|---|---|---|---|---|---|---|---|
| | Percentage | Bus. Results | Percentage | Bus. Results | Percentage | Bus. Results | Percentage | Bus. Results |
| Impersonal, rational | 31.0% | 4.95 | 30.4% | 4.66 | 31.9% | 5.18 | 28.6% | 6.43 |
| Human feelings—oriented | 69.0 | 5.06 | 69.6 | 4.83 | 68.1 | 5.28 | 71.4% | 5.83 |

In smaller Sake brewing companies with annual production amount less than 2,000 kilolitters each, it is hard to improve business results through product diversification; presidents' respect for their subordinates raise their morale, help them display creativity, and thereby improving business performance.

## 5-3-5. Intuition

In a drastically changing environment, it is difficult to foresee the future based on past statistics. This section compares the importance of quantitative thinking and intuition.

*Question*: "On what basis will you estimate for the total sales for five years after?" Answer A: related objective figures and information rather than my intuition. Answer B: my intuition rather than related objective figures and information.

A correlation analysis indicates that the chief executive's quantitative thinking is less related to his major field (0.005), and more related to his enthusiasm toward self-study (0.143*).

*Hypothesis 5-6*: The chief executive's quantitative thinking is related less to his major field, and more to his enthusiasm toward self-study.

Table 5-5 shows the relationship between the president's quantitative and analytical thinking and business performance.

*Hypothesis 5-7*: In the Sake brewing industry which is growing at a low rate, companies with presidents who have excellent quantitative and analytical thinking show a higher level of corporate performance than those whose presidents attach importance to their intuition.

This hypothesis doesn't hold in the case of the rapidly growing electronics and chain restaurant industries mentioned in Chapter 4. In these industries, the top executives can afford to make a prompt decision based on their intuition because a loss resulting from a failing decision can be easily recovered by big profit margins. On the other hand, the stagnant Sake brewing industry cannot afford to make up for any minor loss, for its profit margin is limited. It is very important that quantitative and analytical thinking based on related figures and data makes a

**Table 5-5.** Quantitative Thinking (not intuition) and Business Results

| President's attitude | Whole Sake | | <200kl | | 200~2000kl | | 2000kl≤ | |
|---|---|---|---|---|---|---|---|---|
| | Percent-age | Bus. Results | Percent-age | Bus. Results | Percent-age | Bus. Results | Percent-age | Bus. Results |
| Based on data | 73.6% | 5.13* | 68.6% | 4.93* | 79.3% | 5.27 | 78.6% | 6.06 |
| Based on intuition | 26.4 | 4.73 | 31.4 | 4.43 | 20.7 | 5.19 | 21.4 | 5.94 |

sales estimate in detail. This is especially true with competitive petty firms (annual Sake production amount of less than 200 kilolitters).

## 5-3-6.  Willingness to Do Others a Favor

A Japanese company president is always required to do his subordinates favors and make informal discussions with them on a given subject so that he can make a prompt decision at a formal executive meeting. The president's such practice is important to enable a prompt and innovative decision-making in which many executives participate.

*Question*: "Suppose you drink and eat out with your familiar friends, who will pay the expense?" Answer A: We usually split the account. Answer B: I usually pick up the bill. Those who chose Answer A are considered willing to do others a favor.

The president's willingness to do others a favor is not markedly related to his attributes such as age (correlation coefficient: 0.054), length of period of presidency (0.013), and major field (0.047).

But Table 5-6 shows the relationship between the presidents doing others a favor and business results.

**Table 5-6.** Willingness to Do Others a Favor and Business Results

| President's attitude | Whole Sake | | <200kl | | 200~2000kl | | 2000kl≤ | |
|---|---|---|---|---|---|---|---|---|
| | Percent-age | Bus. Results | Percent-age | Bus. Results | Percent-age | Bus. Results | Percent-age | Bus. Results |
| Split the expense | 55.1% | 4.97 | 57.5% | 4.67 | 54.2% | 5.31 | 32.1% | 6.14 |
| Pick up the bill | 44.9 | 5.10 | 42.5 | 4.93 | 45.8 | 5.18 | 67.9 | 5.98 |

*Hypothesis* 5-8: In the Sake brewing industry, companies with presidents willing to do others a favor always achieve better business performance than those whose presidents are unwilling to do so.

The practice of *"Kashi-Kari"* (give and take) is generally conducted in Japanese businesses including the Sake brewing industry. But this isn't true with medium and large companies producing more than 200 kilolitters of Sake a year. This is because they need not make a prompt and innovative decision on their products which have relatively stable markets.

## 5-3-7. Persuasion

The chief executive is required to have confidence and ability in persuading his fellow executives to agree with his devised proposal; confident attitudes and tenacious efforts to persuade other people are necessary requirements for competent business leaders.

*Question*: "If an executive opposes your new product strategy, what will you do?" Answer A: I will shelve up my plan temporarily, and try to persuade him through occasional contacts with him. Answer B: I will try to persuade him persistently on the basis of objective data.

A correlation analysis shows that the president's persuasion has been developed by such factors as his physical power (correlation coefficient between health and persuasion: 0.119*), enthusiasm about self-study (0.108*) and ability in collecting indirect information (0.118*).

*Hypothesis 5-9*: The chief executive's persuasion is improved by health, ability in collecting indirect information and enthusiasm toward self-study.

Table 5-7 indicates the relationship between the president's persuasion and business results.

**Table 5-7.** Persuasion and Business Results

| President's attitude | Whole Sake | | <200kl | | 200~2000kl | | 2000kl≤ | |
|---|---|---|---|---|---|---|---|---|
| | Percent-age | Bus. Results | Percent-age | Bus. Results | Percent-age | Bus. Results | Percent-age | Bus. Results |
| Shelve up temporarily | 31.1% | 4.93 | 34.2% | 4.80 | 27.6% | ·5.07 | 28.7% | 5.79 |
| Persuade persistently | 68.9 | 5.07 | 65.8 | 4.77 | 72.4 | 5.32 | 71.4 | 6.13 |

From the above table, this hypothesis is available:

*Hypothesis 5-10*: In the Sake brewing industry as a whole, firms whose presidents are able to persuade their fellow executives to agree with their-proposed business strategies enjoy better corporate performances than those with presidents who shelve up their plans temporarily.

The above hypothesis is most effective to large companies with annual Sake production amount exceeding 2,000 kilolitters each, where tenacious efforts are needed to obtain consents of many executives involved.

## 5-3-8.  Health

Health is an indispensable factor required of the president in fulfilling his duties——thinking out a future business vision, making an innovative decision, and conducting management and control.

*Question*: "Do you take good care of your health when work is hard?" Answer A: I work within the limit of my health. Answer B: I give top priority to my duties, irrespective of my health.

A correlation analysis shows that younger presidents (correlation coefficient: −0. 214*) with a shorter period of presidency (−0. 201*) tend to give preference to their duties.

*Hypothesis 5-11*: Young presidents serving for a relatively short period tend to be heal thy and have determination to fulill their duties.

Table 5-8 indicates the relationship between the president's health and business performances.

*Hypothesis 5-12*: The firms whose presidents give top priority to their duties, regardless of their health, show better corporate results than those whose heads work within the limit of their health.

This hypothesis suggests that the president should be vigorous enough to sustain hard work; unhealthy presidents cannot produce satisfactory business results.

**Table 5-8.**    Health and Business Results

| President's attitude | Whole Sake | | <200kl | | 200~2000kl | | 2000kl≤ | |
|---|---|---|---|---|---|---|---|---|
| | Percent-age | Bus. Results | Percent-age | Bus. Results | Percent-age | Bus. Results | Percent-age | Bus. Results |
| Health-conscious approach to work | 39. 5% | 4. 85 | 40. 7% | 4. 56 | 39. 0% | 5. 15 | 28. 6% | 5. 81 |
| Give top priority to work | 60. 5 | 5. 15* | 59. 3 | 4. 92* | 61. 0 | 5. 31 | 71. 4 | 6. 12 |

## 5-3-9. Ability in Gathering Information

The chief executive should constantly collect and understand a variety of information so that he can quickly deal with a changing environment. Especially important are the information on prospects of the future market for the company's main products and on the development of related technology.

*Question*: "What do you think of gathering product-related information?" Answer A: I constantly collect as much information as possible. Answer B: I collect information, considering its possible effects on my company.

A correlation analysis shows that the chief executive of a profitable firm is enthusiastic about gathering information (correlation coefficient: 0. 118*). The president's ability in collecting information is not very much related to his age (0. 001), length of period of presidency (0. 055) and major field (0. 066). Ambitious presidents (0. 107*) with quantitative thinking (0.228*) are active in gathering information.

*Hypothesis 5-13*: President's enthusiasm toward gathering information is related less with his age, period of presidency and field of specialisation, but more with the company's profitability and president's ambitions and quantitative thinking.

Table 5-9 shows the relationship between the president's ability in collecting information and business results.

*Hypothesis 5-14*: The firms whose presidents gather as much information as possible achieve a higher level of corporate performances than those with presidents collecting only those information that will directly affect their companies.

**Table 5-9.**    Information Gathering and Business Results

| President's attitude | Whole Sake | | <200kl | | 200~2000kl | | 2000kl≦ | |
|---|---|---|---|---|---|---|---|---|
| | Percentage | Bus. Results | Percentage | Bus. Results | Percentage | Bus. Results | Percentage | Bus. Results |
| Gather as much as possible | 54.9% | 5.16* | 47.0% | 4.88 | 62.2% | 5.32 | 82.1% | 6.04 |
| Gather select information | 45.1 | 4.86 | 53.0 | 4.68 | 37.8 | 5.13 | 17.9 | 6.01 |

In today's drastically changing society, it is difficult for business enterprises to predict exactly future external impacts on them, so it is necessary to collect information as much as possible and prepare for possible external impacts.

## 5-3-10.    Ability in Gathering Indirect Information

In a bid to cope with the drastically changing environment, the chief executive should always pay attention to factors which may affect his company in the future.

*Question*: "Do you often read newspaper articles on politics, international relations, literature and other issues that appear to have no direct bearing on the company management?" Answer A: No. Answer B: Yes.

The chief executive's ability in gathering indirect information is not markedly related to his attributes. However, it shows high correlations with his persuasion (correlation coefficient: 0.118*), quantitative thinking (0.109*) and showing respects for others (0.099*). Such factors as the president's age (−0.046) and major field (0.052) are not markedly related to the above ability.

**Table 5-10.** Gathering Indirect Information and Business Results

| President's attitude | Whole Sake | | <200kl | | 200~2000kl | | 2000kl≦ | |
|---|---|---|---|---|---|---|---|---|
| | Percent-age | Bus. Results | Percent-age | Bus. Results | Percent-age | Bus. Results | Percent-age | Bus. Results |
| Don't read newspaper articles extensively | 15.4% | 4.84 | 14.3% | 4.60 | 17.0% | 4.98 | 10.7% | 6.94 |
| Read the above often | 84.6 | 5.06 | 85.7 | 4.81 | 83.0 | 5.30 | 89.3 | 5.92 |

*Hypothesis 5-15*: In the Sake brewing industry, firms with the presidents often reading newspaper articles on such issues as politics, international relations, and literature, achieve better corporate performances.

Many presidents of Sake brewing companies are well-educated and an overwhelming number of them often read newspaper articles on issues that are not directly related with their firms. The high corporate performances of such companies are attributed to the fact that sales of Sake are largely affected by people's life styles and thinking modes, as well as by prices and quality of products.

## 5-3-11. Contributions of President's Abilities to Corporate Performance

Figure 5-1 compares contributions of ten president's abilities to better business results. Values for each abilities in Figure 5-1 are the difference between two values of business results in the category of the whole Sake brewing industry in their respective Tables from 5-1 through 5-10. For example, the value for ambitions was obtained in this way: 5.44−4.97=0.47 (See Table 5-1). This difference indicates the degree of contribution of president's ambition to business results.

As indicated in Figure 5-1, ambitions, quantitative thinking, health and ability in gathering information are four major contributors to better corporate performance. It can be concluded that to produce satisfactory business results, presidents of Sake brewing firms are required to: think out a future business vision based on bold ambitions; constantly gather information on the present situation and future prospects of products; use as available statistics as possible in making a sales

**Figure 5-1.** Contributions of President's Abilities to Better Business Results

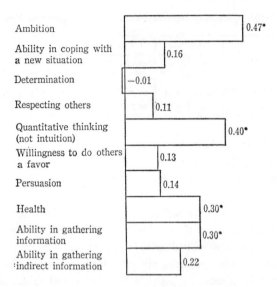

estimate; and be healthy enough to sustain hard work.

## 5-3-12.  Requirement for Company Presidents

I have so far discussed abilities required of the chief executives through their behavior patterns and thinking modes. This section is to examine what the presidents consider important in performing their duties. They were asked to choose three most important requirements for presidency from among those listed below:

1. ambitions,  2. sense of duty,  3. philosophy,  4. belief,  5. intuition, 6. imagination,  7. insight,  8. determination,  9. boldness to run a risk, 10. generosity,  11. personal attractiveness  12. ethics,  13. systematic thinking,  14. effective use of time,  15. quantitative thinking,  16. leadership,  17. sense of responsibility,  18. health,  19. general know- ledge,  20. knowledge of other executives' views,  21. curiosity,

Table 5-11 shows presidents' choice of required abilities (total: 300 percent).

As seen in the Table 5-11, most presidents attach importance to det- ermination, belief, health and sense of responsibility. This is compared

**Table 5-11.** Abilities Required of Presidents

| Ability | 1 | 2 | 3 | 4 | 5 | 6 | 7 | 8 | 9 |
|---|---|---|---|---|---|---|---|---|---|
| | 4.8% | 21.9 | 6.3 | 35.1 | 3.0 | 2.7 | 14.7 | 46.8 | 1.5 |
| Ability | 10 | 11 | 12 | 13 | 14 | 15 | 16 | 17 | 18 |
| | 13.2% | 18.3 | 4.8 | 2.1 | 4.8 | 16.2 | 27.0 | 31.5 | 35.1 |
| Ability | 19 | 20 | 21 | no answer | | | | | |
| | 5.7% | 3.0 | 0.9 | 0.3 | | | | | |

with those ablities which contribute to improved corporate performance described in the previous section; health is the only common ability. The four abilities considered most important for the presidents seem to be necessary conditions, but these abilities alone cannot ensure excellent business results. Other contributors to better business performance: ambitions, and quantitative thinking. are excluded. Compared with the case of the electronics and chain restaurant industries, chief executives of the Sake brewing industry possess more belief and sense of responsibility, and less leadership and personal appeal. This is attributed to the fact that presidents of Sake makers are celebrities in their communities who operate relatively small scale businesses.

The above 21 abilities are classified into three categories: 1. entrepreneurship: abilities numbered 1 (ambitions) through 9 (boldness to run a risk); 2. health; and 3. administratorship: abilities numbered 10 (generosity) through 21 (curiosity) except health (ability number 18). A comparative study says that there is not a large difference in each categories' contributions to better business results; 5.04 for entrepreneurship, 5.00 for administratorship, and 5.03 for health. The slight difference in value between the entrepreneurship and administratorship categories indicates the importance of the former in the stagnant Sake brewing industry. In the rapidly growing electronics industry, administratorship marked more contributions to business performance than entrepreneurship, as mentioned in Chapter 4.

## 5–4.  Decision-Making in Business

This section deals with the decision-making process in business which involves such factors as "external environment"→"attributes of president" →"president's abilities"→"decision-making"→" consequences of decision making"→"business performance". [3] Issues to be discussed here are factors related to the decision-making process such as an objective of the firm and business goals sought by the presidents, their views on business environment, and strength of their companies, as well as patterns of decision-making at the highest decision-making body.

### 5–4–1.  Firm Objectives Thought by the President

Japanese businesses primarily aim at growing for a long period of time, while U.S. firms seek maximization of present values of issued stocks. In other words, Japanese business objectives are set from the corporate viewpoint, whereas U.S. ones from the stockholders'. Medium-large companies in Japan which enjoy prosperity generally cite a long-term corporate growth as one of their objectives, but stagnant petty firms usually aim at retaining their assets. The chief executives of Sake brewing businesses were asked to choose one of these four firms objectives: 1. to earn a living; 2. to earn a living and retain family assets; 3. to secure profits and seek long-term corporate growth; and 4. to seek company growth and accomplish social responsibility.

The objectives with larger numbers in the above list are considered to indicate president's active attitude toward business management. The coefficients of correlation between president's such attitude for firm objectives and his abilities are relatively high; $0.106^*$ for ambitions, $0.215^*$ for ability in coping with a new situation, and $0.171^*$ for ability in gathering information, but relatively low for determination $(0.030)$ and willingness to do others a favor $(0.047)$. This results in the following hypothesis:

*Hypothesis 5–16*: Ambitious presidents, who are enthusiastic about gathering information and quick to respond to changing situations, tend to seek corporate growth for long time and fulfill social responsibility,

---

(3)   Section 6–2.

rather than retaining their family assets.

Table 5-12 shows the relationship between selected business objectives and corporate performance.

**Table 5-12.** Firm Objectives Thought by the President and Business Results

| Objectives of firm | Whole Sake | | <200kl | | 200~2000kl | | 2000kl≤ | |
|---|---|---|---|---|---|---|---|---|
| | Percent-age | Bus. Results | Percent-age | Bus. Results | Percent-age | Bus. Results | Percent-age | Bus. Results |
| To earn a living, to maintain assets | 42.3% | 4.64 | 58.5% | 4.51 | 26.0% | 4.99 | 0.0% | — |
| Long—term corporate growth | 33.1 | 5.39* | 23.6 | 5.31* | 43.0 | 5.40* | 53.6 | 5.77 |
| To fulfill social responsibility | 24.6 | 5.21 | 17.8 | 4.94 | 31.0 | 5.25 | 46.4 | 6.33 |

*Hypothesis 5-17*: Companies which primarily aim at long-term corporate growth enjoys a higher level of performance than those which seek to earn a living or retain their assets.

*Hypothesis 5-18*: The larger the size of a company, the more likely the president primarily aims at long term corporate growth, rather than at retaining his assets.

The president of a large company is not allowed to exclusively aim at retaining his assets. If he keeps to such an objective, it will affect employees' morale and company's vitality, hence deteriorate business results.

## 5-4-2. Business Environment and Strengths of Companies

In devising a business strategy, the top management take into account the ever-changing external environment and regid internal situations. As to the external circumstance, chief executives of Sake brewing firms usually attach importance to factors related to market environment including the growing popularity of whisky and other alcohol and the ever intensifying competitions with their rival companies. However, factors related to production costs such as increases in wages and prices of rice do not attract the attention of the presidents.

With respect to strengths of their companies, presidents of Sake manufacturing firms cite local consumers' support and good relations with their clients as market related-factors, and good quality products as a technical factor. This contrasts with the presidents of the other manufacturing companies most of whom mention excellent ability in new-product development.

**Table 5-13.** Company's Strength and Business Results

| Strength of firm | Whole Sake | | <200kl | | 200~2000kl | | 2000kl≦ | |
|---|---|---|---|---|---|---|---|---|
| | Percent-age | Bus. Results | Percent-age | Bus. Results | Percent-age | Bus. Results | Percent-age | Bus. Results |
| Local consumers' support | 39.4% | 4.97 | 47.5% | 4.87 | 31.6% | 5.07 | 14.3% | 7.10* |
| Good relations with clients | 20.0 | 4.89 | 19.3 | 4.66 | 20.7 | 5.10 | 21.4 | 5.41 |
| Tradition, popularity, brand, assets | 9.7 | 5.02 | 4.8 | 4.52 | 15.2 | 5.12 | 17.9 | 5.83 |
| High quality of products | 16.4 | 5.27* | 14.3 | 4.69 | 18.6 | 5.72* | 21.4 | 6.19 |
| Others | 14.4 | 5.11 | 14.1 | 4.79 | 13.9 | 5.38 | 25.0 | 5.97 |

*Hypothesis 5-19*: In the Sake brewing industry, companies whose chief executives regard technical factors including quality of products as one of their strengths generally achieve satisfactory business results.

The above hypothesis holds with the whole Sake brewing industry, but Table 5-13 also indicates the importance of a market-related factor —local consumers' support.

## 5-4-3. President's Business Goals

In devising concrete business strategies, the chief executive must first set business, goals. Japanese manufacturing businesses usually seek cost reduction during a low economic growth period, and new-product development and share expansion in a high economic growth period. The survey conducted for this section shows that in the Sake brewing

**Table 5-14.** Business Goals and Business Results

| | Whole Sake | | <200kl | | 200~2000kl | | 2000kl≦ | |
|---|---|---|---|---|---|---|---|---|
| | Percent-age | Bus. Results | Percent-age | Bus. Results | Percent-age | Bus. Results | Percent-age | Bus. Results |
| To maintain present sales | 30.0% | 4.88 | 33.2% | 4.61 | 27.6% | 5.25 | 14.3% | 5.80 |
| Sales expansion | 28.7 | 5.14 | 27.9 | 5.06* | 28.8 | 5.16 | 39.3 | 5.85 |
| Reduction of production cost | 6.9 | 4.48 | 7.5 | 4.27 | 6.5 | 4.75 | 3.6 | 5.16 |
| Quality improvement, new— product development | 34.3 | 5.17* | 31.4 | 4.82 | 37.2 | 5.41* | 42.9 | 6.36 |

industry, the presidents place emphasis on keeping or expanding present sales, and quality improvement. Table 5-14 shows the relationship between selected business goals and business results.

As seen in the table, firms with aggressive business goals such as quality improvement, new-product development and sales expansion achieve excellent corporate performance. On the contrary, conservative goals such as reduction in production cost and maintaining present sales result in poor business performance.

*Hypothesis 5-20*: Companies whose presidents pursue aggressive business goals including quality improvement, new-product development and sales expansion produce satisfactory business results, while conservative goals such as production cost reduction result in poor performance.

Aggressive business goals set by the chief executive encourages his employees to display their creativity in the process of challenging them, which in turn provides vitality for the company as a whole, and thereby raising business performance. However, conservative targets such as cost reductions are likely to be set by those companies suffering from poor performances. But such targets contribute to further conservatism of the employees, and negatively affect their creativity, and thus deteriorating the company's vitality.

### 5-4-4. The Highest Decision-Making Body and Decision-Making Pattern

The highest decision-making body in most manufacturing companies listed on the Tokyo Stock Exchange is the board of managing directors. Other highest decision-making bodies include the board of directors and the committee. The dominance of the board of managing directors is an indication of the fact that Japanese business enterprises are not run from the stockholders' standpoint. A majority of Sake brewing companies (50.3 percent), however, have the board of directors and the board of executive officers as the highest decision-making body. This is followed by the chief executive (in 27.9 percent of the companies), the council of chief executive's family (in 20.4 percent), and others (in 1.3 percent). This can be attributed to the small scale of the industry as a whole. There is no clear relationship between the form of the highest decision-making organ and business performance.

The pattern of decision-making at the highest decision-making body falls into three categories: 1) decision-making according to the president's view; 2) decision-making by the president after discussing with executives; and 3) decision-making according to executives' opinions.

In the Sake brewing industry, decisions are made by the president after consulting his family and executives in most companies (53.4 percent). This is followed by the decision according to the president's view (36.7 percent). The smallest percentage of the companies (9.9 percent) make a decision according to opinions of the executives and presidents' families.

A correlation analysis of presidents' attributes and decision-making pattern shows that the older the president, the more likely he accepts opinions of executives and his family (correlation coefficient: 0.212*). This is also true with the president whose successor has already been appointed (0.133*). A similar tendency is seen with the president who shows respect for others (0.162*) and excels in quantitative thinking (0.116*). It can be said that the president who makes a decision based on his view is relatively young, so his successor is not yet decided; he has less respects for others and makes a sales estimate primarily based on his intuition.

*Hypothesis 5-21*: The chief executive who takes initiative in making a decision is relatively young and his successor is not yet decided; he shows less consideration for others, attaching importance to his intuition. On the other hand, the president who makes much of executives' opinions is relatively old and his successor has already been appointed; he shows more respects for others and excels in quantitative thinking.

There is no significant relationship between decision-making patterns and business results.

## 5-5. Consequences of Decision-Making

"Consequences of decision-making" refers to what is produced by decision-making based on business goals which the chief executive worked out, taking account of both external environment and internal conditions into consideration. This section deals with the consequences of decision making in business, which involves these factors: "development of new product," "investment in equipment," etc."

## 5-5-1. Development of New Products and New Market Cultivation

The development of a new product requires employees' ability development, which in turn promotes further development of new products. In this reciprocal process, employees become vitalized and demonstrate their creativity, which is the origin of profit, and thus contributing to corporate growth. If the company makes too light of new product development, it will lead to deterioration of company's vitality and performance. An overemphasis on developing new products could also result in a fall in corporate performance due to the excessive cost incurred. In the Sake brewing industry, sales of new products developed over the past five years account for 1.98 percent of the total sales in the same period. The percentage increases in proportion to the size of business; 1.70 percent registered by companies with an annual Sake production of less than 200 kilolitters, 2.20 percent between 200 and 2,000 kilolitters, and 3.42 percent more than 2,000 kilolitters.

A correlation analysis shows that companies with younger presidents (correlation coefficient: $-0.105^*$), who have received technical education ($0.115^*$) and have enthusiasm about self-study ($0.186^*$) register higher percentages of new products. Such percentage is also high in the firm whose president is excellent in dealing with changing environments ($0.194^*$), healthy ($0.162^*$) and enthusiastic toward collecting information ($0.182^*$). Such factors as ambitions, determination, intuition, quantitative thinking, respecting others, and willingness to do others a favor have less relationship with the percentage of new products. Among other factors, president's aggressive business objectives ($0.229^*$) show a high correlation with this percentage.

*Hypothesis 5-22*: Young presidents with technical education and enthusiasm toward self-study show much interest in developing new products. President's abilities such as health, abilities in gathering information and in coping with new environments also contribute to the promotion of new product development. Furthermore, presidents who primarily aim at long-term corporate growth and assuming social responsibility, rather than at retaining their assets, are active in developing new products. Other factors including ambitions, determination, intuition, quantitative thinking, respecting others, and willingness to do others a favor have less relations with the percentage of new products.

Table 5–15 shows the relationship between the percentage of new products and business results.

*Hypothesis 5–23*: The optimum percentage of new products is between two and five percents in the Sake brewing industry as a whole. Other percentages result in lower levels of corporate performances.

In the Sake manufacturing industry where most products are stable, it is rather difficult to develop other successful products, so it is important to cultivate new markets for conventional stable products. New markets may include big cities for those products which are popular only in limited areas, and beverage shops or hotels for other products. A questionaire survey conducted by the author shows that there are more Sake brewing firms which have failed to find new markets in the past three years than those which have succeeded to do so; the former account for 54.6 percent, and the latter 45.4 percent.

**Table 5–15.**    Percentage of New Products and Business Results

|  | Whole Sake | | <200kl | | 200~2000kl | | 2000kl≦ | |
|---|---|---|---|---|---|---|---|---|
|  | Percent-age | Bus. Results | Percent-age | Bus. Results | Percent-age | Bus. Results | Percent-age | Bus. Results |
| 0% | 36.2% | 4.79 | 43.7% | 4.57 | 29.1% | 5.17 | 10.7% | 5.70 |
| up to 1% | 15.8 | 4.97 | 14.3 | 4.81 | 18.3 | 5.06 | 7.1 | 6.80 |
| between 1 and 2% | 17.0 | 5.21 | 14.6 | 5.20* | 19.8 | 5.27 | 17.9 | 6.39 |
| between 2 and 5% | 15.2 | 5.28* | 14.6 | 4.99 | 13.9 | 5.52* | 39.3 | 5.84 |
| 5% and more | 15.9 | 5.19 | 12.8 | 4.94 | 18.9 | 5.33 | 25.0 | 5.86 |

New market cultivation has few correlations with president's atîribute, for example, 0.001 with the avarage age of presidents. But, it is correlated with president's abilities; ambitions (0.141*), ability in coping with new environment (0.190*), quantitative thinking (0.111*), ability in gathering information (0.211*).

*Hypothesis 5–24*: The ambitious chief executive who excels in abilities in coping with new environment, quantitative thinking and collecting information is eager to find a new market. The ability in collecting information is particularly related to market cultivation. The age and major field of the president have less contribution to cultivation of new markets.

Table 5–16 shows the relationship between new market cultivation and corporate performance.

*Hypothesis* 5-25: Companies which found new markets achieve better business results than those failing to do so.

**Table 5-16.** New Market Cultivation and Business Results

| | Whole Sake | | <200kl | | 200~2000kl | | 2000kl≦ | |
|---|---|---|---|---|---|---|---|---|
| | Percent-age | Bus. Results | Percent-age | Bus. Results | Percent-age | Bus. Results | Percent-age | Bus. Results |
| New markets cultivated | 45.4% | 5.12 | 38.7%˙ | 4.86 | 51.4% | 5.25 | 71.4% | 6.07 |
| No new markets cultivated | 54.6 | 4.95 | 61.3 | 4.72 | 48.6 | 5.24 | 28.6 | 5.95 |

## 5-5-2. Quality Control, Investment in Equipment, Financial Management

For a successful implementation of product strategies, such factors as quality control, standardization of products and investment in equipment for cost reductions are indispensable. Also important is an over-all system of financial management. This section examines companies' attitudes about quality control, equipment investment, and financial management. In a survey, companies were asked to choose what they implemented from among: six measures concerning quality control which include check of products at the time of shipment, check of products sold over, etc.; eight measures concerning equipment investment such as in automatically continuous rice steamers, air chutes, automatic rice malters, etc.; and 15 measures concerning financial management such as long-range business planning, profit planning and break-even analysis, sales planning, budgetary control etc.

The average number of measures implemented by the firms surveyed is 2.58 for quality control, 2.48 for equipment investment, and 6.42 for financial management. Larger companies implement more measures in all of the three fields.

*Hypothesis* 5-26: In the Sake brewing industry, larger companies are stricter in their quality control and financial management, and more active in equipment investment.

President's attributes are not markedly related to the positive implementation of quality control, equipment investment and financial management. However, self-studying presidents are active in management of quality control (correlation coefficient: 0.179*), equipment investment (0.188*), and financial management (0.307*).

*Hypothesis* 5-27: Positive implementation of quality control, equipment investment and financial management are related less to the president's attributes such as his age and major field, but more to his enthusiasm toward self-study.

The above management and control shows a high correlation with the president's such abilities as ambitions, ability to cope with changing environment and gather information, and quantitative thinking. But, it is less related to such abilities as determination, respecting others, and willingness to do others a favor. No conclusion was obtained as to other abilities—persuasion, health, and ability in collecting indirect information. Table 5-17 indicates the relationship between president's abilities and positive management and control.

*Hypothesis* 5-28: President's abilities such as ambitions, abilities to collect information and cope with new situations, and quantitative thinking are evidently related to positive management of quality control, equipment investment and financial management. But, such abilities as respecting others and doing others a favor have less relations with such management and control.

**Table 5-17.** Coefficients of Correlation between President's Abilities and Management and Control

|  | Quality control | Equipment investment | Financial management |
|---|---|---|---|
| Ambition | 0.055 | 0.144* | 0.100* |
| Ability to cope with a new Situation | 0.112* | 0.243* | 0.194* |
| Determination | 0.022 | −0.089 | 0.005 |
| Respecting Others | 0.058 | −0.004 | 0.034 |
| Quantitative thinking | 0.120* | 0.080 | 0.255* |
| Willingness to do others favor | −0.005 | 0.087 | −0.004 |
| Persuasion | 0.053 | 0.090 | 0.093 |
| Health | 0.052 | 0.038 | 0.049 |
| Ability to gather information | 0.143* | 0.173* | 0.281* |
| Ability to gather indirect information | 0.028 | 0.017 | 0.057 |

President's positive objectives of the firm are largely related to the positive implementation of: quality control (correlation coefficient: 0.162*), equipment investment (0.287*), and financial management (0.287*).

*Hypothesis* 5-29: Presidents who primarily aim at corporate growth and fulfilment of social responsibility are positive in quality control, equipment investment and financial management.

Table 5-18 shows the relationship between implementation of quality control, equipment investment and financial management, and business

**Table 5-18.** Positive Implementation of Quality Control, Equipment Investment and Financial Management and Business Results.

| | Whole Sake | | <200kl | | 200~2000kl | | 2000kl≦ | |
|---|---|---|---|---|---|---|---|---|
| The number of quality control measures conducted | Percent-age | Bus. Results | Percent-age | Bus. Results | Percent-age | Bus. Results | Percent-age | Bus. Results |
| 0~1 | 21.5% | 4.81 | 24.9% | 4.73 | 18.3% | 4.85 | 18.3% | 4.85 |
| 2 | 27.5 | 4.99 | 28.6 | 4.75 | 27.6 | 5.27 | 27.6 | 5.27 |
| 3~ | 51.0 | 5.14* | 46.5 | 4.81 | 54.2 | 5.37* | 54.2 | 5.37* |
| The number of equipment investment measures conducted | Percent-age | Bus. Results | Percent-age | Bus. Results | Percent-age | Bus. Results | Percent-age | Bus. Results |
| 0~1 | 38.2% | 4.71 | 63.6% | 4.70 | 10.2% | 4.89 | 0 % | — |
| 2~3 | 32.4 | 5.02 | 29.9 | 4.78 | 37.8 | 5.24 | 7.1 | 5.81 |
| 4~ | 29.4 | 5.43* | 6.5 | 5.54* | 52.0 | 5.33 | 92.9 | 6.05 |
| The number of financial management measures conducted | Percent-age | Bus. Results | Percent-age | Bus. Results | Percent-age | Bus. Results | Percent-age | Bus. Results |
| 0~3 | 20.3% | 4.74 | 28.6% | 4.61 | 11.5% | 5.05 | 3.6% | — |
| 4~7 | 42.7 | 5.01 | 49.7 | 4.85 | 37.5 | 5.27 | 3.6 | — |
| 8~ | 37.0 | 5.20 | 21.6 | 4.82 | 51.1 | 5.28 | 92.9 | 5.96 |

results. This hypothesis is possible:

*Hypothesis 5-30*: In the Sake brewing industry, those firms which conduct stricter quality control and financial management, and active equipment investment show a high level of business results.

It can be said that business results may be improved by those presidents who aim at long-term corporate growth and display such abilities as bold ambitions, and gathering and analysing information in a scientific manner. Aggressive product strategies, strict quality control, rationalization through equipment investment, and over-all financial management may also help improve corporate performance.

## 5-6. Summary

Figure 5-2 shows the relationship between top management factors and business performance. Here, five factors are involved: "external environment and attributes of president", "president's abilities", "decision-making", "consequences of decision-making" and "business performance". Items included in each factor are those verified to be relatively important. Items with a *mark are those which make a statistically significant contribution to better business results. The coefficients of correlations between items connected by an arrow are statistically significant. The small number of arrows between items in the "decision-making" and "consequences of decision-making" factors is due to failure of verifications resulting from a limited scope of analysis of the former items.

As seen in the figure, items in the "consequences of decision-making" evidently contribute to improved business performance, while the contributions of items in the "external environment" are relatively small: contributions of the former items are all statistically significant, whereas there are only two such items in the latter factor.

In order to achieve better business results, (1) it is necessary for companies to keep the average percentage of new products over the past five years between two and five percents, and to constantly cultivate new markets, besides conducting equipment investment for the purpose of rationalization and labor-saving, as well as strict quality control and financial management. (2) The president should primarily aim at long-term corporate growth and fulfilling social responsibility, rather than at retaining his or his families' assets; he must also have quality improvement and new product development included in his business goals. Decision-making patterns have a few effect on corporate performance. An excellent performance is achieved by those presidents who think their companies' strength is good quality of their products, and conduct strict quality control. (3) The ability expected most of the chief executive is the ability to collect information. This is followed by such abilities as ambitions, quantitative thinking and health. The ability in gathering information contributes to the president's positive objectives of the firm, and all items in the "consequences of decision-making" factor. Ambition also help the president seek positive objectives, increase the percentage of new products and raise business performance. Quantitative thinking also contributes to better business results through new market cultivation. The importance of ambitions and quantitative thinking for better corporate performance is indicated in Figure 5–1 described before. Health is considered by many presidents a requirement for presidency, however, it is correlated only with the percentage of new products; its contribution to vitalizing companies is smaller than anticipated. (4) Concerning external environment, "not red figures" affects the president's abilities; the president of a profitable firm has confidence and ambitions beyond his abilities. This helps him further improve his ability to collect information. As to attributes of the president, enthusiasm about self-study, the average age of presidents and period of presidency are important; self-study helps the president improve quantitative thinking. It also make him active in new product development, new market cultivation, quality control, equipment investment and financial management. Obviously, younger presidents serving for a relatively short period are healthy.

It can be concluded that in order to vitalize his company, the chief executive should have such abilities as ambitions, develop his ability to collect information needed to realize his ambitions, and quantitative thinking to analyse the collected information. To achieve these purposes, the company should be profitable and its president should be enthusiastic about self-study.

# 6

# Quantitative Research on Relationship between Top Management Factors and Corporate Growth
——From the Viewpoint of Chief Executive's Ability——

## 6-1. Introduction

The desirable qualities of the chief executive are the abilities to adopt himself to given circumstances and to carry out his functions effectively, thereby contributing to the development of a business firm. These abilities can be described only in broad, abstract terms such as "entrepreneurship" and "administratorship."

The abilities required of chief executives differ depending on the environment in which they are placed or the functions they are to perform. For example, in the electronics industry where the environment is now improving, intuition is the most important requirement[1]; while in the Sake brewing industry chief executives are required to have analytical abilities because of unfavorable changes in its environment[2]. When thinking out the future business vision, the president should excel in intuition, insight and imagination. But, for strategic decision-making, such qualities as belief, determination and generosity assume greater importance. It is a sense of responsibility and an analytical ability that counts most in business management and control.

The desirable abilities of the chief executive differ with the required

(1)  Section 4-3-4.
(2)  Section 5-3-5.

functions and the environment surrounding the business enterprise. Thus, properly speaking it is very difficult to define such abilities by large scale observation. The usual approach is to limit the environment and functions to specific examples and then pursue the desirable abilities within these limits. This method is similar to that adopted in case study and in research on the history of business administration. In this chapter, however, an attempt is made to identify the desirable abilities of top management by large scale observation. Instead of trying to identify abilities directly, I intend to purse them indirectly by observing a large number of objective factors which are related to the chief executive's abilities, i.e., surrogates. Full utilization of these surrogates will hopefully make it possible to obtain general hypotheses in which the special circumstances of individual enterprises are removed.

## 6-2. Framework for Empirical Research in Factors Related to the Chief Executive's Ability

In general, the chief executive displays his ability in three functional processes: thinking out the future business vision, strategic decision-making, and business management and control. The ability of the chief executive and related objective factors are shown in Figure 6-1. A chief executive with certain attributes plans out future business by taking account of conditions both internal and external to the company. He then makes decisions to establish goals and corporate strategies which give birth to corporate structure. Business in the new-born structure yields new business performance. As objective factors which are concerned with the chief executive's ability, such surrogates as "external environment & internal conditions, " "attributes of presidents and executives, " "decision-making" and "consequences of decision-making" are to be measured. In other words, the extent to which these factors contribute to the improvement is corporate performance and employees' morale is studied. An analysis is then conducted to evaluate the ability of top management in an indirect manner. Specific factors are given in Figure 6-1.

For this study, the chief executive's abilities are classified into

**Figure 6-1.** Factors Related to the Top–Management

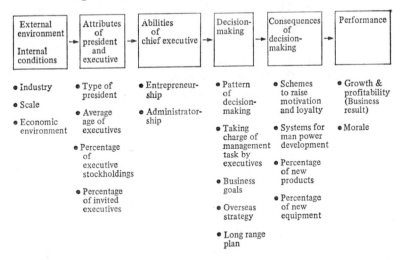

"entrepreneurship" and "administratorship." While some presidents excel in the former, others excel in the latter. The presidents can be divided into four types: founder, successor, company-bred, and *Amakudari* (retired high-ranking official). The founder-president generally posesses a great amount of entrepreneurship in contrast to the company-bred and the *Amakudari*-presidents who abound in administratorship. The company with a higher percentage of executive's stockholdings is relatively new and full of entrepreneurship, whereas the company in which executives hold a lower percentage of stocks boasts a long history and administratorship permeates. Decision-making at the highest decision-making body falls into three types: 1) decision-making according to president's view, 2) decision-making upon discussions with executives, 3) decision-making according to executives view. The company in which the president's opinion dominates decision-making is generally small in scale and imbued with a strong entrepreneurship. In the company where executives, not the president, have a strong voice in decision-making, administratorship is more valued. The company with a higher proportion of new products and new equipment allows the president to bring his entrepreneurship into full play. The company which encourages the development of new products is rich in this ability, while administratorship is predominant in the firm which gives priority to cost reduction. These points will be enlarged upon in latter sections

In order to evaluate the extent to which various factors contribute to better corporate performance, D-value[3] analysis is conducted. The data employed for this study were collected by the Japan Development Bank (JDB) and the Ministry of International Trade and Industry (MITI). From 1973 to 1985 I served as a chief examiner for JDB and Head of MITI's Management Ability Research Committee when they conducted an investigation and analysis of Japanse business. In 1973, data were gathered for 630 companies (JDB), and from 1974 the data were collected by the Ministry of International Trade and Industry. Data were gathered for 472 companies in 1974, 478 companies in 1975, 438 companies in 1976, 540 companies in 1977, 541 companies in 1978, 521 companies in 1980, 473 companies in 1981 and 480 companies in 1982. There was no investigation in 1979 although no reason was given.

During 1973 and 1974 the effect of high economic growth was still lingering. Then came a period of low economic growth which lasted until 1977. From 1979 to 1982 the Japanese economy was in a period of stable growth. By utilizing the long-term data, we can estimate which type of ability is most desirable as the environment changes. Furthermore, by classifying factors according to the sectors of industry, the desirable abilities which vary from one area to another because of different technology and market conditions can be observed.

The dependent variables employed are morale and business result, the latter being the integration of growth and profitability. With regard to the relationship between morale and business result, we assume that when business management is carried out in line with an aggressive strategy to attain corporate goals as determined by the president, employees are inspired and morale increased. This gives free play to their creativity in the process of product strategy implementation and contributes to the improvement of business result.

---

(3)    A sophisticated and very useful statistical measure to analyse the qualitative factors in social science, which has been newly developed by author and his associates. For details, refer to author's book; *The Growth of Firms in Japan*, Keio-Tsushin, 1980, pp. 211~214. Refer section 5-3-11 of this book where a similar analysis is conducted.

# 6-3. Factors Related to the Attributes of Chief Executives

## 6-3-1. Type of President

The type of president is one of the most significant surrogates that explain his attitude and policy toward business management. As mentioned above, there are four types of company presidents: founder, successor, company-bred, [4] and *Amakudari*. [5] The founder-president has a high degree of entrepreneurship, while the company-bred and *Amakudari*-presidents usually have a strong administratorship. Large firms listed in the first section of the Tokyo Stock Exchange are primarily headed by company-bred presidents. while *Amakudari*-presidents are generally found in medium-large firms. The founder-presidents comprise the smallest group in the industry.

The relationship between the type of the president and business results or employees' morale is represented in Tables 6-1, 2, 3, and 4. The following hypotheses are obtained from these Tables.

*Hypothesis 6-1*: The founder president-headed firm enjoys excellent business results due to the high degree of entrepreneurship though employees' morale is not necessarily high. This holds true regardless of scale or external environment.

*Hypothesis 6-2*: The company-bred president-headed firms show a lower degree of business results because of the conservative policies of the strong administratorship. Employee morale however is generally maintained at a higher level.

*Hypothesis 6-3*: The *Amakudari*-president-headed firm experiences a lower level of morale and poorer business results.

Although the founder-president may be successful in improving business results by adjusting the company's policies to a changing environment, his forcible manner sometimes provokes antipathy among employees, resulting in low morale. Conversely, the company-bred president, who

---

(4) Company-bred refers to those presidents who worked themselves up through the company ranks.

(5) *Amakudari* refers to those presidents who were formerly government officials or officials of associated banks or the parent firms.

has learned from experience how to behave toward his subordinates, is better able to win employees' cooperation, because they feel satisfied with the president's compassionate attitude. The lower morale and poorer business results of the company with the *Amakudari*-president can be attributed to the president's failure to familiarize himself with the company's ethos and culture. In addition, the employee's apprehension about his unfairness in personnel management contributes to the lower morale.

The relationship between the type of president and business results categorized by area is described in Table 6-5 through 6-9. This provides us with the following hypothesis.

*Hypothesis 6-4:* In those industries whose growth rate is low, such as textiles and chemicals, the company with the founder-president experiences better corporate achievement. This can be attributed to the entrepreneurship of the president. However, in highly growing areas such as the electric machinery and transport equipment industries, good performance is shown by those companies headed by a company-bred

**Table 6-1.** The Relationship between the Type of President and Business Results (All manufacturing industry)

| | 1973 | | 1974 | | 1975 | | 1976 | |
|---|---|---|---|---|---|---|---|---|
| | Percent-age | Bus. Result | Percent-age | Bus. Result | Percent-age | Bus. Result | Percent-age | Bus. Result |
| Founder | 21.2% | 3.40* | 11.7 | 3.50* | 10.7 | 5.59* | 9.8 | 5.06 |
| Successor | 21.0 | 2.65 | 23.7 | 2.95 | 20.7 | 5.12 | 21.0 | 5.03 |
| Company-bred | 22.4 | 2.66 | 30.3 | 2.63 | 36.2 | 5.00 | 34.7 | 5.08 |
| Amakudari | 35.4 | 2.66 | 34.3 | 2.72 | 32.4 | 4.69 | 34.5 | 4.87 |

| 1977 | | 1978 | | 1980 | | 1981 | | 1982 | |
|---|---|---|---|---|---|---|---|---|---|
| Percent-age | Bus. Result | Percent-age | Bus. Result | Percent-age | Bus. Result | Percent-age | Bus. Result | Percent-age | Bus. Result |
| 10.9 | 5.08 | 9.1 | 5.52* | 8.3 | 5.21 | 6.8 | 5.24 | 5.6 | 5.32 |
| 21.5 | 4.91 | 19.6 | 5.03 | 23.4 | 4.97 | 23.3 | 5.03 | 25.0 | 4.91 |
| 35.7 | 4.99 | 37.7 | 5.07 | 34.9 | 4.91 | 35.9 | 5.01 | 35.4 | 5.00 |
| 31.9 | 4.90 | 33.6 | 4.78 | 33.4 | 4.89 | 34.0 | 5.01 | 34.0 | 4.90 |

In the tables underlined figures indicate note worthy values—that is, maximum values.
The * mark on figures indicates statistical significance for the F-test (5% level).
Figures of 1973 and 1974 are different from the others, due to the different measuring method used

**Table 6-2.** The Relationship between the Type of the President and Employees' Morale (All manufacturing industry)

| | 1974 | | 1975 | | 1976 | | 1977 | |
|---|---|---|---|---|---|---|---|---|
| | Percent-age | Morale | Percent-age | Morale | Percent-age | Morale | Percent-age | Morale |
| Founder | 11.7% | 2.62* | 10.7 | 3.53 | 9.8 | 3.44 | 10.9 | 3.48 |
| Successor | 23.7 | 2.41 | 20.7 | 3.31 | 21.0 | 3.29 | 21.5 | 3.30 |
| Company-bred | 30.3 | 2.49 | 36.2 | 3.54* | 34.7 | 3.57* | 35.7 | 3.49* |
| Amakudari | 34.4 | 2.39 | 32.4 | 3.27 | 34.5 | 3.30 | 31.9 | 3.25 |

| 1978 | | 1980 | | 1981 | | 1982 | |
|---|---|---|---|---|---|---|---|
| Percent-age | Morale | Percent-age | Morale | Percent-age | Morale | Percent-age | Morale |
| 9.1 | 3.52* | 8.3 | 3.45 | 6.8 | 3.27 | 5.6 | 3.37 |
| 19.6 | 3.41 | 23.4 | 3.43 | 23.3 | 3.40 | 25.0 | 3.22 |
| 37.7 | 3.51 | 34.9 | 3.57* | 35.9 | 3.63* | 35.4 | 3.57 |
| 33.6 | 3.21 | 33.3 | 3.26 | 34.0 | 3.24 | 34.0 | 3.21 |

Morale is quantified by SD–Method, utilizing the following questionnaire. "What is the level of morale of your employees compared with other firm in the same field? Please select from the below. 1. Lower, 2. Slightly lower, 3. Almost equal, 4. Slightly higher, 5. Much higher."

Figures of 1974 are different from the others, due to using 3 leves of morale while the others are 5 levels.

**Table 6-3.** The Relationship between the Type of the President and Business Results (Large firms)

| | 1973 | | 1974 | | 1975 | | 1976 | |
|---|---|---|---|---|---|---|---|---|
| | Percent-age | Bus. Result | Percent-age | Bus. Result | Percent-age | Bus. Result | Percent-age | Bus. Result |
| Founder | 12.2% | 3.64* | 8.9 | 3.59* | 7.6 | 5.84* | 7.4 | 5.17 |
| Successor | 12.2 | 2.88 | 20.3 | 2.94 | 17.5 | 5.15 | 15.9 | 5.10 |
| Company-bred | 41.2 | 2.65 | 40.6 | 2.62 | 46.9 | 5.01 | 45.2 | 5.17 |
| Amakudari | 34.3 | 2.52 | 30.2 | 2.77 | 28.1 | 4.88 | 31.4 | 4.81 |

| 1977 | | 1978 | | 1980 | | 1981 | | 1982 | |
|---|---|---|---|---|---|---|---|---|---|
| Percent-age | Bus. Result | Percent-age | Bus. Result | Percent-age | Bus. Result | Percent-age | Bus. Result | Percent-age | Bus. Result |
| 8.2 | 5.22 | 7.3 | 5.57* | 8.0 | 5.18 | 6.8 | 5.22 | 5.2 | 5.26 |
| 18.7 | 4.98 | 16.0 | 5.12 | 20.2 | 5.02 | 19.0 | 5.04 | 21.1 | 5.06 |
| 47.1 | 5.05 | 47.1 | 5.08 | 43.5 | 4.96 | 45.3 | 5.10 | 45.1 | 4.95 |
| 26.0 | 4.90 | 29.7 | 4.90 | 28.3 | 5.00 | 28.9 | 5.03 | 28.6 | 4.94 |

**Table 6-4.**    The Relationship between the Type of the President and Business Results (Medium-large firms)

| | 1973 | | 1974 | | 1975 | | 1976 | |
|---|---|---|---|---|---|---|---|---|
| | Percent-age | Bus. Result | Percent-age | Bus. Result | Percent-age | Bus. Result | Percent-age | Bus. Result |
| Founder | 15.0% | 3.47* | 15.7 | 3.43 | 16.0 | 5.38* | 14.2 | 4.95 |
| Successor | 22.5 | 2.55 | 28.8 | 2.97 | 26.3 | 5.08 | 30.3 | 4.95 |
| Company-bred | 15.5 | 2.79 | 15.2 | 2.66 | 17.7 | 4.94 | 15.5 | 4.60 |
| Amakudari | 46.9 | 2.69 | 40.3 | 2.66 | 40.0 | 4.47 | 40.0 | 4.94 |

| 1977 | | 1978 | | 1980 | | 1981 | | 1982 | |
|---|---|---|---|---|---|---|---|---|---|
| Percent-age | Bus. Result | Percent-age | Bus. Result | Percent-age | Bus. Result | Percent-age | Bus. Result | Percent-age | Bus. Result |
| 15.3 | 4.96 | 12.2 | 5.47* | 8.6 | 5.27 | 6.8 | 5.29 | 6.4 | 5.40 |
| 25.8 | 4.83 | 25.9 | 4.85 | 29.2 | 4.91 | 31.5 | 5.02 | 32.0 | 4.73 |
| 17.7 | 4.72 | 21.3 | 5.05 | 19.5 | 4.72 | 17.9 | 4.55 | 18.0 | 5.18 |
| 41.1 | 4.90 | 40.6 | 4.64 | 42.7 | 4.77 | 43.8 | 4.97 | 43.6 | 4.85 |

**Table 6-5.**    The Relationship between the Type of the President and Business Results (Textiles)

| | 1974 | | 1975 | | 1976 | | 1977 | |
|---|---|---|---|---|---|---|---|---|
| | Percent-age | Bus. Result | Percent-age | Bus. Result | Percent-age | Bus. Result | Percent-age | Bus. Result |
| Founder | 9.3% | 2.00 | 8.3 | 4.96 | 8.3 | 6.27* | 7.1 | 6.21* |
| Successor | 23.3 | 2.30 | 13.9 | 4.32 | 16.7 | 4.54 | 23.8 | 4.40 |
| Company-bred | 37.2 | 2.13 | 38.9 | 3.87 | 38.9 | 4.24 | 35.7 | 4.45 |
| Amakudari | 30.2 | 2.00 | 38.9 | 3.15 | 36.1 | 4.56 | 33.3 | 4.76 |

| 1978 | | 1980 | | 1981 | | 1982 | |
|---|---|---|---|---|---|---|---|
| Percent-age | Bus. Result | Percent-age | Bus. Result | Percent-age | Bus. Result | Percent-age | Bus. Result |
| 4.7 | 5.77 | 7.0 | 5.06 | 7.4 | 5.91* | 6.5 | 4.99 |
| 14.0 | 4.36 | 23.3 | 4.15 | 22.2 | 4.23 | 19.4 | 4.39 |
| 46.5 | 4.82 | 44.2 | 4.20 | 48.1 | 4.36 | 35.5 | 4.34 |
| 34.9 | 4.21 | 25.6 | 3.97 | 22.2 | 3.50 | 38.7 | 4.42 |

or *Amakudari*-president with a strong administrative ability.

In the field where the industry as a whole is stagnant, corporate performance is increased by the enterprising president who encourages the research and development of new products because demand cannot

**Table 6-6.** The Relationship between the Type of the President and Business Results (Chemicals)

| | 1974 | | 1975 | | 1976 | | 1977 | |
|---|---|---|---|---|---|---|---|---|
| | Percent-age | Bus. Result | Percent-age | Bus. Result | Percent-age | Bus. Result | Percent-age | Bus. Result |
| Founder | 9.3% | 3.25* | 8.2 | 6.04 | 9.5 | 5.64 | 6.9 | 5.29 |
| Successor | 23.3 | 2.40 | 25.9 | 5.26 | 21.6 | 5.32 | 26.4 | 5.44 |
| Company-bred | 31.4 | 1.52 | 37.6 | 5.37 | 43.2 | 5.41 | 37.9 | 5.35 |
| Amakudari | 36.0 | 1.68 | 28.2 | 5.54 | 25.7 | 5.46 | 28.7 | 5.32 |

| 1978 | | 1980 | | 1981 | | 1982 | |
|---|---|---|---|---|---|---|---|
| Percent-age | Bus. Result | Percent-age | Bus. Result | Percent-age | Bus. Result | Percent-age | Bus. Result |
| 8.8 | 5.56 | 2.5 | 5.37△ | 2.9 | 6.10△ | 4.5 | 5.61* |
| 23.1 | 5.29 | 26.3 | 5.17 | 30.0 | 5.05 | 19.7 | 4.93 |
| 45.1 | 4.98 | 42.5 | 4.97 | 41.4 | 4.89 | 43.9 | 4.88 |
| 23.1 | 4.91 | 28.8 | 4.88 | 25.7 | 5.04 | 31.8 | 5.19 |

△This figure is insignificant because the percentage is smaller than 5%.

**Table 6-7.** The Relationship between the Type of the President and Business Results (General machinery)

| | 1974 | | 1975 | | 1976 | | 1977 | |
|---|---|---|---|---|---|---|---|---|
| | Percent-age | Bus. Result | Percent-age | Bus. Result | Percent-age | Bus. Result | Percent-age | Bus. Result |
| Founder | 6.2% | 3.20* | 10.6 | 5.62 | 9.5 | 4.25 | 10.5 | 4.62 |
| Successor | 28.4 | 1.87 | 25.8 | 5.47* | 20.6 | 4.77 | 23.7 | 4.38 |
| Company-bred | 24.7 | 1.85 | 25.8 | 5.21 | 27.0 | 4.58 | 28.9 | 4.67 |
| Amakudari | 40.7 | 1.46 | 37.9 | 4.31 | 42.9 | 4.74 | 36.8 | 4.28 |

| 1978 | | 1980 | | 1981 | | 1982 | |
|---|---|---|---|---|---|---|---|
| Percent-age | Bus. Result | Percent-age | Bus. Result | Percent-age | Bus. Result | Percent-age | Bus. Result |
| 8.6 | 5.75* | 7.5 | 5.83 | 6.3 | 4.72 | 4.9 | 6.46 |
| 24.3 | 4.92 | 25.0 | 4.83 | 28.6 | 5.19 | 26.2 | 4.83 |
| 35.7 | 4.83 | 31.3 | 5.15 | 31.7 | 5.63 | 29.5 | 5.30 |
| 31.4 | 4.56 | 36.3 | 5.15 | 33.3 | 5.50 | 39.3 | 5.30 |

otherwise be developed. But when the industry is rapidly expanding due to technological innovation or changes in consumption, new products are further developed without particular effort. In such circumstances, the company should realize the importance of cost reduction and imple-

**Table 6-8.** The Relationship between the Type of the President and Business Resuls (Electric machinery)

| | 1974 | | 1975 | | 1976 | | 1977 | |
|---|---|---|---|---|---|---|---|---|
| | Percent-age | Bus. Result | Percent-age | Bus. Result | Percent-age | Bus. Result | Percent-age | Bus. Result |
| Founder | 20.9% | 2.33 | 13.2 | 5.01 | 16.0 | 4.80 | 14.7 | 4.99 |
| Successor | 39.5 | 2.35 | 22.1 | 4.65 | 22.8 | 4.91 | 17.6 | 4.86 |
| Company-bred | 14.0 | 2.17 | 26.5 | 5.08* | 26.3 | 4.90 | 27.9 | 5.02 |
| Amakudari | 25.6 | 2.36 | 38.2 | 4.29 | 36.8 | 4.62 | 39.7 | 4.63 |

| 1978 | | 1980 | | 1981 | | 1982 | |
|---|---|---|---|---|---|---|---|
| Percent-age | Bus. Result | Percent-age | Bus. Result | Percent-age | Bus. Result | Percent-age | Bus. Result |
| 9.0 | 5.68 | 12.5 | 4.96 | 8.3 | 6.59* | 3.4 | 5.82 |
| 20.5 | 5.12 | 17.2 | 5.05 | 25.0 | 5.16 | 25.4 | 5.32 |
| 30.8 | 5.48 | 32.8 | 5.40 | 25.0 | 5.35 | 40.7 | 5.34 |
| 39.7 | 5.23 | 37.5 | 5.25 | 41.7 | 5.45 | 30.5 | 5.34 |

**Table 6-9.** The Relationship between the Type of the President and Business Results (Transport equipment)

| | 1974 | | 1975 | | 1976 | | 1977 | |
|---|---|---|---|---|---|---|---|---|
| | Percent-age | Bus. Result | Percent-age | Bus. Result | Percent-age | Bus. Result | Percent-age | Bus. Result |
| Founder | 3.2% | 2.00△ | 10.5 | 4.67 | 0 | — | 4.4 | 5.44 |
| Successor | 25.8 | 1.38 | 18.4 | 4.56 | 22.9 | 5.38 | 22.2 | 5.55 |
| Company-bred | 32.3 | 1.40 | 34.2 | 4.82 | 37.1 | 5.37 | 37.8 | 5.21 |
| Amakudari | 38.7 | 1.75 | 36.8 | 4.71 | 40.0 | 5.57 | 35.6 | 5.39 |

| 1978 | | 1980 | | 1981 | | 1982 | |
|---|---|---|---|---|---|---|---|
| Percent-age | Bus. Result | Percent-age | Bus. Result | Percent-age | Bus. Result | Percent-age | Bus. Result |
| 0 | — | 0 | — | 6.3 | 4.50 | 2.2 | 5.89* |
| 26.2 | 5.28 | 25.6 | 4.74 | 18.8 | 5.20 | 26.1 | 5.33 |
| 33.3 | 5.36 | 41.0 | 4.83 | 35.4 | 5.08 | 26.1 | 5.37 |
| 40.5 | 5.23 | 33.3 | 4.77 | 39.6 | 4.77 | 45.7 | 4.76 |

ment policies designed to enable the firm to be more competitive; this is where the role of the president with a long experience in management comes into play.

## 6-3-2. Average Age of Executives

It is generally accepted that younger people are more progressive and more flexible. This also pertains to the company executive. Exceedingly progressive and innovative executives, however, may tend to venture upon ambitious schemes at the expense of employees' "desire for stability". In contrast, elderly executives may lack both an innovative spirit and flexibility and the corporate structure is regidified at the expense of employees' "desire for change." Howerver on the other hand employees' "desire for stability" can be satisfied by the discreet manner of the elder executives. The average age of Japanese business firm executive listed on the Tokyo Stock Exchange is 56.5. The relationship between the average age of executives and business result is indicated in Table 6-10. The following hypothesis can be derived:

*Hypothesis 6-5:* Companies with younger executives achieve a high level of business results as long as the external environment is experiencing a high rate of growth. When the growth rate is lower, companies with elderly executives excel in the level of performance.

During a rapidly expanding external environment, younger executives who tactfully respond to the changing circumstances are more competent in elevating business achievement. In the low-growth period, however,

**Table 6-10.** The Relationship between the Average Age of Executives and Business Results (All manufacturing industry)

| | 1974 | | 1975 | | 1976 | | 1977 | |
|---|---|---|---|---|---|---|---|---|
| | Percent-age | Bus. Result | Percent-age | Bus. Result | Percent-age | Bus. Result | Percent-age | Bus. Result |
| ·<55 years | 23.5% | 3.01* | 24.1 | 4.84 | 19.4 | 4.88 | 21.3 | 5.02 |
| 55 ≦·<58 | 26.7 | 2.76 | 33.3 | 4.95 | 28.3 | 4.90 | 31.1 | 4.89 |
| 58≦·<61 | 32.0 | 2.77 | 31.2 | 5.15 | 36.3 | 5.06 | 32.4 | 4.95 |
| 61≦· | 17.8 | 2.69 | 11.5 | 4.96 | 16.0 | 5.14 | 15.2 | 4.99 |

| 1978 | | 1980 | | 1981 | | 1982 | |
|---|---|---|---|---|---|---|---|
| Percent-age | Bus. Result | Percent-age | Bus. Result | Percent-age | Bus. Result | Percent-age | Bus. Result |
| 20.5 | 5.28* | 23.6 | 5.09 | 23.3 | 5.05 | 21.3 | 5.08 |
| 29.8 | 4.84 | 20.7 | 4.99 | 21.1 | 4.98 | 18.3 | 4.69 |
| 33.8 | 5.01 | 28.8 | 4.89 | 29.6 | 5.05 | 29.8 | 4.95 |
| 15.9 | 4.97 | 26.9 | 4.84 | 26.0 | 5.03 | 30.6 | 4.88 |

cautious and defensive elders lend better themselves to the improvement of corporate performance. The evidence in Table 6-10 indicates that companies with executives 58 years old or older produced, on the average, a higher performance level in 1975 and 1976 when economic growth slackened. This is further confirmed in Table 6-1 which shows that only in 1976 did companies headed by company-bred presidents achieve the highest results.

# 6-4. Factors Related to Decision-Making

## 6-4-1. Decision-Making Pattern in the Highest Decision-Making Body

The highest decision-making body in a Japanese business firm generally takes the form of either a board of managing directors (*Jômukai* in Japanese), a board of directors, or a committee. One of the salient features of the Japanese business organization is that the highest decision-making body in most companies is not a board of directors which comprises the directors designated by stockholders, but rather a *Jômukai* whose members are all managing directors. This practice facilitates the decision-making process, making possible the establishment of business goals from the corporate, not from the stockholders' standpoint. In the Japanese manufacturing sector, a board of managing directors constitutes the highest decision-making body in 55 percent of the companies. This is followed by the board of directors found in 34 percent of firms and the committee or other type of body found in 11 percent of the companies. Based on the scale of business, the board of managing directors as the highest decision-making body is more prevalent in large firms, while a board of directors is more prevalent in medium-large firms(Section 1-1).

The pattern of decision-making at the highest decision-making body falls into three categories: 1) Decisions are made mainly by the president, though executives' opinions are to some extent respected. 2) After all the members of the body participate in the discussion on an equal basis, the president takes the leadership in making a final decision, 3) A decision is made focusing upon constituent members' opinions, which are brought to a conclusion by the president in the final stage. In Japanese business firms, the second type of decision-making is the most popular. This is followed by decision-making of the third type. The relationship between the decision-making patterns and business result is presented in Tables 6–11, 12, and 13. This gives rise to the following hypothesis.

*Hypothesis 6–6*: Companies where decisions are primarily made in accordance with the president's opinion and view are prosperous when the external environment shows a high rate of growth. In the low economic growth period, however, the company where decision-making is based on executives' ideas achieves better results. The scale of business does not have an effect on any of three types of decision-making.

When the rate of economic growth is low, highly prudent decision-making through the full participation of all executives is demanded because reduced profit margin does not permit the company to make even smallest mistake. Consequently, all the constituent members of the highest decision-making body must assume responsibility for their policies which they have decided. In a period of high economic growth, it is essential for business enterprises to surpass the market competition by prompt decision-making rather than by avoiding risks. Since profit margin increases, they need not be apprehensive about committing small mistakes. As Tables 6–12 and 13 indicate, the most suitable patterns of decision-making for the external conditions in large firms and medium-large firms are identical. Although Chandler raised the proposition that functions for adjustment of the top management are important for large scale enterprises and functions for innovation of the top management are important for medium or medium-large firms, the results of our investigation do not attest to his hypothesis. The most appropriate pattern of decision-making depends, not on the scale of business, but on the external environment and, as will be stated later, on the sector of industry.

Tables 6–14 through 6–18 deal with the relationship between the patterns of decision-making at the highest decision-making body and business result in different industries. This provides us with the following hypothesis.

**Table 6-11.** The Relationship between the Patterns of Decision-Making at the Highest Decision-Making Body and Business Results (All manufacturing industry)

| | 1973 | | 1974 | | 1975 | | 1976 | |
|---|---|---|---|---|---|---|---|---|
| | Percent-age | Bus. Result | Percent-age | Bus. Result | Percent-age | Bus. Result | Percent-age | Bus. Result |
| According to president's view | 29.2% | 2.91 | 15.7 | 3.04* | 13.8 | 5.01 | 11.4 | 4.91 |
| Upon discussions with executives | 48.5 | 2.78 | 54.9 | 2.83 | 59.3 | 4.96 | 66.9 | 4.98 |
| According to executives' view | 22.3 | 2.73 | 29.4 | 2.75 | 26.8 | 5.03 | 21.7 | 5.08 |

| 1977 | | 1978 | | 1980 | | 1981 | | 1982 | |
|---|---|---|---|---|---|---|---|---|---|
| Percent-age | Bus. Result | Percent-age | Bus. Result | Percent-age | Bus. Result | Percent-age | Bus. Result | Percent-age | Bus. Result |
| 13.2 | 4.95 | 12.6 | 5.12 | 13.4 | 5.10* | 14.8 | 5.17 | 12.5 | 5.11 |
| 66.9 | 4.96 | 70.8 | 4.99 | 66.4 | 4.98 | 68.5 | 5.00 | 69.4 | 4.95 |
| 19.9 | 4.94 | 16.6 | 5.00 | 20.2 | 4.73 | 16.7 | 5.00 | 18.1 | 4.88 |

**Table 6-12.** The Relationship between the Patterns of Decision-Making at the Highest Decision-Making Body and Business Results (Large firms)

| | 1973 | | 1974 | | 1975 | | 1976 | |
|---|---|---|---|---|---|---|---|---|
| | Percent-age | Bus. Result | Percent-age | Bus. Result | Percent-age | Bus. Result | Percent-age | Bus. Result |
| According to president's view | 28.9% | 2.88 | 11.7 | 2.84 | 11.3 | 5.14 | 8.1 | 5.01 |
| Upon discussions with executives | 49.6 | 2.78 | 59.4 | 2.86 | 60.9 | 5.00 | 69.3 | 5.02 |
| According to executives' view | 21.5 | 2.49 | 28.8 | 2.75 | 27.8 | 5.14 | 22.6 | 5.16 |

| 1977 | | 1978 | | 1980 | | 1981 | | 1982 | |
|---|---|---|---|---|---|---|---|---|---|
| Percent-age | Bus. Result | Percent-age | Bus. Result | Percent-age | Bus. Result | Percent-age | Bus. Result | Percent-age | Bus. Result |
| 10.9 | 4.99 | 12.5 | 5.17 | 11.0 | 5.06 | 15.1 | 5.14 | 10.1 | 5.28 |
| 68.5 | 4.98 | 71.2 | 5.06 | 68.8 | 5.05* | 67.2 | 5.09 | 71.8 | 4.97 |
| 20.6 | 5.13 | 16.3 | 5.11 | 20.2 | 4.79 | 17.7 | 5.00 | 18.2 | 4.88 |

**Table 6-13.** The Relationship between the Patterns of Decision-Making at the
Highest Decision-Making Body and Business Results
(Medium-large firms)

| | 1973 | | 1974 | | 1975 | | 1976 | |
|---|---|---|---|---|---|---|---|---|
| | Percent-age | Bus. Result | Percent-age | Bus. Result | Percent-age | Bus. Result | Percent-age | Bus. Result |
| According to president's view | %<br>28.4 | 2.89 | 21.5 | 3.23* | 18.3 | 4.87 | 17.4 | 4.82 |
| Upon discussions with executives | 48.3 | 2.80 | 48.2 | 2.79 | 56.6 | 4.88 | 62.6 | 4.90 |
| According to executives' view | 23.2 | 2.70 | 30.4 | 2.74 | 25.1 | 4.81 | 20.0 | 4.93 |

| 1977 | | 1978 | | 1980 | | 1981 | | 1982 | |
|---|---|---|---|---|---|---|---|---|---|
| Percent-age | Bus. Result | Percent-age | Bus. Result | Percent-age | Bus. Result | Percent-age | Bus. Result | Percent-age | Bus. Result |
| 16.8 | 4.91 | 12.7 | 5.03 | 17.8 | 5.15 | 14.2 | 5.25 | 16.9 | 4.92 |
| 64.4 | 4.92 | 70.1 | 4.87 | 62.2 | 4.83 | 71.0 | 4.85 | 65.1 | 4.91 |
| 18.8 | 4.60 | 17.3 | 4.81 | 20.0 | 4.62 | 14.8 | 5.00 | 18.0 | 4.88 |

*Hypothesis* 6-7: In the electric machinery industry, the firm whose
president takes precedence over executives in decision-making enjoys
favorable results; in the transport equipment industry, the company
where a decision is made by the president who also considers the
executives' opinions achieves a higher level of business results. In the
fields of textile, chemicals and general machinery, the decision-making
pattern should be adjusted in response to changes in external conditions,
though the most appropriate pattern of decision-making in a given
period might be slightly different from one sector to another. In other
words, decision-making based on the president's view or discussions
with executives helps the firm to raise corporate achievement when an
economy is growing fast, while in the low economic growth period
the decision-making based on executives' view is favorable.

Even when economic growth is slow, good performance is observed
in the electric industry which is constantly subject to technological
innovation. In this sector emphasis should be placed not on the avoidance of risks, but on prompt decision-making by the president's view.
The growth of the transport equipment industry is also generally high,

but not as high as that of the electric machinery industry. Its technological innovation is also less remarkable. Therefore, executives' views as to future risks should be taken fully into account when decisions are made. They should be ready to take a responsible role in the policy implementation process. In the textile, chemical and general machinery industries, the optimum pattern of decision-making changes depending on the external conditions. This can be attributed to the following. In these three fields of industries, profit margin is limited due to the nature of the business. Accordingly, prompt decision-making centering upon the president's opinion is desirable when an economy is growing fast. Once the speed of economic growth has decreased, cost reduction and other measures for which all the executives should take a responsibility are demanded. The time when a certain pattern of decision-making is recommended differs from one industry to another. This is due to either the time lag from decision-making to implementation or the differences in "slacks" which results from the differences in profit margin.

**Table 6–14.** The Relationship between the Patterns of Decision-Making at the Highest Decision-Making Body and Business Results (Textiles)

|  | 1974 | | 1975 | | 1976 | | 1977 | |
|---|---|---|---|---|---|---|---|---|
|  | Percent-age | Bus. Result | Percent-age | Bus. Result | Percent-age | Bus. Result | Percent-age | Bus. Result |
| According to president's view | 25.6% | 2.91 | 11.1 | 3.37 | 16.7 | 4.64 | 16.7 | 4.72 |
| Upon discussions with executives | 51.2 | 3.00 | 63.9 | 3.70 | 63.9 | 4.64 | 76.2 | 4.66 |
| According to executives' view | 23.3 | 2.22 | 25.0 | 4.02 | 19.4 | 4.30 | 7.1 | 4.62 |

| 1978 | | 1980 | | 1981 | | 1982 | |
|---|---|---|---|---|---|---|---|
| Percent-age | Bus. Result | Percent-age | Bus. Result | Percent-age | Bus. Result | Percent-age | Bus. Result |
| 16.3 | 4.58 | 18.6 | 4.03 | 14.8 | 4.64 | 16.1 | 4.60 |
| 72.1 | 4.66 | 62.8 | 4.31 | 63.0 | 4.12 | 71.0 | 4.31 |
| 11.6 | 4.13 | 18.6 | 3.96 | 22.2 | 4.41 | 12.9 | 4.79 |

**Table 6-15.** The Relationship between the Patterns of Decision-Making at the Highest Decision-Making Body and Business Results (Chemicals)

| | 1974 | | 1975 | | 1976 | | 1977 | |
|---|---|---|---|---|---|---|---|---|
| | Percent-age | Bus. Result | Percent-age | Bus. Result | Percent-age | Bus. Result | Percent-age | Bus. Result |
| According to president's view | %<br>15.1 | 2.61 | 15.3 | 5.16 | 5.4 | 5.45 | 10.3 | 5.54 |
| Upon discussions with executives | 52.3 | 2.84 | 48.2 | 5.45 | 67.6 | 5.46 | 66.7 | 5.33 |
| According to executives' view | 32.6 | 2.92 | 36.5 | 5.56 | 27.0 | 5.33 | 23.0 | 5.37 |

| 1978 | | 1980 | | 1981 | | 1982 | |
|---|---|---|---|---|---|---|---|
| Percent-age | Bus. Result | Percent-age | Bus. Result | Percent-age | Bus. Result | Percent-age | Bus. Result |
| 12.1 | 5.28 | 5.0 | 5.03 | 14.3 | 4.90 | 12.1 | 4.77 |
| 64.8 | 5.08 | 70.0 | 5.13* | 67.1 | 5.00 | 65.2 | 4.88 |
| 23.1 | 5.01 | 25.0 | 4.66 | 18.6 | 5.13 | 22.7 | 5.55* |

**Table 6-16.** The Relationship between the Patterns of Decision-Making at the Highest Decision-Making Body and Business Results (General machinery)

| | 1974 | | 1975 | | 1976 | | 1977 | |
|---|---|---|---|---|---|---|---|---|
| | Percent-age | Bus. Result | Percent-age | Bus. Result | Percent-age | Bus. Result | Percent-age | Bus. Result |
| According to president's view | %<br>14.8 | 3.17 | 16.7 | 5.09 | 11.1 | 4.62 | 13.2 | 4.28 |
| Upon discussions with executives | 53.1 | 2.50 | 56.1 | 4.96 | 66.7 | 4.52 | 71.1 | 4.52 |
| According to executives' view | 32.1 | 2.65 | 27.3 | 4.97 | 22.2 | 5.08 | 15.8 | 4.25 |

| 1978 | | 1980 | | 1981 | | 1982 | |
|---|---|---|---|---|---|---|---|
| Percent-age | Bus. Result | Percent-age | Bus. Result | Percent-age | Bus. Result | Percent-age | Bus. Result |
| 20.0 | 4.84 | 21.3 | 5.36 | 15.9 | 5.84 | 18.0 | 5.77* |
| 68.6 | 4.85 | 60.0 | 5.25 | 65.1 | 5.28 | 67.2 | 5.29 |
| 11.4 | 4.82 | 18.8 | 4.42 | 19.0 | 5.47 | 14.8 | 4.32 |

**Table 6-17.** The Relationship between the Patterns of Decision-Making at the Highest Decision-Making Body and Business Results (Electric machinery)

| | 1974 | | 1975 | | 1976 | | 1977 | |
|---|---|---|---|---|---|---|---|---|
| | Percentage | Bus. Result | Percentage | Bus. Result | Percentage | Bus. Result | Percentage | Bus. Result |
| According to president's view | 14.0% | 3.46 | 16.2 | 4.76 | 8.8 | 4.23 | 13.2 | 4.99 |
| Upon discussions with executives | 67.4 | 3.03 | 64.7 | 4.69 | 75.4 | 4.88 | 67.6 | 4.80 |
| According to executives' view | 18.6 | 3.35 | 19.1 | 4.52 | 15.8 | 4.65 | 19.1 | 4.84 |

| 1978 | | 1980 | | 1981 | | 1982 | |
|---|---|---|---|---|---|---|---|
| Percentage | Bus. Result | Percentage | Bus. Result | Percentage | Bus. Result | Percentage | Bus. Result |
| 15.4 | 6.07* | 17.2 | 4.81 | 11.7 | 5.74 | 11.9 | 5.24 |
| 69.2 | 5.12 | 65.6 | 5.30 | 78.3 | 5.44 | 71.2 | 5.42 |
| 15.4 | 5.48 | 17.2 | 5.35 | 10.0 | 5.21 | 16.9 | 5.24 |

**Table 6-18.** The Relationship between the Patterns of Decision-Making at the Highest Decision-Making Body and Business Results (Transport equipment)

| | 1974 | | 1975 | | 1976 | | 1977 | |
|---|---|---|---|---|---|---|---|---|
| | Percentage | Bus. Result | Percentage | Bus. Result | Percentage | Bus. Result | Percentage | Bus. Result |
| According to president's view | 9.7% | 2.79 | 5.3 | 4.49 | 20.0 | 5.21 | 8.9 | 5.07 |
| Upon discussions with executives | 58.1 | 2.50 | 57.9 | 4.82 | 65.7 | 5.54 | 71.1 | 5.42 |
| According to executives' view | 32.3 | 2.36 | 36.8 | 4.59 | 14.3 | 5.33 | 20.0 | 5.25 |

| 1978 | | 1980 | | 1981 | | 1982 | |
|---|---|---|---|---|---|---|---|
| Percentage | Bus. Result | Percentage | Bus. Result | Percentage | Bus. Result | Percentage | Bus. Result |
| 11.9 | 5.06 | 5.1 | 3.41 | 20.8 | 4.72 | 8.7 | 5.29 |
| 76.2 | 5.29 | 66.7 | 4.86* | 60.4 | 5.07 | 67.4 | 5.10 |
| 11.9 | 5.47 | 28.2 | 4.68 | 18.8 | 4.79 | 23.9 | 5.01 |

## 6-4-2. Taking Charge of Management Task by Executives

An executive who is in charge of a division in a functional organization tends to assume the role of a representative of the particular division. Thus he may lose sight of the objectives and the prospects of the company as a whole. Such an attitude adversely affects the decisions in which they participate. It is generally considered, therefore, that the executives who take part in strategic decision-making should preferably be free from the task of division management. And yet, in the Japanese manufacturing sector, executives are usually in charge of divisions; the firms where executives are exempt from division management tasks are so few that they are taken the exceptional rather than the rule. In over 50 percent of the firms in the manufacturing industry in Japan, a majority of executives are responsible for devision management. In about forty percent of the firms a portion of executives are in charge of divisions, while in only three to six percent of the firms all executives are free from the task of division management. The relationship between the division management task of executives and corporate performance is presented in Table 6-19. The following hypothesis is obtained.

**Table 6-19.** The Relationship between Taking Charge of Management Task by Executives and Business Results (All manufacturing industry)

|  | 1973 | | 1974 | | 1975 | |
|---|---|---|---|---|---|---|
|  | Percent-age | Bus. Result | Percent-age | Bus. Result | Percent-age | Bus. Result |
| A majority of executives are in charge of management task | 37.7% | 2.88 | 53.1 | 2.79 | 53.1 | 4.90 |
| A portion of executives are in charge of management task | 34.4 | 2.65 | 40.3 | 2.84 | 41.8 | 5.06 |
| All executives are free from management task | 27.9 | 2.91 | 6.6 | 3.19 | 5.0 | 5.36 |

| 1976 | | 1977 | | 1978 | |
|---|---|---|---|---|---|
| Percent-age | Bus. Result | Percent-age | Bus. Result | Percent-age | Bus. Result |
| 51.6 | 5.05 | 56.1 | 4.89 | 56.7 | 5.03 |
| 43.4 | 4.98 | 40.9 | 5.01 | 40.5 | 4.99 |
| 5.3 | 4.62 | 3.0 | 4.61 | 2.8 | 4.84 |

*Hypothesis 6-8*:  When external conditions are favorable, the firms whose executives do not assume the task of management achieve better results. But, when the economic growth is slow, better results are produced by those companies whose executives are responsible for management task.

During the low-growth period, executives are not permitted to make the smallest mistakes due to the low profit margin. Most executives who take charge of a division are held responsible for management and control. When an economy is enjoying high growth, however, executives need not be mindful of trivials; they should be more concerned with the prospect of the company as a whole, detaching themselves from the task of division management.

### 6-4-3.  Business Goals

In establishing business goals and strategies the chief executive envisages the company's outlook and determines measures and policies to be executed, taking account of both external and internal conditions. The business goals and strategies for accomplishing objectives reveal most clearly the attitude of the president. For this research, I conducted a survey by sending out a questionaire to chief executives. They were asked to choose what they consider to be the most significant of the following eleven business goals. They are: 1. new product development, 2. expansion of the main products' market share, 3. coordination with the regional community, 4. reinforcement of export and overseas investment, 5. cost reduction by rationalization and labor-saving, 6. personnel curtailment, 7. expansion of employees' welfare, 8. diversification and changes in business, 9. improvement of consumer services, 10. reduction of production lines, and 11. increase of the own capital ratio. Ninety percent of those who responded to the survey chose new product development, expansion of the main products' market share, or cost reduction by rationalization and labor-saving; the remaining eight items did not attract the attention of chief executives. With regard to the relationship between business goals and external environment, it can be concluded that most presidents attach importance to the share expansion of main products when economic growth rate is on the rise. When economic growth is low, cost reduction is stressed.

The development of new products is also given more attention when external conditions are favorable, while less attention may be given in a low economic growth period, though the differences is not as marked as with the expansion of main products' market share. Classification of business goals by industry reveals that new product development is highly regarded in the electric machinery and chemical industries where technological innovation is very rapid. The expansion of main products' market share leads the list in textile and general machinery industries where technological innovation is slower.

Tables 6–20 through 26 describe the relationship between the selection of business goals and corporate performance. This gives rise to the following hypothesis.

*Hypothesis 6–9*: The company which vigorously pursues the development of new products constantly enjoys a higher level of achievement regardless of external environment.

The ambitious development of new products gives impetus to manpower development, which, in turn, furthers new product development. Such a reciprocity stimulates the creativity of employees and paves the way for the promotion of corporate performance. Among the various abilities of chief executives, energetic implementation of forward-looking policies backed by a strong entrepreneurship is a major factor contributing to the prosperity of business.

The following hypothesis is possible with regard to the relationship between the selection of business goals and corporate performance.

*Hypothesis 6–10*: In the electric machinery industry, companies which primarily aim at the reduction of cost show good performance, whereas in the chemical industry firms which have new product development as their objective enjoy better results. In the area of textiles, both share expansion of main products' market and new product development should be given similar importance.

Companies in an industry showing rapid development should realize the importance of the administratorship, that is, defensive measures including cost reduction. In a stagnant industry, the entrepreneurship, that is the expansion of main products' market share and new product development is important.

Table 6–26 explains the relationship between the selection of business

**Table 6-20.** The Relationship between the Selection of Business Goals and Business Results (All manufacturing industry)

| | 1973 | | 1974 | | 1975 | | 1976 | |
|---|---|---|---|---|---|---|---|---|
| | Percent-age | Bus. Result | Percent-age | Bus. Result | Percent-age | Bus. Result | Percent-age | Bus. Result |
| New product development | 23.9% | 3.01* | 25.6 | 2.90* | 24.5 | 5.10* | 20.1 | 4.89 |
| Share expansion of main products | 30.0 | 2.67 | 46.8 | 2.89 | 45.6 | 5.03 | 47.7 | 5.19* |
| Cost-reduction | 33.2 | 2.76 | 19.5 | 2.72 | 15.7 | 4.98 | 17.8 | 4.79 |
| Others | 12.9 | 2.81 | 8.1 | 2.64 | 14.2 | 4.67 | 14.4 | 4.74 |

| 1977 | | 1978 | | 1980 | | 1981 | | 1982 | |
|---|---|---|---|---|---|---|---|---|---|
| Percent-age | Bus. Result | Percent-age | Bus. Result | Percent-age | Bus. Result | Percent-age | Bus. Result | Percent-age | Bus. Result |
| 22.6 | 5.03 | 21.1 | 5.29* | 21.9 | 5.36* | 25.1 | 5.17 | 26.0 | 5.29* |
| 52.4 | 4.92 | 47.0 | 5.00 | 46.4 | 4.90 | 47.6 | 5.03 | 49.0 | 4.86 |
| 17.0 | 4.94 | 23.8 | 4.82 | 18.6 | 4.95 | 17.3 | 4.94 | 16.7 | 4.64 |
| 8.0 | 4.99 | 8.1 | 4.87 | 13.1 | 4.41 | 9.9 | 4.81 | 8.3 | 5.13 |

**Table 6-21.** The Relationship between the Selection of Business Goals and Business Results (Textiles)

| | 1973 | | 1974 | | 1975 | | 1976 | |
|---|---|---|---|---|---|---|---|---|
| | Percent-age | Bus. Result | Percent-age | Bus. Result | Percent-age | Bus. Result | Percent-age | Bus. Result |
| New product development | 23.6% | 2.51 | 11.6 | 2.01 | 11.1 | 4.55 | 11.1 | 4.65 |
| Share expansion of main products | 16.7 | 2.73 | 41.9 | 3.16 | 41.7 | 4.13 | 38.9 | 4.67 |
| Cost-reduction | 54.2 | 2.57 | 34.6 | 2.64 | 22.2 | 3.06 | 27.8 | 4.82 |
| Others | 5.5 | 2.71 | 11.6 | 2.77 | 25.0 | 3.34 | 22.2 | 4.07 |

| 1977 | | 1978 | | 1980 | | 1981 | | 1982 | |
|---|---|---|---|---|---|---|---|---|---|
| Percent-age | Bus. Result | Percent-age | Bus. Result | Percent-age | Bus. Result | Percent-age | Bus. Result | Percent-age | Bus. Result |
| 16.7 | 4.77 | 11.6 | 4.86 | 9.3 | 4.75* | 22.2 | 4.12 | 9.7 | 4.28 |
| 50.0 | 4.81 | 39.5 | 4.84 | 41.9 | 4.51 | 25.9 | 3.85 | 51.6 | 4.32 |
| 23.8 | 4.50 | 44.2 | 4.30 | 32.6 | 3.60 | 25.9 | 3.85 | 16.1 | 4.33 |
| 9.5 | 4.15 | 4.7 | 4.50 | 16.3 | 4.22 | 25.9 | 5.14* | 22.6 | 4.78 |

**Table 6-22.** The Relationship between the Selection of Business Goals and Business Results (Chemicals)

| | 1973 | | 1974 | | 1975 | | 1976 | |
|---|---|---|---|---|---|---|---|---|
| | Percent-age | Bus. Result | Percent-age | Bus. Result | Percent-age | Bus. Result | Percent-age | Bus. Result |
| New product development | 36.7% | 3.04 | 36.0 | 2.90 | 29.4 | 5.41 | 25.7 | 5.57 |
| Share expansion of main products | 25.5 | 2.50 | 38.4 | 2.93 | 49.4 | 5.43 | 51.4 | 5.35 |
| Cost-reduction | 16.3 | 2.85 | 11.6 | 2.39 | 8.2 | 6.49* | 8.1 | 5.43 |
| Others | 21.5 | 2.60 | 14.0 | 2.77 | 12.9 | 4.89 | 14.9 | 5.41 |

| 1977 | | 1978 | | 1980 | | 1981 | | 1982 | |
|---|---|---|---|---|---|---|---|---|---|
| Percent-age | Bus. Result | Percent-age | Bus. Result | Percent-age | Bus. Result | Percent-age | Bus. Result | Percent-age | Bus. Result |
| 28.7 | 5.55* | 36.3 | 5.41* | 32.5 | 5.29* | 42.9 | 5.20 | 42.4 | 5.15 |
| 54.0 | 5.28 | 49.5 | 4.93 | 45.0 | 4.99 | 44.3 | 4.87 | 37.9 | 5.16 |
| 11.5 | 5.51 | 9.9 | 4.65 | 11.3 | 4.70 | 8.6 | 4.91 | 13.6 | 4.33 |
| 5.7 | 4.88 | 4.4 | 5.19 | 11.3 | 4.54 | 4.3 | 4.75 | 6.1 | 4.78 |

**Table 6-23.** The Relationship between the Selection of Business Goals and Business Results (General machinery)

| | 1973 | | 1974 | | 1975 | | 1976 | |
|---|---|---|---|---|---|---|---|---|
| | Percent-age | Bus. Result | Percent-age | Bus. Result | Percent-age | Bus. Result | Percent-age | Bus. Result |
| New product development | 33.3% | 2.36 | 33.3 | 2.92 | 30.3 | 5.12 | 28.6 | 4.20 |
| Share expansion of main products | 37.6 | 2.15 | 42.0 | 2.45 | 50.0 | 5.01 | 46.0 | 5.09* |
| Cost-reduction | 26.9 | 2.51 | 18.5 | 2.53 | 9.1 | 5.24 | 11.1 | 4.84 |
| Others | 8.1 | 2.34 | 6.2 | 2.89 | 10.6 | 4.24 | 14.3 | 4.00 |

| 1977 | | 1978 | | 1980 | | 1981 | | 1982 | |
|---|---|---|---|---|---|---|---|---|---|
| Percent-age | Bus. Result | Percent-age | Bus. Result | Percent-age | Bus. Result | Percent-age | Bus. Result | Percent-age | Bus. Result |
| 32.9 | 4.64 | 22.9 | 4.84 | 22.5 | 5.72* | 25.4 | 5.20 | 24.6 | 5.99* |
| 43.4 | 4.33 | 40.0 | 4.65 | 48.8 | 4.86 | 46.0 | 5.50 | 57.4 | 4.93 |
| 19.7 | 4.27 | 28.6 | 5.03 | 16.3 | 5.64 | 19.0 | 5.50 | 11.5 | 5.40 |
| 3.9 | (5.13) | 8.6 | 5.15 | 12.5 | 4.37 | 9.5 | 5.27 | 6.6 | 4.74 |

**Table 6-24.** The Relationship between the Selection of Business Goals and Business Results (Electric machinery)

| | 1973 | | 1974 | | 1975 | | 1976 | |
|---|---|---|---|---|---|---|---|---|
| | Percent-age | Bus. Result | Percent-age | Bus. Result | Percent-age | Bus. Result | Percent-age | Bus. Result |
| New product development | 54.3% | 3.30 | 27.9 | 3.38 | 47.1 | 4.90 | 35.1 | 4.60 |
| Share expansion of main products | 25.4 | 3.26 | 48.8 | 3.14 | 36.8 | 4.38 | 45.6 | 4.91 |
| Cost-reduction | 16.9 | 2.94 | 20.9 | 2.84 | 8.8 | 5.31 | 10.5 | 5.06 |
| Others | 3.4 | 2.23 | 2.3 | 3.61△ | 7.4 | 3.88 | 8.8 | 4.54 |

| 1977 | | 1978 | | 1980 | | 1981 | | 1982 | |
|---|---|---|---|---|---|---|---|---|---|
| Percent-age | Bus. Result | Percent-age | Bus. Result | Percent-age | Bus. Result | Percent-age | Bus. Result | Percent-age | Bus. Result |
| 27.9 | 4.70 | 26.9 | 5.59* | 40.6 | 5.38 | 41.7 | 5.56 | 37.3 | 5.73 |
| 52.9 | 4.77 | 44.9 | 5.11 | 35.9 | 5.19 | 45.0 | 5.29 | 45.8 | 5.03 |
| 17.6 | 5.21 | 23.1 | 5.32 | 15.6 | 5.57* | 8.3 | 5.85 | 6.8 | 4.90 |
| 1.5 | 4.90 | 5.1 | 5.83 | 7.8 | 3.94 | 5.0 | 5.40 | 10.2 | 5.85 |

**Table 6-25.** The Relationship between the Selection of Business Goals and Business Results (Transport equipment)

| | 1973 | | 1974 | | 1975 | | 1976 | |
|---|---|---|---|---|---|---|---|---|
| | Percent-age | Bus. Result | Percent-age | Bus. Result | Percent-age | Bus. Result | Percent-age | Bus. Result |
| New product development | 24.8% | 3.33 | 32.3 | 2.61 | 21.1 | 4.65 | 8.6 | 5.73 |
| Share expansion of main products | 27.1 | 2.98 | 29.0 | 2.56 | 34.2 | 4.64 | 51.4 | 5.30 |
| Cost-reduction | 42.4 | 2.92 | 29.0 | 2.31 | 28.9 | 4.75 | 22.9 | 5.81 |
| Others | 5.7 | 2.87 | 9.7 | 2.36 | 15.8 | 4.92 | 17.1 | 5.24 |

| 1977 | | 1978 | | 1980 | | 1981 | | 1982 | |
|---|---|---|---|---|---|---|---|---|---|
| Percent-age | Bus. Result | Percent-age | Bus. Result | Percent-age | Bus. Result | Percent-age | Bus. Result | Percent-age | Bus. Result |
| 15.6 | 5.37 | 14.3 | 5.37 | 25.6 | 5.26 | 20.8 | 5.28 | 30.4 | 5.24 |
| 57.8 | 5.22 | 54.8 | 5.25 | 35.9 | 5.03 | 47.9 | 5.24 | 37.0 | 5.24 |
| 17.8 | 5.64 | 21.4 | 5.50 | 15.4 | 5.37 | 14.6 | 4.68 | 26.1 | 4.74 |
| 8.9 | 5.65 | 9.5 | 4.86 | 23.1 | 3.49 | 16.7 | 3.91 | 6.5 | 5.03 |

**Table 6-26.** The Relationship between the Selection of Business Goals and Employees' Morale (All manufacturing industry)

| | 1974 | | 1975 | | 1976 | |
|---|---|---|---|---|---|---|
| | Percent-age | Morale | Percent-age | Morale | Percent-age | Morale |
| New product development | 25.6% | 24.3 | 20.7 | 3.42 | 19.4 | 3.39 |
| Share expansion of main products | 46.8 | 2.46 | 34.1 | 3.39 | 36.5 | 3.36 |
| Cost-reduction | 19.5 | 2.39 | 27.4 | 3.43 | 29.2 | 3.42 |
| Others | 8.1 | 2.63* | 17.8 | 3.31 | 14.8 | 3.50 |

| 1977 | | 1978 | | 1980 | | 1981 | | 1982 | |
|---|---|---|---|---|---|---|---|---|---|
| Percent-age | Morale | Percent-age | Morale | Percent-age | Morale | Percent-age | Morale | Percent-age | Morale |
| 21.7 | 3.39 | 28.8 | 3.43 | 38.6 | 3.47 | 46.3 | 3.46 | 26.0 | 3.38 |
| 41.1 | 3.40 | 40.5 | 3.40 | 34.0 | 3.43 | 30.2 | 3.42 | 49.0 | 3.34 |
| 29.4 | 3.23 | 22.9 | 3.32 | 16.9 | 3.35 | 15.0 | 3.18 | 16.7 | 3.26 |
| 7.8 | 3.49 | 7.8 | 3.38 | 10.6 | 3.34 | 8.5 | 3.65* | 8.3 | 3.49 |

goals and employee morale. This provids us with the following hypothesis.

*Hypothesis 6-11*: The selection of business goals does not exert direct influence upon the morale of employees.

Employees' morale cannot be immediately elevated by changing business goals, because it is related to the inheried corporate culture.

## 6-4-4. Overseas Strategies

Today many Japanese business firms operate internationally. The chief executives' positive attitude toward business management is displayed in active and progressive overseas strategies. This in general falls into two categories, export and the establishment of overseas production bases. From the standpoint of a solution to trade friction, the latter is regarded as more positive and enterprising. An investigation was conducted for this paper through the use of the questionaire, by requesting chief executives to choose the most significant of the following four items:

1) No export or foreign foothold.

2) Without establishing overseas production bases, export should be promoted by expanding the market through trading companies and

sales agents.

3)  Without establishing overseas production bases, export should be promoted and the market expanded by establishing business offices and sales subsidiaries.

4)  Production should be fostered abroad by active investment in overseas factories.

In the Japanese manufacturing sector, most companies export their products through trading firms and sales agents. This tendency has remained unchanged in spite of changes in the external environment. The relationship between the overseas strategies emphasized and corporate performances is represented in Table 6–27. The following hypothesis is derived.

*Hypothesis 6–12*: Until the end of the 1970s, companies which placed an emphasis on the establishment of, and investment in, overseas production bases proved more successful in achieving higher level of business results. But in the 1980s companies that promote export through their own business offices and sales subsidiaries have been experiencing better business results.

**Table 6–27.** The Relationship between Overseas Strategies and Business Results (All manufacturing industry)

| | 1973 | | 1974 | | 1975 | | 1976 | |
|---|---|---|---|---|---|---|---|---|
| | Percent-age | Bus. Result | Percent-age | Bus. Result | Percent-age | Bus. Result | Percent-age | Bus. Result |
| No export or foreign foothold | 22.2% | 2.93 | 12.7 | 2.85 | 17.6 | 5.03 | 13.2 | 5.10 |
| Mainly export through trading companies | 36.4 | 2.62 | 46.0 | 2.75 | 45.8 | 4.92 | 50.2 | 4.81 |
| Mainly export through business offices or subsidiaries | 4.1 | 2.62 | 11.9 | 2.83 | 10.7 | 5.07 | 16.4 | 4.98 |
| Positive expansion through production abroad | 37.4 | 2.95 | 29.8 | 2.93* | 25.9 | 5.05 | 29.1 | 5.39 |

| 1977 | | 1978 | | 1980 | | 1981 | | 1982 | |
|---|---|---|---|---|---|---|---|---|---|
| Percent-age | Bus. Result | Percent-age | Bus. Result | Percent-age | Bus. Result | Percent-age | Bus. Result | Percent-age | Bus. Result |
| 14.3 | 4.81 | 17.4 | 4.99 | 15.7 | 4.91 | 12.7 | 5.07 | 8.8 | 4.75 |
| 53.0 | 4.88 | 51.0 | 4.89 | 49.5 | 4.88 | 53.5 | 4.91 | 49.4 | 4.65 |
| 15.0 | 5.09 | 13.5 | 5.29* | 12.7 | 5.15 | 12.9 | 5.35* | 19.0 | 5.42* |
| 17.8 | 5.18 | 18.1 | 5.15 | 22.1 | 5.00 | 20.9 | 5.02 | 22.9 | 5.31 |

Positive strategies utilized by chief executives for the expansion of overseas production and foreign investment serve to vitalize employees. The possibility of an active role abroad and the prospect of company's development enhance employees' morale and creativity, that is, important factors that contribute to favorable performance. In the 1980s, however, life in foreign countries has become less attractive to the Japanese as the standard of living rose in Japan. To be dispatched abroad is no longer an incentive to most employees. This tendency in recent years has forced companies to export their products through their own well-established overseas export networks and as a result better corporate performance has been achieved.

## 6-4-5. Long-Range Plan

In devising a long-range plan, business goals and strategies should be presented with concrete numerical data based on an overall analysis, reflecting a total system concept and scientific attitude of the chief executive. The long-range plan as a total system is comprised of individual strategies and various short-range plans as sub-systems, in reference to which, annual budget, profit plan and others are set up. The period of a long-range plan in most Japanese manufacturing companies listed on the Tokyo Stock Exchange is three years, and about 65 to 75 percent of companies make such long-range plans.

The long-range plan effect on corporate performance is revealed in

**Table 6-28.** The Relationship between the Long-Range Plan and Business Results (All manufacturing industry)

| | 1973 | | 1974 | | 1975 | | 1976 | |
|---|---|---|---|---|---|---|---|---|
| | Percent-age | Bus. Result | Percent-age | Bus. Result | Percent-age | Bus. Result | Percent-age | Bus. Result |
| Have long-range plan | 74.9% | 2.87 | 72.9 | 2.83 | 71.5 | 5.01 | 63.9 | 5.11* |
| No long-range plan | 25.1 | 2.67 | 27.1 | 2.87 | 28.5 | 4.92 | 36.1 | 4.79 |

| 1977 | | 1978 | | 1980 | | 1981 | | 1982 | |
|---|---|---|---|---|---|---|---|---|---|
| Percent-age | Bus. Result | Percent-age | Bus. Result | Percent-age | Bus. Result | Percent-age | Bus. Result | Percent-age | Bus. Result |
| 65.9 | 5.07* | 66.7 | 5.08* | 74.1 | 4.97 | 72.3 | 5.70* | 68.3 | 5.07* |
| 34.1 | 4.72 | 33.3 | 4.88 | 25.9 | 4.87 | 27.7 | 4.80 | 31.7 | 4.71 |

Table 6–28. This gives rise to the following hypothesis.

*Hypothesis 6–13*: Compared with companies without any long-range plan, those which devise scientific, long-range plans always enjoy prosperous achievement, irrespective of changes in external economic conditions.

A long-range plan reflects the scientific attitude of the president who aims at the total system. It helps to coordinate business and to promote growth and profitability.

# 6–5. Factors Related to the Consequences of Decision-Making

## 6–5–1. Percentage of Executives' Stockholdings

For those companies listed on the Tokyo Stock Exchange, the percentage of executives' stockholdings to total stocks issued varies from five to ten percent. The higher the percentage, the greater responsibility the executives assume for business achievement because corporate achievement is directly related to their own income. The proportion of stocks held at executives has recently been changing. This is probably a result of an increase in the number of companies newly listed on the Tokyo Stock Exchange. In these companies the percentage of executives' stockholdings is generally high. The relationship between the percentage of executives' stockholdings and corporate performance is indicated in Table 6–29. The following hypothesis is obtained.

*Hypothesis 6–14*: Regardless of the economic growth rate, good performance is shown by those companies in which the proportion of executives' stockholdings exceeds 10 percent.

The company in which executives hold more than 10 percent of the stock has characteristics of a family enterprise; when many executives are from the same family, there is sufficient mutual understanding among them and decision can be made quickly to cope with changes in external environments. Generally speaking executives of small family enterprises tend to be concerned with their own interest. But when those firms become large scale firms such as those listed on the Tokyo Stock Exchange, opinions and views of the executives and managers who are non-relatives are also respected in long-range planning, in-

**Table 6-29.** The Relationship between the Percentage of Executives' Stockholdings and Business Results (All manufacturing industry)

| | 1974 | | 1975 | | 1976 | | 1977 | |
|---|---|---|---|---|---|---|---|---|
| | Percent-age | Bus. Result | Percent-age | Bus. Result | Percent-age | Bus. Result | Percent-age | Bus. Result |
| ·≤ 1% | 47.5% | 2.67 | 41.2 | 4.82 | 45.4 | 4.99 | 24.3 | 5.02 |
| 1<·≤ 5 | 23.1 | 2.84 | 27.0 | 5.04 | 23.3 | 4.97 | 35.0 | 4.87 |
| 5<·≤15 | 18.9 | 2.86 | 18.4 | 5.08 | 20.8 | 4.94 | 30.4 | 5.00 |
| 15<· | 12.5 | 3.47* | 13.4 | 5.24* | 10.5 | 5.19 | 10.4 | 4.94 |

| 1978 | | 1980 | | 1981 | | 1982 | |
|---|---|---|---|---|---|---|---|
| Percent-age | Bus. Result | Percent-age | Bus. Result | Percent-age | Bus. Result | Percent-age | Bus. Result |
| 29.0 | 4.79 | 23.8 | 4.87 | 25.2 | 4.99 | 24.4 | 4.95 |
| 32.5 | 4.94 | 23.0 | 4.83 | 24.7 | 5.04 | 23.1 | 4.93 |
| 29.0 | 5.28* | 26.9 | 4.98 | 25.8 | 5.00 | 29.0 | 4.92 |
| 9.4 | 5.02 | 26.3 | 5.08 | 24.3 | 5.09 | 23.5 | 5.03 |

cluding fund raising. In other words, the large companies whose executives' stockholdings exceed 10 percent show both merits of a family-owned company and merits of a large company that is managed by scientific thought.

## 6-5-2. Percentage of Invited Executives

Edith T. Penrose argues that the shortage of able executives prevents the growth of firms; a rapidly expanding firms, in order to increase executives, must resort to offering the post to those outside the company, incurring the lack of mutual understanding among the executives and inefficient decision-making. The offering of the post of executive to outsiders has additional disadvantage in Japanese business firms. It discourages and demoralize employees. University graduates join companies with the hope and belief of promotion, step by step through the ranks of middle management to executive according to their ability and seniority. This is based on the life-time employment system. Whatever the reason, it is very disheartening to employees that a firm should offer the post of executive to those who did not belong to the company. Invited executives constitute an average of eight or nine percent of all executives in Japanese companies. This has been showing a very little change in the past several years. Invited executives are non-existent in about 40 to 50 percent of companies and this percentage has also been remaining unchanged. Most of the invited executives in Japanese business enterprises come from parent companies, financial institutions, or government offices. The relationship between the percentage of invited executives and employees' morale is revealed in Table 6-30. The following hypothesis can be deduced.

*Hypothesis 6-15*: If a company offers the post of executive to those outside the company, employees' morale visibly declines regardless of external economic environments. This is statistically significant.

One of the most significant elements to activating a business organization is fair personnel affairs at the level of top. For a majority of employees wishing to be top management, it is unacceptable that the post of executive should be open to outsiders. And a reduction in their morale is a natural consequence. This is confirmed by Table 6-2 which shows that the morale of employees is lower in the company with an *Amakudari*-president. Thus, personnel administration of top management exerts an influence on employees' morale. The following hypothesis can be derived.

*Hypothesis 6-16*: Employees in Japanese firms are highly sensitive to personnel affairs in top management. Their morale is evidently

**Table 6-30.** The Relationship between the Percentage of Invited Executives and Employees' Morale (All manufacturing industry)

|  | 1974 | | 1975 | | 1976 | | 1977 | |
|---|---|---|---|---|---|---|---|---|
|  | Percent-age | Morale | Percent-age | Morale | Percent-age | Morale | Percent-age | Morale |
| $\cdot = 0$   % | 53.2 % | 2.49* | 41.0 | 3.65* | 39.7 | 3.49* | 41.1 | 3.50* |
| $0. < \cdot \leq 12.5$ | 15.9 | 2.47 | 30.0 | 3.51 | 31.3 | 3.42 | 27.2 | 3.35 |
| $12.5 < \cdot \leq 25.0$ | 19.5 | 2.47 | 15.1 | 3.52 | 18.0 | 3.22 | 17.6 | 3.28 |
| $25.0 < \cdot$ | 11.4 | 2.20 | 13.6 | 3.00 | 11.0 | 3.34 | 14.1 | 3.15 |

| 1978 | | 1980 | | 1981 | | 1982 | |
|---|---|---|---|---|---|---|---|
| Percent-age | Morale | Percent-age | Morale | Percent-age | Morale | Percent-age | Morale |
| 45.1 | 3.48* | 43.2 | 3.51* | 43.3 | 3.48 | 45.0 | 3.41* |
| 26.1 | 3.44 | 27.3 | 3.50 | 27.1 | 3.45 | 29.0 | 3.40 |
| 15.3 | 3.28 | 15.0 | 3.24 | 16.3 | 3.40 | 14.6 | 3.24 |
| 13.5 | 3.12 | 14.6 | 3.20 | 13.3 | 3.17 | 11.5 | 3.09 |

affected by the percentage of invited executives, as well as by the type of president.

The relationship between the percentage of invited executives and business results as indicated in Table 6–31 gives rise to the following hypothesis.

**Table 6-31.** The Relationship between the Percentage of Invited Executives and Business Results (All manufacturing industry)

| | 1974 | | 1975 | | 1976 | | 1977 | |
|---|---|---|---|---|---|---|---|---|
| | Percent-age | Bus. Result | Percent-age | Bus. Result | Percent-age | Bus. Result | Percent-age | Bus. Result |
| • = 0 % | 53.2% | 2.96* | 41.0 | 5.25* | 39.7 | 5.09 | 41.1 | 5.01 |
| 0 < • ≤ 12.5 | 15.9 | 2.72 | 30.3 | 5.02 | 31.3 | 5.18 | 27.2 | 4.98 |
| 12.5 < • ≤ 25.0 | 19.5 | 2.85 | 15.1 | 4.75 | 18.0 | 4.77 | 17.6 | 4.92 |
| 25.0 < • | 11.4 | 2.43 | 13.6 | 4.40 | 11.0 | 4.47 | 14.1 | 4.77 |

| 1978 | | 1980 | | 1981 | | 1982 | |
|---|---|---|---|---|---|---|---|
| Percent-age | Bus. Result | Percent-age | Bus. Result | Percent-age | Bus. Result | Percent-age | Bus. Result |
| 45.1 | 5.21* | 43.2 | 5.02 | 43.3 | 5.03 | 45.0 | 5.03* |
| 26.1 | 4.99 | 27.3 | 4.95 | 27.1 | 5.15* | 29.0 | 4.98 |
| 15.3 | 4.86 | 15.0 | 4.81 | 16.3 | 5.11 | 14.6 | 4.92 |
| 13.5 | 4.53 | 14.6 | 4.89 | 13.3 | 4.65 | 11.5 | 4.66 |

*Hypothesis 6–17*: The company with virtually no invited executives and where top management has full communication and mutual understanding enjoys a higher level of corporate performance regardless of the growth rate of the external economy.

The lower percentage of invited executives might be a result, rather than a cause, of satisfactory corporate performance because the company which is favorably developing has no need to call for the help of those outside the firm. Nevertheless, the company with no or very few invited executives has certain advantages such as good communication among top management and quick decision-making to cope with ever-changing external conditions. As Penrose maintains, mutual understanding and the sharing of objectives and goals among executives are important factors necessary to produce higher levels of corporate performance.

### 6-5-3.  Schemes to Raise Motivation and Loyalty

One requirement of an enterprise is to continue promoting employees' morale by means of schemes to raise motivation and loyalty. In implementing such schemes, most business firms institutionalize so-called Japanese management customs and practices which they believe agreeable to employees. The schemes to raise motivation and loyalty of employees involved in this investigation are; employee stock ownership, recreation for employees' families, employee savings and deposit accounts, company housing, house-ownership plan, counseling service, employee's news letter (edited by employees), bonuses for long service, five-day week, private pension, employee's property accumulation savings, profit-sharing, and a mutual aid society. The number of schemes implemented serves as a yardstick to measure the company's efforts to raise motivation and loyalty of employees. In this study, companies which practice more than ten of the above-mentioned schemes are rated "positive", and those which implement more than seven and less than ten are rated "average". Companies which practice less than seven items are rated "negative".

Categorized by scale, large companies are unquestionably more eager to adopt schemes to raise motivation and loyalty. However, the number of schemes implemented by Japanese companies is not constantly increasing probably because some schemes are discontinued. The schemes most widely adopted by Japanese enterprises are typically Japanese: bonuses for long service, company housing, house-ownership plan, employee stock ownership, and employee's news letter. Such systems as a counseling service or profit-sharing are practiced by very few companies.

Tables 6-32 and 33 present the relationship of the number of schemes implemented to employees' morale and corporate performance. The following hypothesis is presented.

*Hypothesis 6-18*: Positive implementation of schemes to raise motivation and loyalty contributes greatly to the enhancement of employees' morale and corporate performance regardless of business scale or the economic growth rate in the external environment.

The implementation of such schemes as bonuses for long service, employee stock ownership, company housing, house-ownership plan,

**Table 6-32.** The Relationship between the Implementation of Schemes to Raise Motivation and Loyalty and Employees' Morale (All manufacturing industry)

|  | 1974 | | 1975 | | 1976** | |
|---|---|---|---|---|---|---|
|  | Percent-age | Morale | Percent-age | Morale | Percent-age | Morale |
| Negative (• < 7) | 23.7% | 2.35 | 12.6 | 2.95 | 15.5 | 3.02 |
| Average (7 ≤ • < 10) | 40.5 | 2.40 | 35.8 | 3.31 | 30.4 | 3.36 |
| Positive (10 ≤ •) | 35.8 | 2.58* | 51.7 | 3.58* | 54.1 | 3.54* |

| 1977 | | 1978 | | 1980 | | 1981 | | 1982 | |
|---|---|---|---|---|---|---|---|---|---|
| Percent-age | Morale | Percent-age | Morale | Percent-age | Morale | Percent-age | Morale | Percent-age | Morale |
| 15.0 | 3.09 | 13.1 | 3.13 | 24.8 | 3.21 | 23.9 | 3.22 | 23.3 | 3.09 |
| 56.7 | 3.30 | 50.6 | 3.28 | 36.7 | 3.40 | 37.0 | 3.39 | 34.4 | 3.29 |
| 28.3 | 3.67* | 36.2 | 3.64* | 38.6 | 3.58* | 39.1 | 3.58* | 42.3 | 3.53* |

**Table 6-33.** The Relationship between the Implementation of Schemes to Raise Motivation and Loyalty and Business Results (All manufacturing industry)

|  | 1974 | | 1975 | | 1976 | |
|---|---|---|---|---|---|---|
|  | Percent-age | Bus. Result | Percent-age | Bus. Result | Percent-age | Bus. Result |
| Negative (• < 7) | 23.7% | 2.81 | 12.6 | 4.64 | 15.5 | 4.57 |
| Average (7 ≤ • < 10) | 40.5 | 2.70 | 35.8 | 4.95 | 30.4 | 4.94 |
| Positive (10 ≤ •) | 35.8 | 3.02 | 51.6 | 5.07* | 54.1 | 5.15* |

| 1977 | | 1978 | | 1980 | | 1981 | | 1982 | |
|---|---|---|---|---|---|---|---|---|---|
| Percent-age | Bus. Result | Percent-age | Bus. Result | Percent-age | Bus. Result | Percent-age | Bus. Result | Percent-age | Bus. Result |
| 15.0 | 4.58 | 13.1 | 4.80 | 24.8 | 4.74 | 23.9 | 4.82 | 23.3 | 4.70 |
| 56.7 | 4.95 | 50.6 | 4.97 | 36.7 | 4.91 | 37.0 | 5.00 | 34.4 | 4.87 |
| 28.3 | 5.16* | 36.2 | 5.14* | 38.6 | 5.12* | 39.1 | 5.18* | 42.3 | 5.17* |

recreation for employees' families, etc. strengthens employees' loyalty and elevate their morale, resulting in more creativity and better performance. No effort should be spared to carry out the schemes to raise motivation and loyalty of employees if the company desires to grow and expand.

## 6-5-4.  Schemes for Human Resource Development

The schemes to raise motivation and loyalty are effective in meeting the economic needs of employees, but their desire for self-realization may not be satisfied. In today's society, it is impossible to elevate employees' morale only by satisfying their economic needs. This realization has led most Japanese companies to practice schemes to develop employees' ability with a view to answering their desire for self-realization. Just as with the schemes to raise the motivation and loyalty of employees, Japanese management customs are manifested also in the human resource development system. This reflects the chief executives' respect for human factors in business organization. The human resource development schemes for middle management involved on this section are as follows: training "camp" program for department and section chiefs, assistance to attend outside lectures, university study, paid holiday for education, establishment of a development center, pay-increase system reflecting ability and capability, periodical seminars for university graduates, examination system for promotion, publishing or report system connected with personnel evaluation, result management by self-reporting, and job rotation. Companies which implement more than five of these items are rated "positive" in their efforts to enhance the human resource development of employees. Those which implement more than three and less than five are rated "average", while firms which adopt less than three of the above-mentioned schemes fall under the category "negative"

Obviously, large companies show more enthusiasm for adoping schemes to develop the abilities of middle management as compared with medium-large firms. Unlike the schemes to raise motivation and loyalty, the number of schemes for human resource development has been constantly increasing in response to employees' desire for self-realization. This is becoming stronger as their economic conditions improve. The schemes most widely adopted by Japanese business enterprises are assistance to attend outside lectures and training "camp" programs for department and section chief. Systems such as the examination system for promotion and publishing or report system connected with personal evaluations are found in few companies. This tendency is a characteristic of the Japanese management system and is often termed "Olympic

System." Just as in Olympic Games, it is not the results but the participation itself that counts. The relationship of the number of human resource development schemes adopted to employees' morale and corporate performance is found in Tables 6–34 and 35. The following hypothesis is obtained.

*Hypothesis 6–19*: The implementation of human resource development systems undoubtedly contributes to the improvement of employees' morale, but not necessarily to corporate performance. In other words, those systems invigorate employees and raise their morale regardless of external economic environment, but they prove effective in improving corporate performance only in a high economic growth period.

It is the chief executive's responsibility to satisfy employees' desire for self-realization and raise their morale. This can be achieved by implementing such systems as training "camp" for middle management, assistance and subsidies to attend outside management courses and lectures, and scholarship for study in the university. However, they should keep in mind that these schemes incur a high cost and consequently lower corporate performance when external conditions are unfavorable. Chief executives are required to be a humanist and scientist at the same time.

**Table 6-34.** The Relationship between the Implementation of Human Resource Development System for Middle Management and Employees' Morale (All manufacturing industry)

| | 1974 | | 1975 | | 1976 | | 1977 | |
|---|---|---|---|---|---|---|---|---|
| | Percent-age | Morale | Percent-age | Morale | Percent-age | Morale | Percent-age | Morale |
| Negative ($\cdot < 3$) | 37.9% | 2.28 | 36.4 | 3.24 | 35.6 | 3.24 | 36.5 | 3.14 |
| Average ($3 \leq \cdot < 5$) | 38.6 | 2.46 | 33.9 | 3.39 | 34.5 | 3.39 | 34.4 | 3.42 |
| Positive ($5 \leq \cdot$) | 23.5 | 2.69* | 29.7 | 3.63* | 29.9 | 3.61* | 29.1 | 3.61* |

| 1978 | | 1980 | | 1981 | | 1982 | |
|---|---|---|---|---|---|---|---|
| Percent-age | Morale | Percent-age | Morale | Percent-age | Morale | Percent-age | Morale |
| 34.6 | 3.21 | 28.0 | 3.21 | 28.5 | 3.19 | 27.5 | 3.16 |
| 32.0 | 3.37 | 34.4 | 3.41 | 31.7 | 3.39 | 35.4 | 3.27 |
| 33.5 | 3.60* | 37.6 | 3.60* | 39.7 | 3.61* | 37.1 | 3.56* |

**Table 6-35.** The Relationship between the Implementation of Human Resource Development System for Middle Management and Business Results (All manufacturing industry)

| | 1974 | | 1975 | | 1976 | | 1977 | |
|---|---|---|---|---|---|---|---|---|
| | Percent-age | Bus. Result | Percent-age | Bus. Result | Percent-age | Bus. Result | Percent-age | Bus. Result |
| Negative (• < 3) | 37.9% | 2.91 | 36.4 | 5.08 | 35.6 | 4.72 | 36.5 | 4.78 |
| Average (3 ≤ • < 5) | 38.6 | 2.83 | 33.9 | 4.94 | 34.5 | 5.06 | 34.4 | 4.97 |
| Positive (5 ≤ •) | 23.5 | 2.74 | 29.7 | 4.93 | 29.9 | 5.24* | 29.1 | 5.15* |

| 1978 | | 1980 | | 1981 | | 1982 | |
|---|---|---|---|---|---|---|---|
| Percent-age | Bus. Result | Percent-age | Bus. Result | Percent-age | Bus. Result | Percent-age | Bus. Result |
| 34.6 | 4.71 | 28.0 | 4.91 | 28.5 | 4.88 | 27.5 | 4.70 |
| 32.0 | 5.14 | 34.4 | 4.90 | 31.7 | 5.04 | 35.4 | 4.88 |
| 33.5 | 5.19* | 37.6 | 4.97 | 39.7 | 5.12 | 37.1 | 5.22* |

## 6-5-5. Percentage of New Products

In the manufacturing sector, the entrepreneurship of the chief executive is most clearly manifested in new product development and new equipment introduction. The former, as a link point between a changing external environment and fixed internal conditions, points the direction the company should take. It is the embodiment of chief executives' qualities of ambition, insight and determination. The development of new products promotes employees' ability development and stimulates their creativity, which, in turn, accelerates the development of new products. By undergoing such a reciprocal process, the development of new products and ability development give an impetus to corporate growth.

The products newly developed by Japanese manufacturing companies in the past three years account for 23 to 15 percent of total sales in the corresponding period. The percentage of new products in large firms becomes a little bit greater than that of medium-large firms recently. The percentage of new products increases when the external economy is growing and decreases as economic growth slackens. In terms of industrial fields, a higher percentage of new product development is observed in assembly industries which includes electric machinery, transport equipment and precision instruments. A lower percentage of new products is developed in process industries such as chemicals, oil, ceramics and steel.

The relationship between the percentage of new products and employees' morale and the relationship between the percentage of new products and corporate performance are shown in Tables 6–36 through 41. The following hypothesis can be derived.

**Table 6-36.** The Relationship between the Percentage of New Products and Employees' Morale (All manufacturing industry)

|  | 1974 | | 1975 | | 1976 | | 1977 | |
|---|---|---|---|---|---|---|---|---|
|  | Percent-age | Morale | Percent-age | Morale | Percent-age | Morale | Percent-age | Morale |
| 0≤·<10% | 58.9% | 2.42 | 62.1 | 3.39 | 60.7 | 3.36 | 20.4 | 3.32 |
| 10≤·<20 | 22.2 | 2.53 | 19.0 | 3.32 | 21.7 | 3.39 | 14.3 | 3.28 |
| 20≤· | 18.9 | 2.47 | 18.8 | 3.54* | 17.6 | 3.57* | 65.4 | 3.41 |

| 1978 | | 1980 | | 1981 | | 1982 | |
|---|---|---|---|---|---|---|---|
| Percent-age | Morale | Percent-age | Morale | Percent-age | Morale | Percent-age | Morale |
| 59.7 | 3.32 | 55.5 | 3.34 | 55.0 | 3.34 | 55.0 | 3.29 |
| 17.2 | 3.45 | 20.3 | 3.47 | 20.1 | 3.47 | 19.6 | 3.31 |
| 23.1 | 3.53* | 24.2 | 3.59* | 24.9 | 3.57* | 25.4 | 3.51* |

**Table 6-37.** The Relationship between the Percentage of New Products and Employees' Morale (Large firms)

|  | 1974 | | 1975 | | 1976 | | 1977 | |
|---|---|---|---|---|---|---|---|---|
|  | Percent-age | Morale | Percent-age | Morale | Percent-age | Morale | Percent-age | Morale |
| 0≤·<10% | 59.4% | 2.50 | 62.4 | 3.50 | 62.9 | 3.50 | 16.6 | 3.57 |
| 10≤·<20 | 21.0 | 2.56 | 20.1 | 3.55 | 20.1 | 3.48 | 17.2 | 3.35 |
| 20≤· | 19.6 | 2.49 | 17.5 | 3.58 | 17.0 | 3.63 | 66.2 | 3.57* |

| 1978 | | 1980 | | 1981 | | 1982 | |
|---|---|---|---|---|---|---|---|
| Percent-age | Morale | Percent-age | Morale | Percent-age | Morale | Percent-age | Morale |
| 60.2 | 3.44 | 57.7 | 3.39 | 53.1 | 3.44 | 55.8 | 3.38 |
| 13.7 | 3.59 | 18.2 | 3.66 | 19.6 | 3.50 | 18.2 | 3.45 |
| 26.2 | 3.68* | 24.1 | 3.65* | 27.3 | 3.69* | 26.0 | 3.62* |

*Hypothesis 6-20*: In those companies whose percentage of new products in total sales exceeds 20 percent, employees' morale remains at the highest level regardless of external economic conditions, although this higher percentage of new products does not necessarily bring about a higher level business results. The percentage of new products should be increased when the economy shows favorable growth and reduced

**Table 6-38.** The Relationship between the Percentage of New Products and Employees' Morale (Medium-large firms)

| | 1974 | | 1975 | | 1976 | | 1977 | |
|---|---|---|---|---|---|---|---|---|
| | Percent-age | Morale | Percent-age | Morale | Percent-age | Morale | Percent-age | Morale |
| 0≤·<10% | 58.1% | 2.29 | 61.7 | 3.19 | 56.8 | 3.09 | 26.3 | 3.06 |
| 10≤·<20 | 24.1 | 2.49 | 17.1 | 2.87 | 24.5 | 3.25 | 9.6 | 3.08 |
| 20≤· | 17.8 | 2.44 | 21.1 | 3.49* | 18.7 | 3.47 | 64.1 | 3.15 |

| 1978 | | 1980 | | 1981 | | 1982 | |
|---|---|---|---|---|---|---|---|
| Percent-age | Morale | Percent-age | Morale | Percent-age | Morale | Percent-age | Morale |
| 58.9 | 3.10 | 51.4 | 3.23 | 58.6 | 31.5 | 53.5 | 3.11 |
| 23.4 | 3.30 | 24.3 | 3.21 | 21.0 | 3.43* | 22.1 | 3.11 |
| 17.8 | 3.13 | 24.3 | 3.48* | 20.4 | 3.24 | 24.4 | 3.30 |

**Table 6-39.** The Relationship between the Percentage of New Products and Business Results (All manufacturing industry)

| | 1973 | | 1974 | | 1975 | | 1976 | |
|---|---|---|---|---|---|---|---|---|
| | Percent-age | Bus. Result | Percent-age | Bus. Result | Percent-age | Bus. Result | Percent-age | Bus. Result |
| 0≤·<10% | 59.1% | 2.76 | 58.9 | 2.77 | 62.1 | 5.11* | 60.7 | 4.93 |
| 10≤·<20 | 17.5 | 2.57 | 22.2 | 2.91 | 19.0 | 4.84 | 21.7 | 5.17 |
| 20≤· | 23.4 | 3.10 | 18.9 | 2.98 | 18.8 | 4.72 | 17.6 | 5.00 |

| 1977 | | 1978 | | 1980 | | 1981 | | 1982 | |
|---|---|---|---|---|---|---|---|---|---|
| Percent-age | Bus. Result | Percent-age | Bus. Result | Percent-age | Bus. Result | Percent-age | Bus. Result | Percent-age | Bus. Result |
| 20.4 | 4.78 | 59.7 | 4.85 | 55.5 | 4.83 | 55.0 | 4.96 | 55.0 | 4.79 |
| 14.3 | 4.95 | 17.2 | 4.93 | 20.3 | 4.97 | 20.1 | 4.83 | 19.6 | 4.99 |
| 65.4 | 5.01* | 23.1 | 5.46* | 24.2 | 5.19* | 24.9 | 5.33* | 25.4 | 5.29* |

in a low-growth period in order that satisfactory corporate performance may always be maintained. This holds true for both large and medium-large firms.

The policy to encourage the development of new products breathes new life into an organization. However, despite the high cost of development, new products may not sell well in the market when

Table 6-40. The Relationship between the Percentage of New Products and Business Results (Large firms)

| | 1973 | | 1974 | | 1975 | | 1976 | |
|---|---|---|---|---|---|---|---|---|
| | Percent-age | Bus. Result | Percent-age | Bus. Result | Percent-age | Bus. Result | Percent-age | Bus. Result |
| 0≤·<10% | 64.6% | 2.70 | 59.4 | 2.78 | 62.4 | 5.10 | 62.9 | 5.02 |
| 10≤·<20 | 18.3 | 2.71 | 21.0 | 2.90 | 20.1 | 5.03 | 20.1 | 5.14 |
| 20≤· | 17.1 | 2.96 | 19.6 | 2.86 | 17.5 | 4.94 | 17.0 | 5.04 |

| 1977 | | 1978 | | 1980 | | 1981 | | 1982 | |
|---|---|---|---|---|---|---|---|---|---|
| Percent-age | Bus. Result | Percent-age | Bus. Result | Percent-age | Bus. Result | Percent-age | Bus. Result | Percent-age | Bus. Result |
| 16.6 | 5.01 | 60.2 | 4.89 | 57.7 | 4.83 | 53.1 | 4.98 | 55.8 | 4.76 |
| 17.2 | 4.93 | 13.7 | 5.02 | 18.2 | 5.13 | 19.6 | 4.83 | 18.2 | 5.14 |
| 66.2 | 5.03 | 26.2 | 5.55* | 24.1 | 5.32* | 27.3 | 5.44* | 26.0 | 5.37* |

Table 6-41. The Relationship between the Percentage of New Products and Business Results (Medium-large firms)

| | 1973 | | 1974 | | 1975 | | 1976 | |
|---|---|---|---|---|---|---|---|---|
| | Percent-age | Bus. Result | Percent-age | Bus. Result | Percent-age | Bus. Result | Percent-age | Bus. Result |
| 0≤·<10% | 55.9% | 2.80 | 58.1 | 2.75 | 61.7 | 5.13* | 56.8 | 4.75 |
| 10≤·<20 | 17.4 | 2.43 | 24.1 | 2.92 | 17.1 | 4.44 | 24.5 | 5.21 |
| 20·≤ | 26.7 | 3.05 | 17.8 | 3.19* | 21.1 | 4.41 | 18.7 | 4.93 |

| 1977 | | 1978 | | 1980 | | 1981 | | 1982 | |
|---|---|---|---|---|---|---|---|---|---|
| Percent-age | Bus. Result | Percent-age | Bus. Result | Percent-age | Bus. Result | Percent-age | Bus. Result | Percent-age | Bus. Result |
| 26.3 | 4.54 | 58.9 | 4.79 | 51.4 | 4.83 | 58.6 | 4.93 | 53.5 | 4.85 |
| 9.6 | 5.01 | 23.4 | 4.85 | 24.3 | 4.76 | 21.0 | 4.82 | 22.1 | 4.77 |
| 64.1 | 4.97* | 17.8 | 5.22 | 24.3 | 4.96 | 20.0 | 5.05 | 24.4 | 5.15 |

external conditions are unsatisfactory. The entrepreneurship of an aggressive chief executive does not necessarily lend itself to the improvement of both employees' morale and corporate performance.

The relationship between the percentage of new products and employees' morale in different industries is shown in Tables 6–42 through 6–46. The following hypothesis is obtained.

**Table 6-42.** The Relationship between the Percentage of New Products and Employees' Morale (Textiles)

| | 1974 | | 1975 | | 1976 | | 1977 | |
|---|---|---|---|---|---|---|---|---|
| | Percent-age | Morale | Percent-age | Morale | Percent-age | Morale | Percent-age | Morale |
| 0≤·<10% | 55.8% | 2.33 | 58.3 | 3.60 | 47.2 | 3.29 | 19.0 | 3.81 |
| 10≤·<20 | 23.3 | 2.60 | 16.7 | 3.50 | 30.6 | 3.64 | 26.2 | 3.00 |
| 20≤· | 20.9 | 2.44 | 25.0 | 3.39 | 22.2 | 3.63 | 54.8 | 3.65* |

| 1978 | | 1980 | | 1981 | | 1982 | |
|---|---|---|---|---|---|---|---|
| Percent-age | Morale | Percent-age | Morale | Percent-age | Morale | Percent-age | Morale |
| 65.1 | 3.50 | 62.8 | 3.40 | 40.7 | 3.46 | 58.1 | 3.28 |
| 20.9 | 3.44 | 4.7 | 4.50 | 22.2 | 4.08 | 19.4 | 3.58 |
| 14.0 | 3.33 | 32.6 | 3.50 | 37.0 | 3.60 | 22.6 | 3.93* |

**Table 6-43.** The Relationship between the Percentage of New Products and Employees' Morale (Chemicals)

| | 1974 | | 1975 | | 1976 | | 1977 | |
|---|---|---|---|---|---|---|---|---|
| | Percent-age | Morale | Percent-age | Morale | Percent-age | Morale | Percent-age | Morale |
| 0≤·<10% | 55.8% | 2.40 | 60.0 | 3.27 | 66.2 | 3.53 | 18.4 | 3.34 |
| 10≤·<20 | 31.4 | 2.39 | 27.1 | 3.30 | 21.6 | 3.34 | 21.8 | 3.47 |
| 20≤· | 12.8 | 2.59 | 12.9 | 3.54 | 12.2 | 3.44 | 59.8 | 3.34 |

| 1978 | | 1980 | | 1981 | | 1982 | |
|---|---|---|---|---|---|---|---|
| Percent-age | Morale | Percent-age | Morale | Percent-age | Morale | Percent-age | Morale |
| 53.8 | 3.31 | 55.0 | 3.22 | 41.8 | 3.21 | 56.1 | 3.42 |
| 24.2 | 3.50 | 32.5 | 3.54 | 38.6 | 3.54 | 24.2 | 3.47 |
| 22.0 | 3.55 | 12.5 | 3.85* | 20.0 | 3.71* | 19.7 | 3.89* |

*Hypothesis 6-21*: In assembly industries such as electric machinery and transportation equipment, companies whose percentage of new products to total sales is over 20 percent are successful in elevating employees' morale. This, though, is not applicable to process industries including textiles and chemicals.

In assembly industries, the necessity of new process control and new

**Table 6-44.** The Relationship between the Percentage of New Products and Employees' Morale (General machinery)

| | 1974 | | 1975 | | 1976 | | 1977 | |
|---|---|---|---|---|---|---|---|---|
| | Percent-age | Morale | Percent-age | Morale | Percent-age | Morale | Percent-age | Morale |
| $0 \leq \cdot < 10\%$ | 50.6% | 2.43 | 47.0 | 3.45 | 49.2 | 3.26 | 15.8 | 2.96 |
| $10 \leq \cdot < 20$ | 22.2 | 2.42 | 22.7 | 3.10 | 17.5 | 3.18 | 5.3 | 3.63 |
| $20 \leq \cdot$ | 27.2 | 2.57 | 30.3 | 3.68* | 33.3 | 3.26 | 78.9 | 3.36 |

| | 1978 | | 1980 | | 1981 | | 1982 | |
|---|---|---|---|---|---|---|---|---|
| | Percent-age | Morale | Percent-age | Morale | Percent-age | Morale | Percent-age | Morale |
| | 51.4 | 3.22 | 45.0 | 3.24 | 47.6 | 3.43 | 49.2 | 3.07 |
| | 18.6 | 3.39 | 26.3 | 3.41 | 19.0 | 3.29 | 21.3 | 3.35 |
| | 30.0 | 3.07 | 28.8 | 3.35 | 33.3 | 3.24 | 29.5 | 3.44* |

**Table 6-45.** The Relationship between the Percentage of New Products and Employees' Morale (Electric machinery)

| | 1974 | | 1975 | | 1976 | | 1977 | |
|---|---|---|---|---|---|---|---|---|
| | Percent-age | Morale | Percent-age | Morale | Percent-age | Morale | Percent-age | Morale |
| $0 \leq \cdot < 10\%$ | 32.6% | 2.00 | 42.6 | 3.19 | 33.3 | 3.18 | 5.9 | 2.75 |
| $10 \leq \cdot < 20$ | 30.2 | 2.23 | 20.6 | 3.07 | 28.1 | 3.47 | 5.9 | 2.88 |
| $20 \leq \cdot$ | 37.2 | 2.16 | 36.8 | 3.64* | 38.6 | 3.73* | 88.2 | 3.37 |

| | 1978 | | 1980 | | 1981 | | 1982 | |
|---|---|---|---|---|---|---|---|---|
| | Percent-age | Morale | Percent-age | Morale | Percent-age | Morale | Percent-age | Morale |
| | 32.1 | 3.30 | 29.7 | 3.21 | 30.0 | 3.17 | 30.5 | 3.08 |
| | 24.4 | 3.47 | 25.0 | 3.34 | 28.3 | 3.29 | 25.4 | 3.07 |
| | 43.6 | 3.75* | 45.3 | 3.57 | 41.7 | 3.50 | 44.1 | 3.44 |

quality control arises as new products increase. As a result, employees are provided with many opportunities to participate in a proposal system, management by objective, QC circle activities and job rotation. Process industries, however, do not afford enough opportunities to raise employees' morale.

In the electric machinery and transport equipment industries, where

**Table 6-46.** The Relationship between the Percentage of New Products and Employees' Morale (Transport equipment)

| | 1974 | | 1975 | | 1976 | | 1977 | |
|---|---|---|---|---|---|---|---|---|
| | Percent-age | Morale | Percent-age | Morale | Percent-age | Morale | Percent-age | Morale |
| 0≤·<10% | 67.7% | 2.21 | 71.1 | 3.30 | 80.0 | 3.36 | 15.6 | 3.43 |
| 10≤·<20 | 12.9 | 2.25 | 13.2 | 3.40 | 11.4 | 3.25 | 15.6 | 3.29 |
| 20≤· | 19.4 | 2.42 | 15.8 | 3.42 | 8.6 | 4.00* | 68.9 | 3.44 |

| 1978 | | 1980 | | 1981 | | 1982 | |
|---|---|---|---|---|---|---|---|
| Percent-age | Morale | Percent-age | Morale | Percent-age | Morale | Percent-age | Morale |
| 73.8 | 3.21 | 53.8 | 3.33 | 52.1 | 3.20 | 39.1 | 3.06 |
| 9.5 | 3.13 | 20.5 | 3.50 | 18.8 | 3.33 | 15.2 | 3.14 |
| 16.7 | 3.57 | 25.6 | 3.85 | 29.2 | 4.03* | 45.7 | 3.45* |

**Table 6-47.** The Relationship between the Percentage of New Products and Business Results (Textiles)

| | 1973 | | 1974 | | 1975 | | 1976 | |
|---|---|---|---|---|---|---|---|---|
| | Percent-age | Bus. Result | Percent-age | Bus. Result | Percent-age | Bus. Result | Percent-age | Bus. Result |
| 0≤·<10% | 52.8% | 2.43 | 55.8 | 2.81 | 58.3 | 4.04 | 47.2 | 4.18 |
| 10≤·<20 | 22.2 | 2.51 | 23.3 | 2.82 | 16.7 | 3.60 | 30.6 | 5.04 |
| 20≤· | 25.0 | 3.00 | 20.9 | 2.73 | 25.0 | 3.15 | 22.2 | 4.78 |

| 1977 | | 1978 | | 1980 | | 1981 | | 1982 | |
|---|---|---|---|---|---|---|---|---|---|
| Percent-age | Bus. Result | Percent-age | Bus. Result | Percent-age | Bus. Result | Percent-age | Bus. Result | Percent-age | Bus. Result |
| 19.0 | 4.04 | 65.1 | 4.53 | 62.8 | 4.31 | 40.7 | 4.11 | 58.1 | 4.17 |
| 26.2 | 4.78 | 20.9 | 4.49 | 4.7 | 3.97 | 22.2 | 4.01 | 19.4 | 4.57 |
| 54.8 | 4.83* | 14.0 | 5.01 | 32.6 | 3.99 | 37.0 | 4.57 | 22.6 | 4.95 |

new product development elevates employees' morale, entrepreneurship of chief excutives is demanded. Such an ability is not necessarily demanded in the textile and chemical industries.

The relationship between the percentage of new products and corporate performance in various areas of industry is represented in Tables 6–47 through 6–51. This makes possible the following hypothesis.

**Table 6-48.** The Relationship between the Percentage of New Products and Business Results (Chemicals)

| | 1973 | | 1974 | | 1975 | | 1976 | |
|---|---|---|---|---|---|---|---|---|
| | Percent-age | Bus. Result | Percent-age | Bus. Result | Percent-age | Bus. Result | Percent-age | Bus. Result |
| 0≤·<10% | 67.3% | 2.62 | 55.8 | 2.74 | 60.0 | 5.52 | 66.2 | 5.39 |
| 10≤·<20 | 15.3 | 2.57 | 31.4 | 2.73 | 27.1 | 5.31 | 21.6 | 5.54 |
| 20≤· | 17.4 | 3.57 | 12.8 | 3.48* | 12.9 | 5.37 | 12.2 | 5.39 |

| 1977 | | 1978 | | 1980 | | 1981 | | 1982 | |
|---|---|---|---|---|---|---|---|---|---|
| Percent-age | Bus. Result | Percent-age | Bus. Result | Percent-age | Bus. Result | Percent-age | Bus. Result | Percent-age | Bus. Result |
| 18.4 | 5.38 | 53.8 | 4.85 | 55.0 | 4.91 | 41.4 | 5.11 | 56.1 | 4.82 |
| 21.8 | 5.42 | 24.2 | 5.15 | 32.5 | 5.14 | 38.6 | 4.73 | 24.2 | 4.83 |
| 59.8 | 5.33 | 22.0 | 5.60* | 12.5 | 5.08 | 20.0 | 5.34* | 19.7 | 5.83* |

**Table 6-49.** The Relationship between the Percentage of New Products and Business Results (General machinery)

| | 1973 | | 1974 | | 1975 | | 1976 | |
|---|---|---|---|---|---|---|---|---|
| | Percent-age | Bus. Result | Percent-age | Bus. Result | Percent-age | Bus. Result | Percent-age | Bus. Result |
| 0≤·<10% | 38.7% | 2.17 | 50.6 | 2.60 | 47.0 | 5.59* | 49.2 | 4.89 |
| 10≤·<20 | 31.2 | 2.10 | 22.2 | 2.40 | 22.7 | 4.65 | 17.5 | 4.20 |
| 20≤· | 30.1 | 2.64 | 27.2 | 2.94 | 30.3 | 4.28 | 33.3 | 4.54 |

| 1977 | | 1978 | | 1980 | | 1981 | | 1982 | |
|---|---|---|---|---|---|---|---|---|---|
| Percent-age | Bus. Result | Percent-age | Bus. Result | Percent-age | Bus. Result | Percent-age | Bus. Result | Percent-age | Bus. Result |
| 15.8 | 3.88 | 51.4 | 4.83 | 45.0 | 4.84 | 47.6 | 5.14 | 49.2 | 5.07 |
| 5.3 | 4.56 | 18.6 | 5.00 | 26.3 | 4.97 | 19.0 | 5.59 | 21.3 | 5.03 |
| 78.9 | 4.56* | 30.0 | 4.77 | 28.8 | 5.69* | 33.3 | 5.68 | 29.5 | 5.65 |

*Hypothesis 6-22*: In growing industries such as electric machinery and transport equipment, the percentage of new products to total sales consistent with favorable corporate achievement is over 20 percent, while in market-sensitive industries such as textiles, chemicals and general machinery, companies are required to adjust new product development to changes in the external environment; i. e. preferably

Table 6-50. The Relationship between the Percentage of New Products and Business Results (Electric machinery)

| | 1973 | | 1974 | | 1975 | | 1976 | |
|---|---|---|---|---|---|---|---|---|
| | Percent-age | Bus. Result | Percent-age | Bus. Result | Percent-age | Bus. Result | Percent-age | Bus. Result |
| $0\leq \cdot <10\%$ | 35.1% | 3.10 | 32.6 | 2.96 | 42.6 | 4.61 | 33.3 | 4.34 |
| $10\leq \cdot <20$ | 22.0 | 3.00 | 30.2 | 3.57 | 20.6 | 4.50 | 28.1 | 4.84 |
| $20\leq \cdot$ | 42.4 | 3.36 | 37.2 | 2.99 | 36.8 | 4.83 | 38.6 | 5.13 |

| | 1977 | | 1978 | | 1980 | | 1981 | | 1982 | |
|---|---|---|---|---|---|---|---|---|---|
| | Percent-age | Bus. Result | Percent-age | Bus. Result | Percent-age | Bus. Result | Percent-age | Bus. Result | Percent-age | Bus. Result |
| | 5.9 | 4.29 | 32.1 | 5.14 | 29.7 | 5.07 | 30.0 | 5.25 | 30.5 | 5.38 |
| | 5.9 | 4.65 | 24.4 | 5.03 | 25.0 | 5.21 | 28.3 | 5.51 | 25.4 | 5.13 |
| | 88.2 | 4.88 | 43.6 | 5.63* | 45.3 | 5.34 | 41.7 | 5.56 | 44.1 | 5.49 |

Table 6-51. The Relationship between the Percentage of New Products and Business Results (Transport equipment)

| | 1973 | | 1974 | | 1975 | | 1976 | |
|---|---|---|---|---|---|---|---|---|
| | Percent-age | Bus. Result | Percent-age | Bus. Result | Percent-age | Bus. Result | Percent-age | Bus. Result |
| $0\leq \cdot <10\%$ | 67.1% | 3.01 | 67.7 | 2.32 | 71.1 | 4.78 | 80.0 | 5.45 |
| $10\leq \cdot <20$ | 16.5 | 3.31 | 12.9 | 2.59 | 13.2 | 4.49 | 11.4 | 5.32 |
| $20\leq \cdot$ | 16.4 | 2.87 | 19.4 | 3.00* | 15.8 | 4.65 | 8.6 | 5.51 |

| | 1977 | | 1978 | | 1980 | | 1981 | | 1982 | |
|---|---|---|---|---|---|---|---|---|---|
| | Percent-age | Bus. Result | Percent-age | Bus. Result | Percent-age | Bus. Result | Percent-age | Bus. Result | Percent-age | Bus. Result |
| | 15.6 | 5.26 | 73.8 | 5.34 | 53.8 | 4.60 | 52.1 | 4.76 | 39.1 | 5.25 |
| | 15.6 | 5.26 | 9.5 | 4.43 | 20.5 | 4.44 | 18.8 | 4.63 | 15.2 | 5.30 |
| | 68.9 | 5.40 | 16.7 | 5.55* | 25.6 | 5.45* | 29.2 | 5.49 | 45.7 | 4.89 |

over 20 percent in a high economic growth period and lower than 10 percent in a low-growth period.

In the growing areas of industry including electric machinery and transport equipment, corporate performance can be increased by the development of new products through the enhancement of morale, for they can develop new technological or marketable products in accordance with the trend of demand. The situation is different in market-sensitive industries where new product development entails reduced business achievement, because even if they develop new products, these products do not always increase sales and increase cost when demand is in ebb.

## 6-5-6. Percentage of New Equipment

As stated in the previous section, the introduction of new equipment is also a manifestation of the chief executives' entrepreneurship. When the life cycle of products goes into a stable period, innovative presidents change the stable product to the new marketable products and introduce new machines and equipment to maximize quality and minimize the cost. Such as innovative attitude on behalf of the president revitalizes employees' future hopes and improves their morale. This, coupled with the high efficiency of new equipment, gives birth to a high level of corporate performance. Based on the total amount of equipment used in Japanese companies, new equipment introduced in the last three years constitutes 22 to 27 percent. The percentage increases in a high economic growth period and decreases when the growth rate is low, though a three year time lag is usually found between economic fluctuations and change in the percentage. Compared with medium-large firms, the proportion of new equipment in large firms is 0.5 to 1 percent larger. Broken down by industrial field, the proportion of new equipment in such growing industries as electric machinery and transport equipment is eight to twelve percentage larger than that in relatively stagnant industries such as textiles, chemicals and general machinery.

Tables 6-52, through 6-57 represent the relationship between the percentage of new equipment and employees' morale, or corporate performance. The following hypothesis is derived.

*Hypothesis 6-23*: Firms with a higher percentage of new equipment show proportionately higher morale. After the introduction of new equipment, employees' morale is raised and corporate performance is improved. The improvement in corporate performance is usually subject to one year time lag.

The chief executives' positive attitude toward promoting the introduction of new equipment vitalizes employees and raises their morale, that is consisted of a will for work and sense of belonging. The

**Table 6-52.** The Relationship between the Percentage of New Equipment and Employees' Morale (All manufacturing industry)

|  | 1974 | | 1975 | | 1976 | | 1977 | |
|---|---|---|---|---|---|---|---|---|
|  | Percent-age | Morale | Percent-age | Morale | Percent-age | Morale | Percent-age | Morale |
| 0≤·<20% | 30.7% | 2.41 | 38.3 | 3.30 | 43.4 | 3.30 | 48.9 | 3.29 |
| 20≤:<30 | 29.9 | 2.43 | 24.7 | 3.46 | 23.3 | 3.44 | 22.6 | 3.41 |
| 30≤·<40 | 21.2 | 2.50 | 18.6 | 3.52* | 18.0 | 3.52* | 13.7 | 3.43 |
| 40≤· | 18.2 | 2.52 | 18.4 | 3.44 | 15.3 | 3.51 | 14.8 | 3.52* |

| 1978 | | 1980 | | 1981 | | 1982 | |
|---|---|---|---|---|---|---|---|
| Percent-age | Morale | Percent-age | Morale | Percent-age | Morale | Percent-age | Morale |
| 47.5 | 3.29 | 43.0 | 2.23 | 43.8 | 3.36 | 46.7 | 3.34 |
| 27.7 | 3.42 | 29.8 | 2.54 | 27.7 | 3.39 | 26.3 | 3.35 |
| 13.1 | 3.51 | 14.8 | 2.71 | 14.4 | 3.56* | 11.9 | 3.26 |
| 11.6 | 3.58* | 12.5 | 2.99* | 14.2 | 3.55 | 15.2 | 3.42 |

**Table 6-53.** The Relationship between the Percentage of New Equipment and Employees' Morale (Large firms)

|  | 1974 | | 1975 | | 1976 | | 1977 | |
|---|---|---|---|---|---|---|---|---|
|  | Percent-age | Morale | Percent-age | Morale | Percent-age | Morale | Percent-age | Morale |
| 0≤·<20% | 28.1% | 2.46 | 38.9 | 3.41 | 40.3 | 3.48 | 46.5 | 3.46 |
| 20≤·<30 | 31.7 | 2.48 | 24.1 | 3.64* | 26.1 | 3.55 | 26.8 | 3.60 |
| 30≤·<40 | 23.1 | 2.63 | 21.1 | 3.58 | 19.8 | 3.58 | 13.6 | 3.50 |
| 40≤· | 17.1 | 2.49 | 15.8 | 3.55 | 13.8 | 3.49 | 15.1 | 3.67 |

| 1978 | | 1980 | | 1981 | | 1982 | |
|---|---|---|---|---|---|---|---|
| Percent-age | Morale | Percent-age | Morale | Percent-age | Morale | Percent-age | Morale |
| 45.9 | 3.45 | 40.5 | 2.26 | 43.1 | 3.41 | 45.8 | 3.43 |
| 29.4 | 3.56 | 32.7 | 2.61 | 26.7 | 3.52 | 27.3 | 3.51 |
| 13.4 | 3.57 | 13.7 | 2.82 | 16.4 | 3.70* | 13.6 | 3.39 |
| 11.3 | 3.71 | 13.1 | 2.87* | 13.8 | 3.66 | 13.3 | 3.48 |

creativity of employees, combined with the physical accuracy of new equipment, contributes to a higher level of corporate achievement though with a time lag.

*Hypothesis 6-24:* The companies which pursue a policy of maintaining the percentage of new equipment (introduced in the previous three years) at over 30 percent enjoy good performance irrespective of

**Table 6-54.** The Relationship between the Percentage of New Equipment and Employees' Morale (Medium-large firms)

| | 1974 | | 1975 | | 1976 | | 1977 | |
|---|---|---|---|---|---|---|---|---|
| | Percent-age | Morale | Percent-age | Morale | Percent-age | Morale | Percent-age | Morale |
| 0≤·<20% | 34.6% | 2.35 | 37.1 | 3.11 | 49.0 | 3.03 | 52.6 | 3.06 |
| 20≤·30 | 27.2 | 2.33 | 25.7 | 3.16 | 18.1 | 3.16 | 19.1 | 3.04 |
| 30≤·40 | 18.3 | 2.26 | 14.3 | 3.36 | 14.8 | 3.37 | 13.9 | 3.33* |
| 40≤· | 19.9 | 2.55* | 22.9 | 3.30 | 18.1 | 3.54* | 14.4 | 3.27 |

| 1978 | | 1980 | | 1981 | | 1982 | |
|---|---|---|---|---|---|---|---|
| Percent-age | Morale | Percent-age | Morale | Percent-age | Morale | Percent-age | Morale |
| 50.3 | 3.05 | 47.6 | 2.19 | 45.1 | 3.26 | 48.3 | 3.19 |
| 24.9 | 3.12 | 24.3 | 2.39 | 29.6 | 3.15 | 24.4 | 3.04 |
| 12.7 | 3.40* | 16.8 | 2.55 | 10.5 | 3.15 | 8.7 | 2.90 |
| 12.2 | 3.38 | 11.4 | 3.18* | 14.8 | 3.33 | 18.6 | 3.34* |

**Table 6-55.** The Relationship between the Percentage of New Equipment and Business Results (All manufacturing industry)

| | 1973 | | 1974 | | 1975 | | 1976 | |
|---|---|---|---|---|---|---|---|---|
| | Percent-age | Bus. Result | Percent-age | Bus. Result | Percent-age | Bus. Result | Percent-age | Bus. Result |
| 0≤·<20% | % | 2.30 | 30.7 | 2.59 | 38.3 | 4.78 | 43.4 | 4.61 |
| 20≤·<30 | 34.9 | 2.86 | 29.9 | 2.85 | 24.7 | 5.00 | 23.3 | 5.07 |
| 30≤·<40 | (average) | 2.93 | 21.2 | 2.94 | 18.6 | 5.02 | 18.0 | 5.51* |
| 40≤· | | 3.09 | 18.2 | 3.11* | 18.4 | 5.36* | 15.3 | 5.35 |

| 1977 | | 1978 | | 1980 | | 1981 | | 1982 | |
|---|---|---|---|---|---|---|---|---|---|
| Percent-age | Bus. Result | Percent-age | Bus. Result | Percent-age | Bus. Result | Percent-age | Bus. Result | Percent-age | Bus. Result |
| 48.9 | 4.71 | 47.5 | 4.74 | 43.0 | 4.60 | 43.8 | 4.78 | 46.7 | 4.73 |
| 22.6 | 5.00 | 27.7 | 5.18 | 29.8 | 5.02 | 27.7 | 5.03 | 26.3 | 4.90 |
| 13.7 | 5.36* | 13.1 | 5.23 | 14.8 | 5.23 | 14.4 | 5.39 | 11.9 | 5.21 |
| 14.8 | 5.32 | 11.6 | 5.39* | 12.5 | 5.61* | 14.2 | 5.41* | 15.2 | 5.56* |

changes in the economic growth rate. This is particularly true of large firms, which should preferably keep the proportion around 40 percent. Medium-large firms are advised to adjust their percentage of new equipment to external conditions, maintaining it at over 40 percent in high-growth periods and reducing it to about 30 percent once the

**Table 6–56.** The Relationship between the Percentage of New Equipment and Business Results (Large firms)

|  | 1973 | | 1974 | | 1975 | | 1976 | |
|---|---|---|---|---|---|---|---|---|
|  | Percent-age | Bus. Result | Percent-age | Bus. Result | Percent-age | Bus. Result | Percent-age | Bus. Result |
| 0≤·<20% | % | 2.39 | 28.1 | 2.61 | 38.9 | 5.01 | 40.3 | 4.67 |
| 20≤·<30 | 30.2 | 2.92 | 31.7 | 2.82 | 24.1 | 4.74 | 26.1 | 5.11 |
| 30≤·<40 | (average) | 2.76 | 23.1 | 2.88 | 21.1 | 5.08 | 19.8 | 5.41 |
| 40≤· |  | 2.98 | 17.1 | 3.09* | 15.8 | 5.65* | 13.8 | 5.49* |

| 1977 | | 1978 | | 1980 | | 1981 | | 1982 | |
|---|---|---|---|---|---|---|---|---|---|
| Percent-age | Bus. Result | Percent-age | Bus. Result | Percent-age | Bus. Result | Percent-age | Bus. Result | Percent-age | Bus. Result |
| 46.5 | 4.78 | 45.9 | 4.80 | 40.5 | 4.62 | 43.1 | 4.84 | 45.8 | 4.76 |
| 24.8 | 5.00 | 29.4 | 5.22 | 32.7 | 5.10 | 26.7 | 4.98 | 27.3 | 4.87 |
| 13.6 | 5.36* | 13.4 | 5.30 | 13.7 | 5.41 | 16.4 | 5.46 | 13.6 | 5.31 |
| 15.1 | 5.42 | 11.3 | 5.61* | 13.1 | 5.50* | 13.8 | 5.57* | 13.3 | 5.66* |

**Table 5–57.** The Relationship between the Percentage of New Equipment and Business Results (Medium-large firms)

|  | 1973 | | 1974 | | 1975 | | 1976 | |
|---|---|---|---|---|---|---|---|---|
|  | Percent-age | Bus. Result | Percent-age | Bus. Result | Percent-age | Bus. Result | Percent-age | Bus. Result |
| 0≤·<20% | % | 2.13 | 34.6 | 2.57 | 37.1 | 4.37 | 49.0 | 4.51 |
| 20≤·<30 | 34.8 | 2.77 | 27.2 | 2.92 | 25.7 | 5.43* | 18.1 | 4.97 |
| 30≤·<40 | (average) | 3.02 | 18.3 | 3.06 | 14.3 | 4.86 | 14.8 | 5.76* |
| 40≤· |  | 3.15 | 19.9 | 3.14* | 22.9 | 5.01 | 18.1 | 5.14 |

| 1977 | | 1978 | | 1980 | | 1981 | | 1982 | |
|---|---|---|---|---|---|---|---|---|---|
| Percent-age | Bus. Result | Percent-age | Bus. Result | Percent-age | Bus. Result | Percent-age | Bus. Result | Percent-age | Bus. Result |
| 52.6 | 4.60 | 50.3 | 4.65 | 47.6 | 4.57 | 45.1 | 4.67 | 48.3 | 4.69 |
| 19.1 | 4.99 | 24.9 | 5.08 | 24.3 | 4.84 | 29.6 | 5.12 | 24.4 | 4.95 |
| 13.9 | 5.35* | 12.7 | 5.24* | 16.8 | 4.96 | 10.5 | 5.18 | 8.7 | 4.91 |
| 14.4 | 5.16 | 12.2 | 5.04 | 11.4 | 5.84* | 14.8 | 5.14 | 18.6 | 5.43* |

economy becomes slack.

Large firms favored with marketable, stable products and a relatively sufficient amount of fund do not experience much difficulty undertaking investment for the purpose of rationalization, labor-saving and the increased precision of machines. The resultant lower manufacturing

**Table 6-58.** The Relationship between the Percentage of New Equipment and Business Results (Textiles)

| | 1974 | | 1975 | | 1976 | | 1977 | |
|---|---|---|---|---|---|---|---|---|
| | Percent-age | Bus. Result | Percent-age | Bus. Result | Percent-age | Bus. Result | Percent-age | Bus. Result |
| 0≤·<20% | 39.5% | 2.21 | 58.3 | 3.76 | 55.6 | 4.58 | 47.6 | 4.77 |
| 20≤·<30 | 30.2 | 3.29 | 16.7 | 3.80 | 27.8 | 4.69 | 31.0 | 4.15 |
| 30≤·<40 | 20.9 | 2.93 | 19.4 | 3.56 | 5.6 | 5.64 | 14.3 | 5.37* |
| 40≤· | 9.3 | 3.39 | 5.6 | 4.03 | 11.1 | 3.73 | 7.1 | 4.80 |

| 1978 | | 1980 | | 1981 | | 1982 | |
|---|---|---|---|---|---|---|---|
| Percent-age | Bus. Result | Percent-age | Bus. Result | Percent-age | Bus. Result | Percent-age | Bus. Result |
| 72.1 | 4.52 | 67.4 | 3.98 | 63.0 | 4.47 | 64.5 | 4.54 |
| 14.0 | 4.21 | 18.6 | 4.35 | 29.6 | 3.87 | 25.8 | 4.19 |
| 11.6 | 5.37 | 7.0 | 5.57* | 7.4 | 4.02 | 3.2 | 3.52 |
| 2.3 | 4.81 | 7.0 | 4.45 | 0 | – | 6.5 | 4.61 |

**Table 6-59.** The Relationship between the Percentage of New Equipment and Business Results (Chemicals)

| | 1974 | | 1975 | | 1976 | | 1977 | |
|---|---|---|---|---|---|---|---|---|
| | Percent-age | Bus. Result | Percent-age | Bus. Result | Percent-age | Bus. Result | Percent-age | Bus. Result |
| 0≤·<20% | 30.2% | 2.47 | 36.5 | 5.20 | 43.2 | 5.08 | 35.6 | 5.22 |
| 20≤·<30 | 29.1 | 3.01 | 25.9 | 5.50 | 17.6 | 5.85* | 26.4 | 5.39 |
| 30≤·<40 | 24.4 | 2.65 | 21.2 | 5.67 | 23.0 | 5.66 | 13.8 | 5.54* |
| 40≤· | 16.3 | 3.48* | 16.5 | 5.59 | 16.2 | 5.56 | 24.1 | 5.42 |

| 1978 | | 1980 | | 1981 | | 1982 | |
|---|---|---|---|---|---|---|---|
| Percent-age | Bus. Result | Percent-age | Bus. Result | Percent-age | Bus. Result | Percent-age | Bus. Result |
| 36.3 | 4.84 | 40.0 | 4.88 | 41.4 | 5.06 | 51.5 | 4.85 |
| 34.1 | 5.20 | 36.3 | 5.07 | 31.4 | 4.78 | 30.3 | 4.95 |
| 13.2 | 5.36 | 13.8 | 4.85 | 12.9 | 5.14 | 10.6 | 5.13 |
| 16.5 | 5.18 | 10.0 | 5.00* | 14.3 | 5.23 | 7.6 | 6.31* |

costs and higher quality give their products a more competitive edge. However, medium-large firms with less fund and less selling power should be cautious when introducing new equipment in an unfavorable external environment. An excessively positive investment can increase capital cost and lower corporate performance.

**Table 6-60.** The Relationship between the Percentage of New Equipment and Business Results (General machinery)

| | 1974 | | 1975 | | 1976 | | 1977 | |
|---|---|---|---|---|---|---|---|---|
| | Percent-age | Bus. Result | Percent-age | Bus. Result | Percent-age | Bus. Result | Percent-age | Bus. Result |
| 0≤·<20% | 35.8% | 2.49 | 45.5 | 4.74 | 58.7 | 4.30 | 59.2 | 4.18 |
| 20≤·<30 | 34.6 | 2.58 | 25.8 | 4.97 | 14.3 | 5.21 | 23.7 | 4.61 |
| 30≤·<40 | 13.6 | 3.18 | 10.6 | 5.62 | 15.9 | 5.03 | 7.9 | 5.06 |
| 40≤· | 16.0 | 2.70 | 18.2 | 5.23 | 11.1 | 5.24 | 9.2 | ·5.25* |

| 1978 | | 1980 | | 1981 | | 1982 | |
|---|---|---|---|---|---|---|---|
| Percent-age | Bus. Result | Percent-age | Bus. Result | Percent-age | Bus. Result | Percent-age | Bus. Result |
| 58.6 | 4.65 | 43.8 | 4.58 | 39.7 | 4.89 | 45.9 | 4.97 |
| 27.1 | 5.16 | 30.0 | 5.35 | 27.0 | 5.64 | 32.8 | 5.13 |
| 11.4 | 5.10 | 15.0 | 5.02 | 14.3 | 5.84 | 8.2 | 5.56 |
| 2.9 | 4.92 | 11.3 | 6.74* | 19.0 | 5.79* | 13.1 | 6.22* |

**Table 6-61.** The Relationship between the Percentage of New Equipment and Business Result (Electric machinery)

| | 1974 | | 1975 | | 1976 | | 1977 | |
|---|---|---|---|---|---|---|---|---|
| | Percent-age | Bus. Result | Percent-age | Bus. Result | Percent-age | Bus. Result | Percent-age | Bus. Result |
| 0≤·<20% | 27.9% | 2.73 | 27.9 | 4.38 | 31.6 | 4.31 | 44.1 | 4.60 |
| 20≤·<30 | 32.6 | 3.21 | 30.9 | 4.64 | 28.1 | 4.55 | 23.5 | 4.76 |
| 30≤·<40 | 27.9 | 3.38 | 25.0 | 4.55 | 22.8 | 5.40* | 17.6 | 5.07 |
| 40≤· | 11.6 | 3.47 | 16.2 | 5.42* | 17.5 | 5.24 | 14.7 | 5.38* |

| 1978 | | 1980 | | 1981 | | 1982 | |
|---|---|---|---|---|---|---|---|
| Percent-age | Bus. Result | Percent-age | Bus. Result | Percent-age | Bus. Result | Percent-age | Bus. Result |
| 32.1 | 5.09 | 20.3 | 4.39 | 20.0 | 5.10 | 23.7 | 4.86 |
| 32.1 | 5.29 | 29.7 | 5.33 | 35.0 | 5.47 | 33.9 | 5.34 |
| 19.2 | 5.50 | 23.4 | 5.23 | 18.3 | 5.67* | 15.3 | 5.68 |
| 16.7 | 5.65 | 26.6 | 5.75* | 26.7 | 5.55 | 27.1 | 5.67 |

**Table 6-62.** The Relationship between the Percentage of New Equipment and Performance (Transport equipment)

| | 1974 | | 1975 | | 1976 | | 1977 | |
|---|---|---|---|---|---|---|---|---|
| | Percent-age | Bus. Result | Percent-age | Bus. Result | Percent-age | Bus. Result | Percent-age | Bus. Result |
| 0≤·<20% | 16.1% | 3.26* | 7.9 | 4.79 | 20.0 | 4.59 | 28.9 | 4.86 |
| 20≤·<30 | 41.9 | 2.44 | 34.2 | 4.64 | 31.4 | 5.08 | 37.8 | 5.37 |
| 30≤·<40 | 16.1 | 1.91 | 28.9 | 4.86 | 28.6 | 6.04* | 17.8 | 5.61 |
| 40≤· | 25.8 | 2.43 | 28.9 | 4.66 | 20.0 | 6.01 | 15.6 | 5.95* |

| 1978 | | 1980 | | 1981 | | 1982 | |
|---|---|---|---|---|---|---|---|
| Percent-age | Bus. Result | Percent-age | Bus. Result | Percent-age | Bus. Result | Percent-age | Bus. Result |
| 35.7 | 5.03 | 30.8 | 3.81 | 35.4 | 4.28 | 32.6 | 4.86 |
| 33.3 | 5.22 | 17.9 | 5.08 | 22.9 | 5.06 | 10.9 | 5.29 |
| 14.3 | 5.30 | 23.1 | 5.34* | 18.8 | 5.46* | 21.7 | 5.46 |
| 16.7 | 5.96* | 28.2 | 5.21 | 22.9 | 5.45 | 34.8 | 5.02 |

The relationship between the percentage of new equipment and corporate performance in different industries is indicated in Tables 6-58 through 6-62. This makes it possible to propose the following hypothesis. *Hypothesis 6-25*: In the electric machinery industry, companies with a higher percentage of new equipment enjoy a higher level of corporate performance. In the transport equipment, textile and chemical industries, companies are recommended to adjust the introduction of new equipment in response to the external environment.

Since advanced technology is most essential to electronic products, the reduced cost and the improved quality resulting from the introduction of new equipment lead to the enhancement of corporate performance in the electronic equipment industry. This is irrespective of the conditions in the external economy. By contrast, companies manufacturing products which are immediately affected by market factors such as apparels in textile, basic material products in chemicals, and automobiles in the transport equipment industry should adjust investment in new equipment depending on external economic conditions. With regard to the introduction of new equipment, aggressive chief executives with a vigorous entrepreneurship are desirable in the electronic equipment industry, whereas administrator-oriented presidents knowledgable on various phases of the business operation are valued in the transport equipment industry.

Incidentally, the relationship between the percentage of new equipment and employees' morale is not as clear as that between the percentage of new equipment and corporate performance. Therefore, it could be concluded a higher level of corporate achievement is a direct result of the introduction of new equipment. This effect does not occur indirectly through the enhancement of morale.

## 6-6. Summary

The factors related to the top management in this section are broken down into two groups: 1. those whose desirable states remain unchanged in spite of environmental changes and 2. those whose desirable states depend on the external economic environment. This makes it possible to review these factors in the light of morale and business result as set forth in Table 6-63. Whatever growth rate the economy mights show, the company whose top management comprises only company-bred executives, has no invited executives, and manages in a fair personnel affairs can maintain higher morale. The important factor necessary to increase business results independent of economic conditions is the introduction of new equipment. This should preferably be kept at over 30 percent. One factor whose desirable condition depends on the external environment is the pattern of decision-making. The company which makes decisions based on the president's opinion is more profitable in a high economic growth period, whereas decisions should be put in the hands of executives when economic growth is slow. The following hypotheses can be formed from Table 6-63.

*Hypothesis 6-26*: For the purpose of elevating employees' morale, the chief executive should always strive to improve both their administrative ability based on fairness and humanity, and the entrepreneurship which keeps businesses in progress.

*Hypothesis 6-27*: In order to attain high business results, the chief executive has to always maintain fairness of personnel management, and to promote the mutual understanding in the firm and scientfic attitude for decision-making, besides continuing to make efforts to be an excellent entrepreneur who has a positive attitude toward setting business goals, developing business strategies and introducing new

**Table 6-63.** Factors Related to Top Management of Which Desirable States are Independent of Environmental Changes and Those of Which Desirable States Depend on External Environment (All manufacturing industry)

| | Morale | | Business Results | |
|---|---|---|---|---|
| | Factors related to top management | Desirable states | Factors related to top management | Desirable states |
| Factors whose desirable states are independent of environmental change. | Percentage of invited executives | 0% | Type of president | Founder |
| | Schemes to raise motivation and loyalty | Positive | Business goals | New-product development |
| | Systems for human resource development | Positive | Overseas strategies | Positive production abroad |
| | Percentage of new products | More than or equal to 20% | Long-range plan | Have the long-range plan |
| | Percentage of new equipment | More than or equal to 30% | Percentage of executives' stockholdings | More than or equal to 10% |
| | | | Percentage of invited executives | 0% |
| | | | Schemes to raise motivation and loyalty | Positive |
| | | | Percentage of new equipment | More than or equal to 30% |
| Factors whose desirable states depend on environmental change. | | | Average age of executives {Period of high growth | Less than 55 years |
| | | | Period of low growth} | More than or equal to 58 years |
| | | | Patterns of decision-making {Period of high growth | According to president's view |
| | | | Period of low growth} | According to executives' view |
| | | | Taking charge of management task {Period of high growth | Free from management task |
| | | | Period of low growth} | Many executives in charge of it |
| | | | Percentage of new-products {Period of high growth | More than or equal to 20% |
| | | | Period of low growth} | 10~20% |

equipments. In addition, to cope with environmental changes by changing decision-making patterns, the chief executive should make decisions according to his own view in the highest decision-making body in which younger executives participate, who are free of divisional management task, in a high economic growth. And also, the proportion of new product is advised to be higher than 20 percent in a high economic growth period. In a low economic growth period, however, the decision-making should be done according to executives who are elder and take charge of division management task. And the chief executive's prudent business attitude such as from 10 to 20 percent proportion of new product is also advised in this period.

The following hypotheses are possible with regard to the five different areas of industry.

*Hypothesis 6-28*: In the electric machinery industry, the enhancement of corporate performance is always realized in the company where decisions are based on the opinion of an administratively superior company-bred or *Amakudari*-president, who attaches importance to cost reduction as a business goal. Though cost reduction should be the aim of the company, the company should be innovative enough to maintain the proportion of new products and new equipment at over 20 percent and 30 percent, respectively.

*Hypothesis 6-29*: In the transport equipment industry, higher level of corporate performance is always achieved by the company where decisions are made by the administratively skilled company-bred or *Amakudari*-president who bases his decisions on executives' opinions. And the proportion of new products should be maintained over 20 percent. Meanwhile the introduction of new equipment should be adjusted in response to changes in the external economy.

*Hypothesis 6-30*: In the the textile industry, the company where decisions are made by the founder-president with a superior entrepreneurial ability who attaches importance to development of new products or the expansion of market share as a business goal, always attains a high level of corporate performance. However, flexibility is required to raise the percentage of new equipment, as well as that of new products in high growth period, and to reduce them in low growth period.

*Hypothesis 6-31:* The desirable factors for the chemical industry are nearly the same as that of the textile industry, that is, decision-making by the enterprising founder-president and aggressive business goals such as the development of new products are always desirable. Just as in the textile industry, however, flexibility is necessary in adjusting the percentage of new equipment and new products, to the external economic environment.

*Hypothesis 6-32:* In the general machinery industry a founder-president with a strong entrepreneurial ability always achieves good performances. But flexible policies to adjust the percentage of newoequipment and new products to the external economic condition should be adopted.

# 7

# Summary and Conclusion

## 7-1. Growth Process of a Firm

The Japanese business management aims at long-term survival and growth of firm itself, rather than at benefiting stockholders, such as American or European companies do. Although the latter attaches importance to stock prices and dividend rate as financial indicators, the former cites growth rate and profit.

### 7-1-1. Origin of Business Profit

The first postulate I would like put forward is that profits are derived from the creativity of constituent members of a firm.

For example, the president exhibits creativity in strategic decision-making which advances the company into new business fields; the researcher and engineer, in developing new techniques and products; the section and department chiefs, in contriving means to encourage subordinates; and the worker, in improving operational methods which improve yield rates.

### 7-1-2. Importance of Product Strategy

The company's product is a central factor for a firm's growth. Actual business management revolves around products. This is because they serve as a link between the fluid external environment and the relatively fixed internal conditions of the firm. Any failure in product strategy will make the firms growth uncertain. This is the case no matter how excellent the top management of the organization may be, or however efficient the company's financial base.

New products accelerate a firm's growth. New product strategy is decided by top management and successful strategy gives top management self-confidence. Generally, as a result, this self-confidence increase human ability and desire to succeed again. It also increases top management's ability in creating for himself discontinuous tension and this becomes a driving force to break off an inertia in conventional management practices. This can be referred to as the entrepreneurial spirit.

Moreover, when new products are developed or a new strategy is deployed, organizational efficiency rises. The execution of positive and fresh strategies leads people to continuous idea changing, promotes active inter-communication, fosters the abilities of the team, and consequently raises the overall organizational efficiency and productivity.

### 7-1-3. Hindering Factor of Firm Growth

I would suggest the growth of firms in Japan is impeded by the mental aging of top management. This is a different phenomenon from Western theories which suggest that the growth of firms is hindered by a shortage of funds. In Japan, most banks are very financially supportive of large firms, if they have had a period of successful growth and specially during the periods of economic growth.

## 7-2. Function of Top Management

The function of top management consists of the three factors: firstly, thinking out future business vision; secondly, strategic decision-making; and thirdly, management and control. The following will explain briefly the meaning of these functions.

### 7-2-1. Thinking out Future Business Vision

The president of a firm must be always thinking of the state of the business in another ten to twenty years. Generally, Japanese presidents think out long-range business visions comparatively. This is because Japanese business management aims at long-term survival and growth of the busiess itself, rather than short-term benefits for stockholders.

Even when there is a drop in a company's profit and stock prices due to management decision to make a large scale investment for the purpose of rationalization or cost savings in the long-term, top management is not reprimanded by the stockholders or forced to retire.

### 7-2-2. Strategic Decision-Making

Some characteristics of the Japanese enterprise decision-making process are *Kashi-Kari* (give and take), *Nemawashi* (informal talks behind the scenes) and Ceremonial Decision-Making. These are expanded upon below.

a) The Logic of "*Kashi-Kari*"

A Japanese company president always does favors for his subordinates to increase their feeling of "indebtedness." These favors may include such things as to help the executives gain promotions or retain their posts. Sometimes he may assist the executives find their daughters prospective husbands. This "indebtedness" promotes trust and loyalty. It has been found by research that company presidents carrying out such practices have good business results.

b) "*Nemawashi*"

Japanese managers practice *Nemawashi* (or informal discussions) behind the scenes before making a decisions. For example, a Japanese company president sometimes proposes a plan at informal breakfast or luncheon meetings with executives. This is *Nemawashi* of what is called the "open type" in which the president's plans and thoughts are communicated to executives openly. Opposite to the open style is the "closed type" where the president will entertain individually the executives who will be shocked by the new plan, for example at a Japanese style restaurant. Here the executive is presented with the president's views in detail with the intention of gaining his full support.

*Kashi-Kari* and *Nemawashi* are important business practices in Japanese decision-making.

c) Ceremonial Decision-Making in Formal Meetings

Therefore, subjects discussed using the above mentioned informal processes and supported by mutual trust are promptly approved at the highest decision-making body such as the Board of Managing Directors.

The above mentioned characteristic features of Japanese decision-making results in innovative and prompt decision-making involving all executives. The phrase "innovative and prompt" would usually contradict to the phrase "involving all executives" in a decision-making process. Where a president accepts many executives opinion it would often result in the decision being "watered down" or suffering from mediocracy. This would not generally be innovative. However, if the president persists with his own opinion, the executives will not collaborate with him with management and control of the decision. Thus the foregoing three steps of the decision-making process are indispensable to the firm which aims to survive and grow responding quickly to the changing environment in Japan.

### 7-2-3. Management and Control

In many Japanese companies the functions of management and control are readily accomplished. This is firstly because the highest decision-making body is also usually the highest executive organ especially in large organizations. The top managers, as a group particpate in all strategic decision-making. In Japanese organizations, it is commonly found that the Board of Managing Directors (*Jômukai* in Japanese), is the highest decision-making and executive organ in the company. Secondly it is because department chief's and even section chief's opinions are reflected in a long-range business plan by the socalled "U" shaped decision-making process that is different from usual "Top-down" or "Bottom-up".

This management and control process is not so important as the above mentioned systematic thinking through of future business vision and strategic decision-making processes. Deciding the future direction of the firm is a more critical problem than contriving the way to reduce production costs and control budgets in rapidly changing Japan.

## 7-3. Abilities of Top Management

This point is very important. I am always saying to bankers that when you appraise a firm, they should examine the financial indicators in the short term; product strategy in the medium term; and, top management abilities in the long term.

### 7-3-1. Ability in Collecting Information

Many cognitive abilities are always necessary for determining future business visions, making strategic decisions and management and control.

However, to maximise effectiveness top priority should be given to collecting information, for example, on the present and future viability of the market for the company's main product as well as technical problems.

To collect useful information, the president must always make efforts to increase or renew "memories built in himself" which, responsive to a new information, are the first criterion for selecting necessary information. If the company head does not renew "memories built in himself", he may have a prejudice and thus fail in dealing with a new situation.

### 7-3-2. Ambition and Insight

Ambition and insight are important human qualities necessary when considering future business vision. Ambition is a desire which is not satisfied with the status quo but pushes one to and beyond the limits of one's abilities. Ambitious presidents generally reflect a better business performance. I would suggest that very often ambition in top management stems from an inferiority complex they felt when young.

Insight is the power to see things beyond the obvious. The true nature of something cannot be seen by analysing related data alone. The company president must not pass judgement on what is right or wrong, profitable or unprofitable, but based upon natural or unnatural.

### 7-3-3. Determination

Determination is one of the most significant factors in strategic decision-making. Presidents who have a firm determination achieve good business results.

Determination is the ability to decide on something with confidence and boldness based upon insufficient information. The decision of the president may be simplier than expected but it is a choice of three principles. 1) To go ahead, 2) cancel, or 3) maintain the status quo. To apply more sophisticated techniques only complicates the decision process.

### 7-3-4. Readiness to Do Others a Favor

Readiness to do others a favor is a indispensable trait in top management decision-making. It includes the practice of trying to understand other's feelings and helping them achieve their goals. Further extending the practice of *Kashi-Kari*, the company head must be aware of the needs of the executives. If one of the executives has a domestic problem, for example, getting his daughter married, the president is expected to help find a prospective husband. To extend this a little, while the executive's daughter is young and attractive, the president's assistance is not effective. However, if the executive's daughter is past the marriageble age and is not so beautiful, the president's help becomes very effective and desired.

### 7-3-5. Ability to Praise a Person

Motivation is necessary to make workers exhibit their creativity. Generally, praising is a good way to motivate a person. Subsequently, the best way to motivate company worker is to praise not only their good performance but also their earnest attitude. In order to praise executives, a president must abandon his sense of rivalry with them. He must make an effort to swallow his pride and praise them. This should be readily achieved if the president considers how he has already reached the peak position in the organization and has a higher and wider responsibility to the organization than those persons beneath him.

## 7-4. State of Desirable Growth Factors

The state of desirable growth factors such as top management ability, their attributes, decision-making patterns and strategies alter according to environmental changes. These factors can be further divided into two groups. Firstly, those whose desirable states remain unchanged in spite of environmental changes, and, secondly, those whose desirable states depend upon the external environment.

## 7-4-1.  Unchanged Growth Factors

Generally, the factors classified in the first category are mainly those which are related to top management's ability. Capability in gathering large amounts of information, strong ambition, capacity to cope quickly with new situations, willingness to extend assistance to others (*Kashi*), belief in what one is doing, persuasive power, and good health are all desirable top management abilities. Ambition and the capacity to cope with new situations are entrepreneurial activities; willingness to extend assistance to others and persuasion are administerial; gathering information and good health are the foundation to both. All these activities are required in combination for the survival of firms.

In addition, a founder-president, coming from a low social class background, having a business goal of new product development, having a long-range plan and a business which has a large ratio of new equipment have been found to be desirable characteristics of a firm despite environmental changes.

Founder-presidents of companies that have grown to be among the large successful classification, have usually an ability for developing new products that are keeping with environmental changes and consumer needs. Otherwise, he had not been able to come up to the present position. The president with a low social status childhood are shown to have an intense drive to be entrepreneurial and do favors to those people around them.

Having a business goal of new product development accelerates the development of new products which stimulates constituent's idea-switching and develops human resources, that inturn, furthermore develops new products. In this reciprocal process constituents display their creativity and it contributes to raising profits and growth of the firm. Having a long-range plan exemplifies the systematic thinking of the president, which inevitably contributes to the success of the firm. Finally, the large ratio of new equipment is the result of the aggressive and scientific attitude of the president which in turn raises business performance.

7-4-2.   Changeable Growth Factors

On the other hand, factors classified in the second category in which desirable states depend prodominantly on the environment are mainly related to strategy, except top management's some ability such as intuition. Business goals of new product development are welcome in any periods, whereas cost reduction is acceptable in periods of low growth or recession. Although intuition is required in a decision-making in rapidly growing industries such as electronics or restaurant chain, quantitative and analytical ability is required in a stagnant industry like Sake brewery.

High and conversely low, new product strategy ratios are respectively followed in high and low growth periods. This comes from the fact that the president's aggressive attitude is required in the former period and defensive in the later.

It is also established that top management decision-making according to the president's viewpoint is best during periods of high growth for innovative and expedient reasons. On the other hand, during low growth periods shared executive decision-making is more appealing to minimize the chances of failures.   Junior, energetic executives are required during high growth cycles, whereas, senior, more experienced executives are desirable while economic growth is low. This is justified on the grounds that during high growth, aggressive attitudes of top management is most fruitful.   Opposite to this, cautious attitude is believed to benefit the company most while periods of stagnated expansion are prevalent.

In conclusion, it can be seen that both an entrepreneural and administerial spirit are continually necessary for effective and flexible top management decision-making. More explicitly, it either requires an aggressive strategy based upon the president's opinion in a favorable environment or a cautious strategy founded on the view of senior executives in an unfavorable environment.

# Index